MW00928760

My Journey through Grief into Grace

Kathleen B. Duncan

Cover photo by Gary Cosby, Jr.

Copyright © 2015 Kathleen B. Duncan

ISBN-13: 978-1516976638

ISBN-10: 1516976630

Published by R and K Publishing,
PO Box 3233 Wichita Falls, TX 76301-0233

Edited by Casey Pitts

All rights reserved. No part of this publication may be reproduced, stored in a retrieval system, or transmitted in any form or by any means — for example, electronic, photocopy, recording — without the prior written permission of the publisher. The only exception is brief quotations in printed reviews.

Scripture quotations marked (ESV) are from The Holy Bible, English Standard Version® (ESV®), copyright © 2001 by Crossway, a publishing ministry of Good News Publishers. Used by permission. All rights reserved.

Scripture quotations marked (NIV) are taken from the Holy Bible, New International Version®, NIV®. Copyright © 1973, 1978, 1984, 2011 by Biblica, Inc.™ Used by permission of Zondervan. All rights reserved worldwide. www.zondervan.com The "NIV" and "New International Version" are trademarks registered in the United States Patent and Trademark Office by Biblica, Inc.™

DEDICATION

To all who have experienced the death of a child,
whether by miscarriage, stillbirth, illness, accident, murder, or suicide.
And to those who love those who have lost a child.

May you find healing and peace.

CONTENTS

Kathleen .Duncan

ACKNOWLEDGMENTS

I have made it through the pain of losing a child in no small part because of the love of friends and family. It is because of them that I wrote this book.

Our friends who loved us well through our grief. You know who you are. I cannot name you all or list all the things you have done for us. I did not see everything you did, but God saw it all. He saw your good deeds. He heard your kind words. He received your prayers. May you be greatly blessed both here on earth and in the life to come.

Those who walked this road before us. Thank you for letting us into your lives. As you walked your journey of grief with grace and strength, you showed me that I could survive the intense pain. May God continue to comfort you all.

My While We're Waiting friends. Many of you I will never meet until we join our children in Heaven, but I consider you my brothers and sisters. Thank you for your friendship and for introducing your children to me at WWW events and on the Group Page. Your stories and honesty bless me. Your words, encouragement, and prayers help me. Let us live well while we wait for that great reunion.

My adult children. Meredith, Lyz, David, Adam, Peter and Margaret. I love you all. I'm glad I get to be your mom. And Mark, thank you for loving our family. I'm glad you married my daughter.

Ron, my husband. I am grateful that I get to walk through life with you. You bring me joy, laughter, and peace. I love you.

Kathleen .Duncan

Preface

On August 12, 2013, six young people got in a car to drive back to Canyon, Texas, after a day-long cast party at a ranch north of Dumas, Texas. All six were part of the show TEXAS, an outdoor musical performed in Palo Duro Canyon each summer. The driver sped through a stop sign. An 18-wheeler going 75 miles per hour hit the Ford Taurus. Five of the six were killed. One survived and spent months in the hospital.

Our son Andrew was one of the five.

The Accident happened about 11:45 pm Monday night. Due to the remote location, they were not pronounced dead by the Medical Examiner until 12:30 am on August 13, 2013. We learned about The Accident when a police officer came to our door about 5:45 morning of the 13th.

Over the next few days we planned our son's memorial service, cleaned out his apartment, and began to deal with pain no parent ever wants to face.

As I posted about what was going on and how I was dealing with my grief on social media, friends suggested I start a blog. I did. My posts were raw and honest. Now, two years later, some of those same people suggested I turn my story into a book. I did.

The following pages contain my posts, thoughts, and essays just as I wrote them. I have changed very little. It will give you a glimpse into my grief journey as it happened.

My prayer is that my words honor my family, glorify my Lord, and help those who are grieving begin to heal. I pray also that my words help those who love those who grieve.

Chapter One

The Day My Life Changed Forever

The Day My Life Changed Forever - August 13, 2013

5:47 am Tuesday, August 13, 2013

There was a knock on the door. I looked out the window and saw a cop car. Not good. Never a good thing to have a cop at your door. Worse this time of day.

I grabbed my bathrobe; Ron got up to get dressed.

Officer Wiggins had seen the news on the police wire and volunteered to come to our home with the news. He knew our family. His son had graduated from high school just a few months before with our son Peter.

Officer Wiggins came in and told us our 20-year-old, Andrew, had been in a car wreck. Our son was dead.

I sat in the corner of the couch. Numb. My son was dead.

Our three children living at home had heard the door and the noise in the living room, and one by one they came in to ask what was happening. One by one we told them. One by one they each got off the couch and went back to their room. Their brother was dead.

I sat on the couch. Numb. My son was dead

Ron called our other children to give them the news. One daughter on vacation with her family. Our former Marine in Denver. Our gymnastic coach son in Michigan. Their brother was dead.

While Ron called the kids, I got on Facebook to see if I could learn more. The local police knew very little. The Troopers were still processing the scene. All they knew was that our son was dead.

One young man had posted kind words on Andrew's page. I sent him a message asking him to call me. He told me they had all been at the end-of-the-season cast party for TEXAS the day before. (This had been Andrew's second year to be in the outdoor musical. Andrew loved that show. He loved being a professional actor and dancer. He loved the cast and crew of the show.) On the way home from the cast party, about 11:30 pm, six

2

young people had been riding back to Canyon, Texas, when the driver ran a stop sign and pulled out in front of a semi. Andrew was killed along with four of his friends, including the driver. They were pronounced dead at the scene by a justice of the peace at 12:30 am. One person survived and was in critical condition. The driver of the semi was in serious condition. I had one question: "Was Andrew driving?" He was not driving, but he was dead.

I called my step-mom. Her grandson was dead.

Ron called more family. Their nephew, cousin, etc. was dead.

Ron contacted our pastor. A member of his congregation was dead. A youth from his youth group was dead.

I posted on Facebook and sent out an email to tell people their friend was dead:

"Our sweet, funny and talented Andrew Raymond went to be with Christ this morning about 12:30.

He was riding in a car going back to Amarillo from the annual End of the Show Ranch BBQ with other cast members from TEXAS. He and four others were killed when the car they were in was struck by a semi. One person in the car is in surgery. We do not know any other details at this time.

Please pray for our family as we deal with this loss. Pray for the families of the others involved, including the driver of the semi involved. I pray that somehow, God will be glorified in this."

The next few moments were quiet and still. It would be a little while before anyone arrived at the house, before we could really do anything but wait.

Ron and I talked a bit. We had plans to make. Arrangements for our son's funeral needed to be made. We talked quietly.

A few decisions were made:

1. We would not blame the driver. It could have as easily been Andrew. They took turns driving to events all summer. He could have been driving. Blame would not change things. It did not matter to us if alcohol was involved. That would not change the results.

2. We would make it through this. We WILL make it through this together.

3. The most important thing we discussed was this: OUR SON WAS NOT DEAD! Andrew was and is still alive!! He is alive in our memories, in our love, in our home, in the thousands of pictures we have of him, in the hundreds of hours of video of him. He is alive!

The reality is that Andrew is not dead. He is now living in Heaven. He is dancing and worshiping before the throne of his Savior! He is even more alive than he ever was on earth. And Andrew lived well! He lived life to the fullest here on earth. But now he is living eternally with Our Heavenly Father.

My life had changed forever that day. I have to deal with grief in a way I never dreamed. We had lots of things to take care of. Lots of details: legal stuff, funeral stuff, closing accounts, shutting off his phone, cleaning his apartment, finding his car!

But one thing in my life will never change: God is the same yesterday, today and forever.

On August 12, God was a loving, compassionate God. He cared for me. He loved me. He had begun a work in me and promised to carry it on to completion until the day of Christ Jesus. He sent His Son to die for me. He promised to never leave me or forsake me. He was the King of Kings, the Lord of Lords, Creator, Redeemer, Messiah and my Friend.

On August 13 those things were still true.

They still are true. They will be true forever.

Even on remarkable days, some things don't change.

What the Day Was Like –
According to My Facebook Posts

5:56 am This cannot be happening.

6:45 am My sweet, sweet Andrew is with Christ. We are hurting and ask for prayers. We are also praying for the families of the other TEXAS young people killed in the crash. I pray, too, for all those involved in the show. I know they are hurting today, having lost so many friends on one brief moment. I pray that we all find comfort in our Lord and Savior Jesus Christ.

7:55 am I cannot say anything. I know Jesus is Lord. That is all I know right now.

10:20 am "Luke 7:50. Your faith has saved you: GO IN PEACE" Just saw this post from my Camp in July. Andrew went in peace. He did what he loved. He sang and danced on stage full of good friends and beautiful women.

2:55 pm Thank you all for your prayers. Andrew is dancing at the throne of God today. Way too soon for me, but God had Andrew's days planned before the creation of the world.

8:24 pm For those who want to attend the memorial service for Andrew:

Graveside service at 2 pm at Rosemont Cemetery. All are welcome.

All are also welcome to join us that evening. Celebration of Andrew Raymond Duncan's life Friday night at 6 pm at the Wichita Theater. We will have food and time to simply be together after the memorial service at the theater.

8:42 pm   I am reading all these posts about my wonderful, wacky son. THANK YOU!! Thank you for - Loving him. Laughing with and at him... Acting with him. Singing with him. Dancing with him. Encouraging him. Not encouraging him, sometimes. Teaching him. Being kind to him. Remembering him. The stories and pictures help us through our pain.

11:46 pm   I had been telling people all day that I knew God was in control. He knew about this day even before Andrew was born, and that He would be glorified somehow.

I did not speak with our grown children until they each arrived at our home. The Holy Spirit confirmed for me the truth when our oldest son David arrived late this evening.

When my son David arrived tonight:

Me (while hugging him tightly and crying): You have lost lots of buddies over the past couple of years (in the Marines). How do you make it through this?

David: You know, Momma, that God is in control. He had a plan for Andrew's life. He knew about this from before the world began. And He will be glorified through it.

Amen and amen.

11:53 pm   For those with great pictures of Andrew: could you have some of these printed and bring them to the memorial Friday evening? So many great pics that I don't have. I cannot seem to keep up with all the posts! So glad others love my son as much as I do. Not did.

August 14

The Day After

Ron and the boys (David, Adam, and Peter) drove to Canyon to clean out Andrew's apartment. One son said he was doing okay until he found a pair of his little brother's worn out ballet shoes. Two little shoes brought my strong young man to his knees. They all cried while packing up their brother's things. Ron looked crushed when he got home. We held each other while we cried.

Our oldest daughter, Meredith, and her husband, Mark made arrangements to fly in tomorrow. I look forward to seeing them. My grandsons, Elijah and Colin, will be fun to have around. They love coming to Texas.

Our other daughters, Lyz and Margaret, live here. They helped me with some of the arrangements. They have been gathering pictures. I'm not sure what can be done without Ron here, but we are working on a few things.

Three friends are helping me with plans as well. One from church, one from theater and Scouts, one from the homeschool community. Others are working on the slide show. Mostly I cry.

**"Blessed are those who mourn,
for they shall be comforted."**

Matthew 5:4 | ESV

August 15

Family Arrives

Mark and Meredith arrived today. When they got here, four year old Elijah came up to me and said in his sweet, innocent voice, "Andrew is dead. He is in Heaven. We don't have to be afraid."

No we don't, Elijah. No, we do not need to be afraid.

After they got everyone settled in, Meredith came and sat down next to me. She told me not to worry if I see her looking sick. She is expecting a baby! Such wonderful news! I am so grateful for joyful news this week. I am grateful that all of my other children are now with me.

We did not know when Andrew's body would be ready for viewing. They sent it to Ft. Worth for an autopsy. Alcohol was involved in The Accident, so they are investigating it as a crime scene.

Today, Ron's brother and sister-in-law arrived. Friday, the day we will bury our son, is the eight year anniversary of when they lost their twenty year old son Todd. Ron went with them to view Todd's body eight years ago. A few minutes after they arrived, the funeral home called to tell us Andrew's body was ready for us to view. They went with us. I am grateful.

On the way, my sister-in-law told me not to touch him. "He will be cold and hard. But his hair will feel the same as always. Touch his hair." That is what I did. She knows me. She knew our son. She knew what would be helpful for me. I am grateful for friends like these who have walked this road before us to help us.

My step-mom and siblings are also here. Kadion and Kevin and their adult children from OKC. Kris from San Francisco. Uncle Bob, as my kids call him, flew in from Tahiti after being at sea for 41 days. I am grateful that he was in port and could get here. He will help my sons. I am grateful my family is here.

Ron said he wished his mom was here. Then he said, "No, I guess it's a good thing she is not here. This would have crushed her. Losing a second grandson."

Glen and Rita are in Heaven with their two grandsons. I am thankful they are together.

August 16

A Note from My Son David

This is what my 24 year old son wrote today:

> When I got to the house Tuesday, I was asked what seems like an unanswerable question. Mom came up and asked me, "What do we do now?" And at the time all I could do was hug her. Then she asked another one, "Why did this happen?"
>
> These seem the hardest questions ever to answer. I didn't sleep for almost three days thinking about these two questions. Then last night it finally came to me. Why? And what do we do now? I finally was shown last night the answers.
>
> When I lost Marines, I could always justify it by saying he had saved someone's life. But Andrew? How could it be justified? The same way. The answer to these two questions is really one answer.
>
> Everywhere I look I see people talking about how much they love him and how he touched everyone's life. Well guess what? He's not done. That is the answer. In life he made everyone's lives funnier, happier, worth living. Now in death he will do the same thing. His legacy WILL change lives, and it is our responsibility to take that legacy and have it live through us.
>
> That is our charge. That is what we do now. Our lives are not just our own anymore. Andrew always did everything to the fullest. It didn't matter if he was good at it or not, he still gave it his fullest until he was good at it. Now that his time on earth is over, we must live our lives to the fullest.
>
> Whenever we want to give up, whenever we feel like a failure, we must push on. He can't push on, so we must, do not neglect his legacy.
>
> So why? And what do we do now? We must push on, make our lives a living memorial, and enable his legacy to continue to change lives. That is our charge. That is the only way we will make it through this.
>
> I love you brother.

The Memorial

We had a graveside service at the cemetery at 2 pm Friday afternoon. Hundreds were there. Our pastor spoke. It was short. It was serious. It was beautiful.

They could not bury him yet, the ground is too wet, and so they took the casket back to the funeral home. He will be buried next week.

We went back to the house for a quick bite. Our friends the Burtons are here. Their family has been fasting and praying for us. They and so many others love us well.

Friday evening we held a memorial service at the Wichita Theatre, where Andrew had performed in nearly twenty-five shows. It was beautiful. Fellow cast members sang while video of him played on the big screen. Scouts did a color guard. Ron spoke. He was amazing. Worship team from our church led worship. Our pastor shared the Gospel. We laughed a lot. We cried. We worshiped.

The service ended with a video of Andrew dancing a duet to "I Won't Give Up on Us." There was a standing ovation.

The theater was open for hours afterwards. One mom had arranged for an open mic upstairs so his friends could share stories. Ron and I finally left about 11:00 pm. I found out later that some of Andrew's friends spent the night on the stage.

The slide show of Andrew and video of the Memorial Service can be found on Vimeo. In the comments of the memorial service is an order of service if you want to skip some parts.
https://www.youtube.com/watch?v=2hP6MP9B3Tc

It was a most unusual service. Friends helped us plan it. It was exactly what Ron and I wanted. Andrew was honored, our Lord was glorified, the Gospel was shared and people began to heal.

Here a few comments friends posted about the memorial.

Josh - I have never been more proud and humbled to be part of the Wichita Falls Theatre arts and music community. Andrew Raymond Duncan's memorial service was incredible. The combined choruses from many theaters pulled together and learned nearly an entire show in the 4 days since Andrew's death, and performed it today in his honor. But I must say I am absolutely blown away by the spirit of Ron and Kathleen. What I witnessed today, in Andrew's family, can only be explained by faith in Jesus Christ. Thank you, Duncan family, for teaching me so much about faith today. What a celebration!

Sherine - What an amazing celebration of Andrew's life! Yes we laughed through the tears and you went out in true Andrew fashion... In the spotlight with a packed house!! And now we enjoy the wonderful memories and begin to heal while we rest assured that you Sir have arrived at the destination of your Faith! God is so good!

Diane - The memorial was so amazing Kathleen! Know that I will be praying for you and Ron and the kids in the days and weeks to come. What an amazing thing Ron did tonight as well. I know you're proud as you should be. ((Hugs)) my friend.

Jean - I've never been to a memorial service quite like Andrew's. But then...we all know there was no one else quite like Andrew. I sobbed and laughed and sobbed again. And I got lots of hugs, because I was surrounded by theater people.

Garrett - It meant everything to be a part of Andrew Raymond Duncan's memorial service, as it was an amazing celebration of his life and all that he had accomplished. It is abundantly clear that God used him to impact an incredible amount of people, for he has left an amazing legacy. Thank you Kathleen, Ron, Adam, Peter, Margaret, and all of your beautiful family, because you are wonderful examples of the Father's everlasting strength and love.

Karlene - Andrew's parents "led out" in celebration of their son's life. They are model examples of how we can all celebrate Jesus in spite of the troubles that come our way. Bless you Duncans. Andrew, I know you are smiling and dancing with the angels.

Sheryl - What a beautiful service. Ron and Kathleen you blessed us all with the testimony of your family's faith. We will continue to lift you up in prayer through the days ahead!

Dexter - It was an honor to get to have a part in Andrew's amazing celebration of life tonight. I will never forget him or the legacy he has left.

Jeree - Your bravery and humor in the midst of such a difficult time set off the floodgates of my tears at the graveside service. You were amazing! Bless you and will continue to lift you up in prayer! Praying for you all.

August 18

A Message from Adam

My son Adam posted this:

People keep asking if there's anything they can do to help, if there's anything my family needs. I want to ask if they can bring my brother and those four young people back. But to you who asked and continue to ask what you can do: I thank you so much for your support of my family in this terrible, disgusting heart wrenching time in our lives. I ask you to continue praying. I ask you to wake up every day, and live your life a little better than you did yesterday. I ask you to call that friend or family member you're holding a grudge against. For the sake of those who can no longer live and walk and have life on this horrible, angry, despicable, beautiful wonderful world we live in, I ask you to LIVE.

I ask that you remember my brother and those four kids by doing something for somebody else today. I ask you to wake up and take a deep breath because you are alive. I ask that do something with the life that you still have. I ask that you grieve for my family and my brother by making something of yourself. I ask you to live as my brother lived: doing what he loved. This world is far too cold a place to spend it hating every waking moment, or hiding from fear and insecurity. I ask that you make a decision to "be the change you want to see in the world." I ask that reach out a hand to someone you know who needs a friend. I ask you to smile, and laugh. And I pray that I will be able to do the same.

My Posts from the First Six Weeks after The Accident

August 14

    Can I wake up now?

August 15

    One question:

    Do I have to shave my legs tomorrow? Will anyone notice or care??

August 16 (day of memorial service)

    I'm so tired but I don't want this day to end. I am afraid of the silence to come.

August 17

    Never once did I ever walk alone.

    Never once did you leave me on own.

    You are faithful God. You are faithful.

August 17

    All that is helping me right now is trusting God to get me through one day at a time.

August 19

Bible Study Starts Tonight

Bible study friends, Ephesians study starts tonight.

Rule 1. Be here by 6:45.

Even if you have not signed up for the study. I have extra books.

Rule 2. Get your homework done. If you don't have your homework done, just read Ephesians and come anyway.

Rule 3: Do not ask me how I am doing or mention Andrew.

Rule 4: Ignore rules 2 and 3. Just show up.

August 20
One week.

My friend Pam flew in from North Dakota. She will be here for a week. I'm glad. She will help me. She will clean house and cook. But mostly she will love me.

August 21
Wondering what my first thoughts of the day used to be. Made it to the Y today. Cried through low impact aerobics and stretch class. Now to get my nails done with my girls.

August 22
Can I just take a moment to say how much I love my kids? And my friends. And my kids' friends.

August 23

I had no idea I could sob in my sleep. I wake to a wet pillow each morning. My chest hurts. I had no idea. The physical pain of grief…

August 24
Ron and I are heading to West Texas A&M University for a memorial service for Andrew and the other two WT students killed in The Accident last week. Pray that this will begin to bring healing for the students and faculty who lost friends last week.

August 25
I told Ron that I could not believe our pastor never came by the day we learned of our son's death. I thought he would care since we had been in that church for more than seven years. Ron told me he did come by with the whole staff. They stayed for more than an hour.

I wonder who else came by that I don't remember. I guess I don't remember a lot that happened that day.

August 26

Behold, I long for your precepts;
in your righteousness give me life!
Psalms 119:40 | ESV

I have spent so much time in His word this past year. I know His truth. I know His comfort. In the midst of this terrible tragedy, I can rest in His promises.

August 27

Two weeks ago my life changed forever. The lives of my whole family changed forever. The lives of Andrew Raymond Duncan's friends changed forever.

August 28

Have I mentioned that my son Peter is now an MSU cheerleader?

August 29

A friend introduced me to While We're Waiting (WWW) today. It is a support group for bereaved parents. They are Christ-based. I hope they help me. I need help.

August 30

I had to take Andrew off our auto insurance and called BSA Hospital in Amarillo to discuss the $30 they billed Andrew from a June visit. He can't talk to them about it because he is not alive. This day sucks already.

Me: This day sucks

Lyz: Have you prayed about it? Praying seems to help me on those kinds of days.

August 31

Margaret is baking!! Who can be sad with that going on their kitchen?

15

September 2
Just pray.

No major issues here - my family is amazing and loving to me. Just having to do some of the hard stuff - like washing his bedding and getting copies of forms to the lawyer helping us with all the legal stuff. (Praising God for such a nice man to help us with all that, but it is hard.) I keep reminding myself what an awesome and loving God we serve. I know He is good. He is kind. He is loving. He knows exactly what it feels like to lose a son. He freely gave His so that mine could dance before His throne! I have a picture in my mind of Andrew dancing before the throne of the King of Kings and Lord of Lords! And God is smiling as He is watching this amazing young man dance with his whole being!

September 2
Attention all ladies!!

We will begin the Precept Upon Precept Genesis II Study on September 17! This study covers chapters 3-11 – The Fall through the Tower of Babel. 7-9 pm at my home on Tuesday evenings. Please email or text me off loop if you want to join us. I will be ordering books this week.

September 4
For you formed my inward parts; you knitted me together in my mother's womb. I praise you, for I am fearfully and wonderfully made. Wonderful are your works; my soul knows it very well. My frame was not hidden from you, when I was being made in secret, intricately woven in the depths of the earth. Your eyes saw my unformed substance; in your book were written, every one of them, the days that were formed for me, when as yet there was none of them.

Psalms 139:13-16 | ESV

Our Father knew every one of our days even before we were formed in our mother's womb. (I'm trying to remind myself of truth. The enemy wants to fill my head with lies.)

September 5

I got really angry yesterday when I saw "some random girl" post a picture of herself with MY son! Then I reminded myself that she was his friend and loves him, too. She is hurting, as are so many others who know and love my Andrew. I am grateful he is so loved.

September 6

Ron wants to know if I want to get up at 5:45 to drive to LETRA to do a triathlon with him tomorrow. Should I do it?? Total bike rides in 2013 – 2. Total distance in a pool in 2013 - 350 meters. Total distance run (walk/jog) in 2013 - 15 miles. I have not exercised much. But we signed up for this weeks ago.

What do ya'll think? Should I?

September 6 3:24 am

Can't Sleep. Yuck!

"They" Said
    It will take time.
    You are in shock now, in 3-4 weeks it will hit you. HARD.
    You will get angry.
    You will find it hard to function.
    This will be harder than anything you have ever done.
    You will need help.
    "They" were right.

"They" also said:
    We will pray for you.
    God will hold you up.
    The Holy Spirit will comfort you.
    You are loved.
    We will help.
    It will get better.
    You will make it.

I hope "They" were right about those things as well.

September 7

We did the triathlon. Well, Ron did. Ron was awesome. Trail run was a zigzag uphill - steep uphill - in the sun the whole way. Proud he finished. I did AquaBike. I beat the guy who got a flat a mile from the transition to the run. I cried on the bike. But, as Andrew used to say, "Hey! I was in the show!"

September 9

On the While We're Waiting page I wrote: Only four weeks into this journey. I am already feeling the fatigue of being "on". The Accident was on the national news. It seems that everywhere we go we see someone who wants to talk with us, tell us a story of their time in a show with Andrew, or ask about details of The Accident or about our other children. Thank you for the encouragement to lay down my burden. I am glad so many want to remember him, but it feels like a Band-Aid being ripped off my heart.

September 10, 10:30 am

My life the past four weeks since Andrew arrived in Heaven:

God, some of the things that happened today were hard and I don't like them. I will praise You because You alone are worthy of honor and praise.   Amen

September 10, 10:00 am

On this day nineteen years ago I went to bed wondering if I would have the baby soon. And would it be a Margaret baby or Peter baby?? Peter was born the next day making it an even two girls and four boys. Seventeen months later, we got the Margaret baby. I love you both. And Meredith, Lyz, David, Adam, and Andrew. So blessed to be Momma to you all.

September 12

Reading posts from others who have experienced the loss of a child is so encouraging to me. I know that I am not alone in feeling the way I do. It helps me to feel more normal when I read that even a year out others are hurting. (I have been told by well-meaning friends that I should be doing better by now. After all, it has been a month.) I pray more now than I ever have. And often it is for the pain of those on this group. I had no idea before Andrew died what this is like.

September 13

Pray for my children. They are missing their brother. Thanks for your prayers. Tough day. It ended with a great conversation with a mom who loved my son as one of her own. I love talking with friends who try to understand and who love me. Tomorrow will be better. Blessings on you all.

September 14

Y-Tri at Bill Barkley YMCA!!! My third year doing this event. Starts at 8:00. If you want to cheer me across the finish line, be here by 9:45. That will give you time to get coffee, set up your lawn chair, and watch everyone else cross before me.

Later that day - I finished!!! Fastest time ever for this event (for me that is): 2:11!! Whootwhooooooooot! After the Y-Tri, we drove to Dallas to see Peter cheer in Cowboy Stadium. Yes, life goes on. I'm glad.

September 16 10:45 pm

Made it through today without crying! I still miss Andrew so much…Oh, wait. Dang it! Crying now. I'll try again tomorrow.

To all our West Texas A&M peeps, for all those who loved these guys involved in The Accident, and who are struggling:

I encourage you to take advantage of grief counseling available to you on WT campus. The counseling center can help you deal with the pain of the loss you are feeling and help you understand the grief process. There are other grief counseling resources in all communities; often local Hospice organizations have grief counseling available. Don't hurt alone, ask for help.

Ask the Creator to help you. He will give you the great Comforter, the Holy Spirit, to lead, guide and comfort you. Pray and ask for His love and comfort. Seek Him now. I know Clint, Eric and Andrew would tell you the same thing if they were here. They know Him face to face now. You can know Him, too.

I pray God's peace be with us all as we go on with our lives though we are still hurting. Be blessed and encouraged today.

September 17

Today is hard. I can't seem to stop crying.

Lord, I need your loving comfort. Amen

September 18

So far it has been a good day. Carpets got cleaned this morning, grocery shopping and cooking for first time since before The Accident. Great talk with a couple of my kids and hubby (who is a stud, by the way).

Thanks for prayers yesterday.

September 20

Listening to John Michael Talbot station on Pandora while reading "The Thief" and watching the rain. Quiet house. I love my life!

Song "Come to Jesus" is playing. This was in the slide show for my mother-in-law's service. Love this song! Love knowing that Andrew is with Glen and Rita, my nephew, my parents, and so many more saints. More importantly, he is with Christ.

So now, if you have not yet, COME TO JESUS!! And live!!!

September 25

Dear Andrew,

I am sorry, but I had to turn your phone off. It was one of the hardest things yet. I so wish you were still on the other end so I could call you to tell you I love you just I one more time.

Love, Momma

September 28

Ron and I went to a Christian conference this weekend in Wichita, KS. It is a small group. We met most everyone here. The first discussion session opened with a man talking about how he loves the scene in Les Miserable where the bishop gives the main character the silver, the best silver. It illustrates God's extravagant grace to us. I started weeping. Ron had to explain why: Thenardier was Andrew's first big lead in a show. He told them about Andrew's death. They loved us well.

Mark Shultz is participating in the conference. He led worship tonight. So many of his songs tell stories of love. And of pain. He sang "Love Has Come" last and looked at Ron and I while he sang. We cried and worshipped. Ron said it was like getting his chest ripped open for ninety minutes. It was awesome. It was healing. It was painful. It was beautiful. This was the first time we had really wept together.

I am grateful that my husband has encouraged me to go through with things we had planned before The Accident like the two triathlons and this conference. I wanted to stop everything. He reminds me that we must go on living. Even through the pain of grief.

September 29

Came home from a wonderful weekend away with my husband and a few hundred godly people to find my kids had cleaned the whole house. Then spent an hour alone reading some of the many kind cards we have received the past seven weeks.

Thank you, Lord, for loving me through amazing people you have placed in my life. Help me to always be grateful for Your many blessings even in the midst of suffering. Amen

September 30

I was just wondering when I will stop counting the weeks since I saw Andrew last, since The Accident, since the knock on the door at 5:30 am, since we buried his body. The good news is that for those of us who know the Lord, we are seven weeks closer to joining him in Heaven.

One of my fears is forgetting. Forgetting his laugh, his voice, conversations, and his hugs. We have video of him acting in plays and dancing, but it's not the same as just remembering normal day stuff.

I am so grateful for all of my children and the blessings they are to me. I want to hang on to everything about every one of them.

Chapter Two

I Started a Blog

October 1

Someday I will like Tuesdays again. Not today. But someday.

~~~~~~

October 3

After losing a child, we do hard things. Today I took a dozen cans of chili to the Food Bank.

Andrew was the only one in the family who ate that brand of chili.

I cried as I handed them the cans. I could not explain to them why I was crying. I just left.

Then I sat in my car and sobbed.

~~~~~~

October 4

I cry every day. Almost all day. This still hurts so badly.

~~~~~~

October 5

Note to self: Never again go weeks without touching your checkbook register or entering transactions in Quicken. Balancing the account is much easier when done every few days. Thank goodness for overdraft protection.

Yep, Dave Ramsey envelope system went out the window August 13. Praise God we had an emergency fund.

I suppose it is a sign that I am finally begin to function normally again (I balanced all three accounts to the penny!! And refilled envelopes.)

Oh, and I started a blog.

October 6

Surrender

Sometimes we in the church talk about surrender. As if we have a choice.

"I SURRENDER, LORD!"

This was my cry months ago. Before The Accident. We had faced some ugly trials. Now, even more so, I cannot stand.

Lord,

I surrender, Lord, I surrender.

Take my life and let it be what You want it to be. Only through Your strength can I stand, or sit, or breathe. Take my yoke. Give me Yours.

Help me as I face another night. Wake me tomorrow and remind me how Your mercies are new each day.

Amen

<div align="center">~~~~~~</div>

October 10

I spent a few days in Michigan with Adam and my stepmom.

Missing Andrew right now. And mostly all the time.

Not sure how anyone gets through the grief of losing a child or spouse without surrendering. Some surrender to depression, some to addiction, some to anger and bitterness. I choose to surrender to Christ. He is my All in All. He WILL sustain me through this. He will sustain my life, my marriage, my joy and my peace.

October 13

Thank you, Lord, for those who walked this road before me.

God is good, and His provision is always enough.

We had a wonderful day yesterday with Jeff and Susan and their family. They are so encouraging to me. They walk this road of grief with grace and faith.

I hate that they know this road, but I am grateful that I was a part of their lives when they began their journey of grief. I saw Jesus in them and in their healing. I still do. Jesus is a huge part of who they are and what their family does.

Thank you, Lord, for all the godly people You have put in our lives who have walked this road before us. Seeing Your truth in their lives helps me believe Your truth in my life. Bless them for their transparency and for allowing me to watch their walk.

Help me, O Lord, to believe Your truth when I have doubts, when I am weak or tired, when the voices of others try to drown out Your voice. Help me remember the truth of Your Word.

Holy Comforter, comfort and lead me.

In the name of the Glorious Son of the Creator Jesus Christ,

Amen

~~~~~~

October 17

Ron and I went for a bike ride in the Wichita Mountains. We stopped for a break and I began to cry. "Don't you think this has changed us all?" I asked my husband.

"Yes. It has. But it has affected you more. You carried him for nine months. You nursed him for a year. You homeschooled him for twelve years. You are his momma. It will affect you more than anyone else. And that's okay. I am here with you."

I love my husband. I am thankful for the man I do life with.

October 18

Andrew,

We are going to see Lion King today. You were supposed to be here to go with us. I miss you. So many things I have to do without you now. Your memory will go with me instead.

I am grateful that Lyz is here to go in your place. Margaret, Caitlin, Lyz and I will have fun. We will remember you.

I know you are in a place of great peace, joy, worship and celebration of the King of Kings! I can't image the beauty of His majesty and glory! You get to see it! Experience it!

Nothing on earth, not even the great sets dreamed up by Broadway or special effects of Hollywood, compares to what you now experience every moment.

Dance, Andrew, dance! Dance with all of your heart, soul, and strength. Dance before the throne. Worship the Creator and the King.

We will do the same; we will worship Him, here until we meet again in Heaven.

Love you,
    Momma

~~~~~~

October 24

To the cast and crew of TEXAS:

Please know that I have been praying for all of you since the day we heard of The Accident. I cannot imagine how you all feel losing so many friends at once. Hang on to all the great memories. Love each other. Take each day as it comes.

God will get us all through this. He can and will heal our hurts.

Love,
    Momma Duncan

October 25

In the first few weeks, I loved looking at his pictures. Now, ten weeks out, I want to throw something when one of his friends posts a new picture of him on Facebook. I can't find joy in pictures right now. They make me miss Andrew's smile and laugh and voice. I am glad to hear I am not alone in avoiding pictures sometimes; other grieving moms have told me they experienced the same thing. I know I will find joy in them again someday. Just not today.

~~~~~~

October 26

A New Overcoat

A dear friend of mine lost six family members in a plane crash a few years ago, including children and grandchildren.

Rene told me that the loss of a child is like putting on a very heavy overcoat that you will wear the rest of your life. It changes you forever. You still function and go on with life. But the coat is always there. Some days it is heavy, other days it is lighter.

Over time, it does get lighter.

This helps me a lot. It also gives me a shorthand I can use when people ask how I am doing. For example, tonight when our oldest daughter called, I could tell her the last couple of days have been "very heavy coat days" and she understands what that means.

I have had a few "light coat" days, like when Ron and I have gone biking or running in the beautiful fall weather. Or when I came home to a surprise of all my fall decorations out!

But the coat of grief is always there. I will wear it always.

October 27

God's Provision

I was talking with Meredith last night. I told her how great it was to come home from Michigan to a clean house with all my fall decorations.

Meredith reminded me that it will be hard for me to decorate for Christmas this year, but God had provided for me. (I love the "But God" passages in the Bible) He had Lyz move back home in June. She loves decorating!!! When it is time to put away the fall and scarecrow décor, Lyz will be here to help me with my Christmas and snowman collections.

Have I mentioned lately how much I love my Kids!!!!

Thank you Lord for bringing Lyz to Wichita Falls in Your timing. And thank you for the blessings that all my kids are to me. Amen

I love that Meredith was kind enough to acknowledge how hard Christmas will be while reminding me of God's provision. I love that she loves Jesus enough to be able to love me enough. Just when I need the love of both my kids and the love of Jesus!!

A few days ago I had texted Ron to tell him I was really struggling. He texted back:

"Not only that, but we rejoice in our sufferings, knowing that suffering produces endurance, and endurance produces character, and character produces hope, and hope does not put us to shame, because God's love has been poured into our hearts through the Holy Spirit who has been given to us. Romans 5:3-5 | ESV

Hope does not disappoint us because of God's love.

I love you."

I am grateful for the family God has provided for me.

October 27

Anger

Amazingly, I have never been mad at God or the driver of the car.

The day we found out about The Accident, Ron and I talked with each other about how Andrew's life was complete. It was completed the moment he died; it was also complete every day. He lived life to the fullest. He was doing what he loved and doing it well. He had launched into adulthood well. He knew Jesus. What more could a parent ask for? There was no one to be angry with.

We were sad and disappointed, but not angry.

I have had times of anger over the past couple of months. I wasn't angry at a person. More like being angry at the whole situation. But each time anger about The Accident and my son no longer being present on earth tries to creep into my mind; scripture quickly pops into my head reminding me of truth. The Holy Spirit gently and kindly reminds me of truth.

Anger is not sin. It is not wrong. But it is also not helpful for me. I could park myself there and go about life filled with anger, which would result in my being hateful and hurtful to others.

I am so grateful for all the time I have spent in the Word over the years. I know truth and truth has set me free. Free from anger, bitterness, fear, regret, worry. Free to trust God even when I do not understand why He is doing things or why He allowed this.

We live in a broken and fallen world. Bad things happen. It rains on the just and the unjust, but we serve a good and beautiful God!! And who can be angry about that?

Record my misery; list my tears on your scroll — are they not in your record? Then my enemies will turn back when I call for help. By this I will know that God is for me.

Psalms 56:8-9 | NIV

October 28

Abundant Life

There are so many Christians out there full of bitterness and anger over their loss. How I wish I could help them see the beauty in trusting Jesus! Really trusting Him! Not just for fire insurance, but for the good and beautiful life, the abundant life He came to give us on earth. Yes, the earth is fallen and corrupt as it states in Genesis, but He came to give us LIFE!! Our life begins now, the moment we got saved, the moment we were born into His Kingdom of light!

Because I know He came to give me abundant life on earth and eternally, I can trust Him with my children. Even in Andrew's death. Even if He takes them all. We are here for His glory, not our own story. But He is so compassionate that He allows my story to be part of the big story.

The Spirit of the Lord God is upon me,
because the Lord has anointed me
to bring good news to the poor;
he has sent me to bind up the brokenhearted,
to proclaim liberty to the captives,
and the opening of the prison to those who are bound;
to proclaim the year of the Lord's favor,
and the day of vengeance of our God;
to comfort all who mourn;
to grant to those who mourn in Zion—
to give them a beautiful headdress instead of ashes,
the oil of gladness instead of mourning,
the garment of praise instead of a faint spirit;
that they may be called oaks of righteousness,
the planting of the Lord, that he may be glorified.

Isaiah 61:1-3 | ESV

October 29

Fear

A few years ago, I almost lost my husband to a serious staph infection. We went through four years of more surgeries and Ron using crutches and a cane before he was able to walk or jog normally again.

My oldest son spent two tours in Afghanistan with the US Marine Corps. One of those was the well-known Dark Horse Unit often mentioned on social media because of the high number of casualties they had in such a short time.

We almost lost one of our children to an illness in the last year.

I was fearful for weeks at a time that I would actually lose one of children or my husband. It did not show to the world, but I was afraid.

Over the past year, I finally came to believe that God is in control; that all the days of our lives are written in His book before one of them came to be; that He knows the time and the hour of our death; and that there was nothing I could do to prevent death at the appointed time. I began to have a lasting peace once again.

Within moments of finding out that Andrew was dead, God tapped me on the shoulder and asked, "You believed it to be true for your husband and other children. Do you believe it for Andrew?"

What choice did I have? I have to believe. I believe that He is a good and beautiful God, slow to anger abounding in love. He is compassionate and gracious. He works all things for our good. He has a plan for our lives. He is faithful and true. He is the Way, the Truth, and the Life.

I am so grateful that He took me through the trials this spring so that my faith was built up and I had studied the Word intensely over the past few years so I know the TRUTH!

I do not understand all He is doing, but I know His character. I can trust Him.

Note: I wrote this in an email to a Jill Sullivan, co-founder of While We're Waiting. Here is her response:

"What a beautiful statement of faith you just made. Everything you said is exactly what While We're Waiting is about. We always talk about Psalms 139:15-16 at our parent retreats. We discuss it in terms of our children's lives, that God had every one of their days planned before they were born, and that His plan for their lives was perfectly fulfilled in the number of days He gave them. And we also discuss this passage in terms of our own lives ... that God has our days numbered as well, and that His plan for us is NOT yet complete. He left us here for a reason, and we need to be about serving Him and seeking to glorify Him while we're waiting to be reunited with our children one day.

And you're so right ... even when we don't understand what He is doing; we can trust Him because He is good. That's the bottom line."

For you formed my inward parts; you knitted me together in my mother's womb. I praise you, for I am fearfully and wonderfully made. Wonderful are your works; my soul knows it very well. My frame was not hidden from you, when I was being made in secret, intricately woven in the depths of the earth.

Your eyes saw my unformed substance; in your book were written, every one of them, the days that were formed for me, when as yet there was none of them.

Psalms 139:13-16 | ESV

~~~~~~

October 29

Today's forecast calls for a "light jacket"!!!

I've been wearing a "heavy coat" the past few days. In prayer, I realized that I can choose, sometimes, to exchange it for a "lighter jacket" with God's help.

You have turned for me my mourning into dancing;
you have loosed my sackcloth and clothed me with gladness,
that my glory may sing your praise and not be silent.
O LORD my God, I will give thanks to you forever!

Psalms 30:11-12 | ESV

October 30

"They" Said

I was looking back to September 6 and reading what "They" said. "They" were right about those things.

We will pray for you. -- People have prayed for us and continue to do so. I am praying for the families and other folks affected not only by this accident, but by any loss.

God will hold you up. -- He is faithful and true. He sustains me.

The Holy Spirit will comfort you. -- I have felt His comfort daily.

You are loved. - I AM LOVED! So many have shown me that. My friends, strangers, my husband, my children, my family. Thank you all for loving me. And for loving Jesus by loving me.

We will help. - You have helped! Your words, kind glances, cards, emails, FB posts, pictures you post and stories of Andrew. We could not have pulled off such an amazing memorial service without your help.

It will get better. -- It is better. We will always miss Andrew. But the pain is not constant. The weeping is not daily. The sorrow is not so unbearable.

You will make it. - Yes, Lord, yes.

As a prisoner for the Lord, then,
I urge you to live a life worthy
of the calling you have received.
Be completely humble and gentle;
be patient, bearing with one another in love.

Ephesians 4:1-2 | NIV

October 30

Clues of Things to Come?

"**But this I call to mind, and therefore I have hope: The steadfast love of the Lord never ceases; his mercies never come to an end; they are new every morning; great is your faithfulness. ...**

The Lord is my portion," says my soul, "therefore I will hope in him." The Lord is good to those who wait for him, to the soul who seeks him. It is good that one should wait quietly for the salvation of the Lord. It is good for a man that he bear the yoke in his youth. Let him sit alone in silence when it is laid on him; let him put his mouth in the dust— there may yet be hope; let him give his cheek to the one who strikes, and let him be filled with insults. For the Lord will not cast off forever, but, though he cause grief, he will have compassion according to the abundance of his steadfast love; for he does not willingly afflict or grieve the children of men.

Lamentations 3:21- 33 | ESV

Back in May of 2013 I wrote, "Sometimes we just have to take it one hour at a time instead of one day at time. Fortunately, His mercies are new every morning."

God was teaching me to trust Him long before I really needed to.

Thank you, Lord, for teaching me to trust You so that when I had to trust in You (for there was nothing else I could trust) I knew You and I knew that You alone are worthy.

Amen

~~~~~~

October 30

The young man who survived the crash that killed my son and four others is out of the hospital this week. He is headed to a rehab hospital. Each time I see him post about his recovery, I get sad, angry, frustrated, etc. I know I should be joyful that Tim is recovering, but I so wish it was my Andrew. I simply have to turn it over to God or I would find myself drowning in pain and bitterness.

October 31

12 Second Warriors

The group of young people involved in the 2013 Musical TEXAS are remarkable. Not only are they remarkable actors, singers, dancers, and crew, they are remarkable people who made it through a remarkable event that no young person should ever have to deal with. They lost five friends in one horrible moment on August 12. A sixth was injured and faces months of recovery. On August 14 they performed the show in front of friends and family. Through tears and pain they gave it their all. They performed for the public a few more times that week to finish out the last 12 seconds of the most difficult summer of their lives.

They have taken on the motto of "12 Seconds Left." Here is an explanation of what that means written by one of their own. Please take time to read it.

What does "12 Seconds Left" mean?

By Victoria Olivier

I have never seen so much rain during a TEXAS summer as I have this season. Three - count 'em, THREE - shows were rained out. Unbelievable. During the Overture of the second of these shows, the rain began to pour down. The cast, instead of groaning and forcing the smile to stay on our faces, began to laugh and enjoy ourselves. We were out there, we might as well make the most of it. We performed the entire overture in the rain. Well, almost the whole overture.

At the top of the "We Invite You All To Come To Texas" Reprise, the last number in the overture, the lights went out on us. After we had danced the hardest choreography in the overture for one of the most supportive audiences we had ever performed for, management cut the lights on us. We understood it was for our safety, but we had already come so far, and we just wanted to finish the song! Many chorus members and dancers continued performing even as they ran offstage, hoping to give this wonderful audience the show they came to see. As we ran off stage, soaking wet and panting, we simultaneously laughed and vented our frustrations.

"Come on!" we yelled. "We only had twelve seconds left!"

Early on the morning of Tuesday, August 13th, we were told that five of our cast members had died in an accident with a tractor-trailer coming back from the cast party, Julian Arredondo, Clint Diaz, Andrew Duncan, Eric Harrison, and Amanda Starz. The sixth, Tim Johnson, was in critical condition in the hospital. The news was absolutely crushing. For a few solid hours, we held each other up as we cried for the loss of our friends - not even friends, our family. Our bodies and our souls ached. I will never forget the screaming and the sobbing I heard and contributed to that night. As I recall the communal anguish of the cast, crew, and friends of those involved in the crash, my heart is pounding and my chest feels like there is a cinder block sitting on it. No one should ever have to feel what we felt. All I could think about was the regret. I thought of how Clint and I only really hung out once over the whole summer, even though we had talked about it for ages. I thought of the coffee date Julian and I had set up for Tuesday morning. I thought of the heart to heart Andrew and I had at the cast party, and how I felt our friendship had truly started on that day. I thought of how Eric had asked if he could ride back to Canyon with me from the party, and chose to ride with Clint instead. I thought of how Tim always wanted to have me come to more of his dance classes, and I didn't. But worst of all, I thought of how I barely even knew Amanda. I was angry, sorrowful, and in shock. And I was not alone. The TEXAS family hurt as one that night. Thankfully, we allowed ourselves to smile and even laugh a little before we finally crawled home to try and sleep. Most of us were not successful in that endeavor.

The next day, the cast was called together to decide the future of the season. We only had four shows left, since the one for that night was cancelled. When I walked into that room, I was under the impression that we were all on the same page. After all, if theater people are famous for anything, it is for our perseverance in the face of adversity - "the show must go on." I was surprised to discover that this was not the case. Many people did agree that the show indeed must go on, but some only wanted to do one show. Some did not want to continue at all. More tears were shed, tempers flared, and pleas for understanding were both heeded and ignored. Eventually, we decided to perform one private show for friends and relatives, and the rest of the season would go as planned. No one was required to stay for any of these shows.

One of my friends stood up and reminded us of the night the overture was cut short before we could finish. This guy is happy all the time, and to see him hurting caused me even more pain. However, smiling through his tears, he recounted the events of that night, and said "We only have twelve seconds left. Let's finish it for them." If I wasn't completely convinced that I had to finish out the season before, I was then. I knew at that moment that I had no choice. Had any of those six people been in our place, and any of us in theirs, I know for a fact that they would want to finish the show for us. This could not have happened to six more loving, talented, dedicated, and passionate people, and I know that they would have pushed through to the end for us. In fact, the families of each of the five people we lost was so happy that we had decided to continue the show - they said that it's what their child would have wanted.

Wednesday night, we showed up to the canyon, terrified of the show we were about to attempt. I know I was shaking almost the whole time I was getting ready. Before the show, the chorus always has a "hands in" moment, and the phrase is always something funny or motivational to get us going. That night, it was "12 seconds left." And it was for every night following.

No one was ready for the emotions that flowed out of us, like the rain that poured down all night. Performing a show with empty spots and stand-ins only reminded us of who should have been there. Certain moments of the show felt almost impossible to complete without our lost friends. Andrew wasn't there to wink at me in Folklorico. Watching DJ dance without Amanda was heartbreaking. Every moment without Tim left me feeling lost and sad. Even backstage, their absence was painfully obvious. Before every show, Clint always gave me a hug and he looked for some way to compliment my makeup or my voice or just say how much he loved me. I ran offstage after Plum Pickers and fell to the ground, knowing Julian wouldn't be there to unhook my dress and comment on how lucky he was. I almost expected Eric to be hanging out backstage to hug us and tell us how well the show was going, and how much he missed doing Twelfth Night with me. The audience cheered for us through their own tears, knowing that at times, their support was the only thing getting us though the moment. Everyone was emotionally compromised. We held each other, knowing that if we didn't we might break apart.

But we made it. Even with the rain, the tears, the heartache, and the pain, we actually made it through what turned out to be the most beautiful and the hardest performance of our lives. More people left the next day. We banded together and promised to finish the season - to bring ourselves peace, to give the audience a show they'd never forget, and to honor the lives of our angels. We learned Tim was doing better, and it spurred us on. The shows got easier to do. We learned to use and push through our feelings. Before every show, we renewed our promise - 12 seconds left. When the end of the season came, we knew none of us would ever be the same, but we knew we were a strong, loving, and resilient family. I will forever hold each member of the TEXAS 2013 cast and crew in my heart. I know our angels were with us every step of the way, and I know they are still with me now. They will be with me always. Tim gets better every day, and it makes my heart soar to get updates from him. I cannot wait for the day that he dances again, and I know Clint, Julian, Andrew, Eric, and Amanda will be there to hold him up and inspire him.

So when you see the hashtag #12secondsleft on Facebook, this is what it means. It means sticking with it when the going gets tough. It means finishing strong, even when you feel like you've got nothing left. It means supporting your family when they are in need. It means smiling bigger, singing louder, and dancing harder. It means never taking your friends for granted. It means loving the people in your life, no matter how often you get hurt.

But most importantly, it means never forgetting. Clint, Julian, Andrew, Amanda, and Eric - my angels. I will never forget you. Thank you for being my inspiration.

I am not okay. Not yet. But I will be, because I know you will be there for me. I can push through this. After all ... it's only 12 seconds.

October 31

After reading about the 12 Second Warriors, think about your own life. What have you struggled with? What challenges do you face today? Can you make it through for just 12 more seconds? If so, can you make it for 12 more after that? Take it moment by moment, day by day. You can make it through.

In the days after The Accident, when asked how I was doing, I often answered, "I am breathing." I had to take it moment by moment, breath by breath. Soon I was taking life moment by moment and a day at a time. I still have my moments when I am overcome with grief and sadness.

But I know God is with me every step of the way. He will be with you as well if you ask Him to be. Will you ask now?

How else will you make it through the next 12 seconds?

~~~~~~~

Not that I have already obtained all this, or have already arrived at my goal, but I press on to take hold of that for which Christ Jesus took hold of me. Brothers and sisters, I do not consider myself yet to have taken hold of it. But one thing I do: Forgetting what is behind and straining toward what is ahead, I press on toward the goal to win the prize for which God has called me Heavenward in Christ Jesus.

Philippians 3:12-14 | NIV

November 1

In response to a comment about how we grieve and about others thinking we should be done in a few weeks or months –

I have a different reaction from some. I have laughed and enjoyed activities my other children are involved in. My husband and I did a triathlon just a few weeks after Andrew's death. Friends have expressed concerned because my husband was able to get through the eulogy without tears. They ask, "Are you guys grieving?" Of course we are!!!!!

Just last night I cried for quite a while. I teared up numerous times today as I helped my stepmom pack up a home that has been in my family since it was built 1933. I am still - and always will be - filled with sorrow at Andrew's death.

But I also have to go on with life. I have to show my other children that I care about them; life did not stop the day their brother went to Heaven. It would not be fair to them for me to sit at home and weep or to show up at their events weeping. I enjoy life with my kids and husband. I also weep with my husband. My kids know we are sad but trying to continue living.

I am not sure how to respond to folks who worry we are not grieving enough.

Bottom line: No one knows if they have not been there. Each one grieves at a unique pace and in a unique way. God will carry each of us through.

~~~~~~

November 4

My stepmom gave me a book yesterday. Les Miserable. 1915 edition. It was a gift to my granddad Bailey when he was a little boy.

Les Mis was one of Andrew's favorite shows. He made an awesome Thenardier.

She was with me the last time I saw Andrew on August 9. We saw TEXAS the night before, and we took Andrew to breakfast and then grocery shopping on Friday. Less than four days later he went Home.

I miss that kid.

November 4

Missing Loved Ones

Tonight, I am missing so many people I have loved. Rita, Glen, Daddy, Andrew, Mom, Grandmother Estes and Papa, my grandparents, and many more.

The phone my dad had since 1975 was turned off today. The house I grew up in is leveled and another house full of memories is empty. I should go to sleep now.

> **But we do not want you to be uninformed, brothers, about those who are asleep, that you may not grieve as others do who have no hope. For since we believe that Jesus died and rose again, even so, through Jesus, God will bring with him those who have fallen asleep. For this we declare to you by a word from the Lord, that we who are alive, who are left until the coming of the Lord, will not precede those who have fallen asleep. For the Lord himself will descend from Heaven with a cry of command, with the voice of an archangel, and with the sound of the trumpet of God. And the dead in Christ will rise first. Then we who are alive, who are left, will be caught up together with them in the clouds to meet the Lord in the air, and so we will always be with the Lord. Therefore encourage one another with these words.**
>
> 1 Thessalonians 4:13-18 | ESV

~~~~~~

November 4

One of my well-meaning friends suggested that I should be better. I should be functioning better. I should no longer be crying so much or be so sad. Perhaps I needed to see a psychiatrist or go on anti-depressants. She does not understand. I hope she never does.

Grieving the loss of a child will take me a lifetime. I am sorry that my children see me sad and crying. But I am dealing with my grief in healthy ways. I am not drinking, drugging, over eating, or indulging in other self-destructive behaviors. I am talking with other bereaved parents who have walked this road before me and have healed. I am exercising, eating right, and resting. I am praying, reading, and worshipping.

I don't know when the tears will become healing tears. They are still tiring. I still weep and hurt. I don't know when death will stop being in my every thought. But I know my Redeemer lives. And He will help me. That is enough. For now.

~~~~~~

November 5

Moving Day

I have been helping my step-mom Evelyn organize and pack her household items the past few days. She is moving from the house my grandparents built back in 1932 to live with her sister in Denver. This is a very good thing for both of them. I am glad for her and her sister.

This is God's plan for her in this time. But it is very hard for me.

I rode my bike to that house almost weekly growing up. I got to see my Grandmother when I wanted to; she always welcomed us to drop by for cookies or a sandwich. We had lots of family dinners there. This is where we had Easter egg hunts in the yard, Thanksgiving dinners in the dining room, and Christmas under a twelve-foot tree in the living room. We played dress up in the bedroom my dad grew up in. Grandmother read "Little Women" to us on her bed upstairs. We watched Miss America Pageants with my sisters and cousin on Grandmother's bed.

Twenty-five years ago, my dad and his wife moved in to help my grandmother. More memories were made there. My kids remember their Granddad and Grandmother Bailey living only in that house. That is where we visited them. Where they opened Christmas stockings and played with my dad's Beanie Baby collection. Where they played in the Lamb Room with all of Grandmother's lambs.

About 15 years ago, I designed a master suite addition which my parents built when my dad could no longer climb the stairs. It was so cool to help my dad with the design and then to come to visit to see the room actually built! So many sweet memories in that home.

Now the house sits empty. No pictures on the walls or junk in the basement. No toys or dress up clothes. Only a hollow shell.

This all made me think of Andrew. Like Evelyn, he has moved.

She is moving to Denver and I will get to see her again soon. I only have to hop on a plane or get in my car and I will see her in a few hours. I don't have to wait long to see her again.

I cannot hop in a plane or get in a car to drive to see Andrew. I have to wait. I have to wait until God's timing, but I will see him again.

Like my family's house, Andrew's body is empty. He is not there. There is no life, no dance, no laughter in his body anymore. But those things have not passed away. We still have memories of him. And he is still alive, doing those things in Heaven.

In God's timing, we will join him before our Savior in worship. We will make new memories together that will last eternity.

On my Moving Day, I will appear before the throne of God and fall down in worship of the Creator of the universe. I will worship Him in Heaven on my Moving Day.

I can worship Him now as well because He sent His Son to take upon Himself my sin and to die on a cross so that I may live.

On your Moving Day, where will you be going?

~~~~~~

November 8

Camp for Bible Nerds, as I call it, continues starting Monday in Chattanooga. It is the Fall Study Program at Precept Ministries. I don't have my homework done for the first day. Looks like a late night in the hotel tonight. I can't do it after tonight because I will be with my grandkids tomorrow and Sunday. We are doing Luke Part II. We did Part I in July.

Thank you, Lord, for the opportunity to study your Word with amazing people. And thanks for having it near my daughter so I can drop in on the way. Amen

November 12

Three months. Seems like forever. Thank you, Lord, for your peace.

I'll be off social media for a while. I'm going to Chattanooga for a study program. Then I'm meeting Ron in Florida for a business meeting. I am glad we had things planned before The Accident. I need to do these things. Or else I would be sitting in my chair weeping. I must live my life in order to go on living.

~~~~~~

November 16

I just spent a week finishing Luke, Part Two. The crucifixion was so much more real to me. Especially thinking about Mary as she was watching her son die. Fortunately, everyone in the room understood my weeping as we discussed it.

His death, burial, and resurrection give us HOPE!! And eternal life that begins NOW! The moment we turn to Him and trust Him we begin to truly live. And we begin to heal.

~~~~~~

November 22

Sometimes the pain seems almost unbearable. I wonder if this could be part of His plan.

~~~~~~

November 23

I got home to find that my friend painted my front door and hung family pictures in our Hall of Fame! Thank you, Diane, for blessing me while I was away!

Chapter Three

The Holidays Begin

November 26

Thanksgiving

I am so wishing Andrew was on his way home for thanksgiving today.

I choose to be thankful that he knew Jesus while here on earth and is with Him in Heaven now. I choose to be thankful for the 20+ years we had him with us. I choose to be thankful for a loving God who gave His Son for me.

Will you choose Christ this Thanksgiving? Will you meet Him now? He is waiting and willing to heal you from all your hurts and pain. Ask Him. He is faithful. He is love. He is the Way and the Truth and the Life.

~~~~~~~

November 26

To my friends who think I am strong: I am not strong. I am weak but He is strong in me.

I have times of doubt and fear and sorrow, but I do not often post those thoughts. I choose to take control of those thoughts and give them to Him at the foot of the cross. I choose to believe the truth of God's Word, even when I am not sure.

I hurt and cry and suffer. But God is able to care for me and handle my doubts.

November 27

Count It All Joy

Many years ago, God had me memorize some books of the Bible. James, Philippians and Ephesians. Three amazing books so full of helpful and healing truth.

In the past few months, He has brought many of these verses to me when I doubt or fear or am just plain feeling like life is unfair.

Here is truth from James chapter one:

> **Consider it pure joy, my brothers and sisters, whenever you face trials of many kinds, because you know that the testing of your faith produces perseverance. Let perseverance finish its work so that you may be mature and complete, not lacking anything. If any of you lacks wisdom, you should ask God, who gives generously to all without finding fault, and it will be given to you. But when you ask, you must believe and not doubt, because the one who doubts is like a wave of the sea, blown and tossed by the wind. That person should not expect to receive anything from the Lord. Such a person is double-minded and unstable in all they do.**

> James 1:2-8 | NIV

I will consider this trial joy and ask God for wisdom as I travel this road of grief and pain. I will believe and have faith and not doubt that God will answer my prayers. I know that, though it may not feel like it right now, God is good. He is able. He will complete what He started in me.

December 1

Thank you all for the birthday wishes.

I had a great day with family and friends. Fifty-one. I am getting old. Looking forward to eternity. But I still have work to do here on earth.

Come, Lord Jesus, come!

~~~~~~

December 2

I just realized I may miss church for the next three Sundays. Each week a different kid is flying in or out of Dallas Airport on Sunday morning. I am glad David will be home in two weeks and Adam in three weeks. Adam and Margaret leave in four weeks. Anyone else notice that my family travels a bunch??

~~~~~~

December 9

Thank you Liz Sanderson for telling me truth when the enemy was speaking lies.

~~~~~~

December 10

I haven't been exercising regularly, but I have been eating well, staying hydrated and taking proper supplements. I also have done two triathlons and three 5K's since September first. I walk much of the distance.

As of today, I have lost 19 pounds since 9/1! So excited! When I get down a few more, I am calling my trainer to start working out again!

Many of you have asked how we are doing. So I wanted to give you an update and tell you that Ron and I are taking care of ourselves physically and spiritually.

December 12

A Story of Friendship and Forgiveness

May I share a story?

A few years ago, a woman in our town did something outrageous to our Andrew, who was underage at the time. No details needed. She had been a friend of mine and of my kids. We did what we needed to do to protect others while also protecting our son. We made sure she would not work with teens again. We also chose to walk in forgiveness.

Late last July, I was driving past her street and knew God was telling me to stop and talk to her: "Today was the day for reconciliation," I knew. I told her that we had completely forgiven her and I wanted to check on her. She had confessed her sin to her husband, and to her church.

Their marriage was now strong and she was glad we had done what we did; it resulted in her repentance.

Less than three weeks later, Andrew was in Heaven. We told her she was welcome at the service, but she chose not to come out of respect for others who were grieving; she did not want to cause others discomfort. She did drive past the cemetery and sat in a park across the street during the burial. I love her for that.

I had a wonderful lunch with her today. We parted with hugs and tears of joy for a marriage restored, a momma now doing the right things

I am glad I stopped by when I was led to do so. I am glad we forgave her and she knew it before Andrew's Heaven day.

Our time on earth is too short to walk in bitterness and unforgiveness.

Forgive others. Free yourselves from the poison of bitterness. During this time of year, remember the extravagant forgiveness offered to you by the grown up Jesus. He did not stay a baby. He grew to become a man. He suffered and died. He died to give you life and freedom. His death brought us forgiveness and life. Freely share what was bought for you at such a high price.

I am glad I forgave this friend - yes, she is my friend - before our son's death. I want to walk in forgiveness!!

December 12

Two Weeks Until ...

This week. Many Americans are thinking, "Oh no! Less than two weeks until Christmas!"

I am sitting here thinking, "He would have been 21 in twelve days."

I miss my kid.

But I am grateful for the time I had with him. I am grateful that he knew Jesus Christ as Savior. I am grateful that we will meet again and spend eternity worshiping our Heavenly Father together.

Will you join us? Do you know Christ? He came to heal us and set us free. He came to show us how to love and care for the broken. He came to seek and save the lost.

~~~~~~

December 14

Dance

Watching the Dance, Etc. Christmas recital was hard. Andrew learned to dance and to love dance through his classes at Dance, Etc.

Margaret was beautiful! I am so glad she is dancing. I am rejoicing with her and others.

I am grieving for those not here.

I am excited that she and friends are heading to Amarillo to see the Nutcracker. I just can't. Not yet. Maybe next year.

To those in Nutcracker in Amarillo this weekend: Dance sweet dancers! Dance for joy and beauty! Dance before our God! Enjoy the thrill of performance. And do everything for the glory of the Lord.

December 14

My Faith Has Not Always Been Strong

My faith has... I'm not sure how to describe it.

There are times in the past four months that I quote truth. I know it to be truth. I know it is God's Word. I KNOW it is true.

But I am not sure I believe it. I know I don't understand what happened or why.

I know my son is not here. He is with Christ. I know Jesus died for us and Andrew knew Him. He is caring for my son and my son knows Him face to face.

I know God is love and He is compassionate and gracious. I know His grace is sufficient for me.

Sometimes, that is all I know. But that is enough to hold me up and keep me strong.

Hold on to the truth you know. We cannot understand all that God is doing. But we can trust that He loves us. For me, that has to be enough sometimes.

Blessed be the God and Father of our Lord Jesus Christ, the Father of mercies and God of all comfort, who comforts us in all our affliction, so that we may be able to comfort those who are in any affliction, with the comfort with which we ourselves are comforted by God. For as we share abundantly in Christ's sufferings, so through Christ we share abundantly in comfort too. If we are afflicted, it is for your comfort and salvation; and if we are comforted, it is for your comfort, which you experience when you patiently endure the same sufferings that we suffer. Our hope for you is unshaken, for we know that as you share in our sufferings, you will also share in our comfort.

2 Corinthians 1:3-4 | ESV

December 16

For Those Who Think I Am Always Strong...

For those who think I am always strong, here is a very raw post...

Excuse me if I am rambling. I need prayer. I am struggling tonight.

Our son was killed in a car wreck near Amarillo in August. This weekend our youngest daughter took her first Big Girl Road Trip with friends to see the Nutcracker in Amarillo. Andrew was a lead in that show last year.

I have been crying all weekend I think in many ways because the show being this weekend makes me miss him even more. He should be on his way home tonight. But he is no longer here.

And my husband left town for a week today.

Then tonight Margaret decided to stop at a friend's on the way home. I could not reach her. I was so scared for hours. I tried not to let my mind imagine what might have happened. She apologized when she got home. She just did not think. She is a great kid who rarely does wrong.

And my dishwasher broke tonight!!

I hate being scared. I hate crying. I hate that my kids see me sad like I have been the last few days. I want to trust God. I want to be joyful. I hate that grief seems to make the little things bigger - like a dishwasher that won't stop beeping!!!!!

I guess I need to pray, put earplugs in, and go to sleep. Thanks for listening.

Did I mention my son - you know the one, the world traveler, the sailor, the one who has been sailing with his Uncle Bob since a couple of weeks after The Accident - got home yesterday!! I'm glad to have David back in the USA and living in my house!!

December 20

Remember back in April when I posted that I needed jelly beans, chocolate, or a nap? Then a huge box of chocolate appeared without a clue who sent it? I am in need of more chocolate today. Or prayers. Or hugs. Or for my husband to come home today instead of tomorrow. Thanks for listening. And praying. Praying is good for you and me.

~~~~~~

December 20

I Have Amazing Friends!

Thank You, Lord, for giving me such amazing friends!

A while back I shared the Heavy Coat of Grief analogy. A friend sent me this yesterday and I want to share it with you:

> "I wish I could be there with you this week to carry your coat a little while. While I was thinking this, I imagined you with this big black coat.
>
> He took it and aired it out...making sure there was no guilt or lies to weigh it down. You took it back....it is yours to wear for this time. You wear it because you love Andrew. It is yours.
>
> Then I saw that you started to sew beautiful pieces of colored fabric onto it....maybe signifying memories of him. Your coat of many colors is special and I pray that God gives you comfort this week as you feel all the feelings that come your way.
>
> I will continue to hold you up in prayer and I will carry your coat for you anytime you need me to. I love you!"

I love the part about God airing it out to be sure there was no guilt or lies. What a sweet picture of His redemption, His forgiveness. We cannot let the enemy lie to us as we grieve. Know the truth, sweet friends. Know HIS truth!

His truth is love, peace, comfort, forgiveness, healing, compassion and joy.

I love that we have friends like this. I pray for you all that you, too, have dear friends who lift you up in kindness and prayer. Joy to you all.

December 21

What Were They Thinking?

As we approach Andrew Raymond Duncan's 21st birthday, I am missing him so very much.

But tonight I am thinking -- As her delivery date approached, what was Mary thinking? How did she feel about what was happening to her? What was Joseph thinking? Were they afraid of a future that involved raising the Son of God? Were they completely at peace, knowing they were in the will of God and He would care for them?

What was God thinking? Just days away from the moment He would be born a man. No turning back now. He would live as a little boy, an adolescent, a young man and finally a grown man. He would teach, perform miracles, and have many followers who would love Him. And others would hate Him.

Did Jesus ever wonder what the Father had planned? Did He question this plan? Of course not! He did what the Father sent Him to do. "Not my will, but Yours be done."

I clearly am not God. I do not know all the Father has planned. I do not understand what He is doing in some things, many things. But my prayer is this:

Father, let my answer be as Mary answered in Luke chapter One.

**"Behold, I am the servant of the Lord;
let it be to me according to your word."**

Luke 1:38 | ESV

~~~~~~

December 21

Oh, I forgot to mention - For my birthday, my youngest daughter gave me a beautiful journal. The first page said, "This is your Andrew Journal. It's for you to write down all the things you would tell him if he were still here."

I love my kids!

December 22

My Prayer for Today

Lord,

I miss Andrew. I miss his smile, joy, and laughter. Thank you for letting me have him in my life. Help me to trust You. Help me to trust that You are God and you have this.

Amen

~~~~~~

December 23

All My Kids Are Home

All of my kids are home!

Lyz, Peter, and Margaret live here with me. Adam arrived at our house today. David got here last week. Meredith is staying at her home with her family. I am glad she has such an awesome husband and two sweet darling little boys!

Andrew is Home. How wonderful for him to celebrate his 21st birthday in Heaven! And then to celebrate Jesus' birthday with Him.

I pray that our family will know peace and grace over the next few days. I pray that for your family as well.

Love one another. Enjoy time together. Ignore the junk that happens and laugh. Life is short. Hug your family and tell them you love them.

~~~~~~

December 24

Andrew's birthday. My husband was in tears when I woke. Firsts are hard.

December 24

Andrew's first birthday in Heaven

I thought about just staying in my warm comfy bed cuddling with my love all day. Then I remembered: We have to celebrate!! Andrew is 21 today!

Happy Birthday, sweet Andrew-son!
Enjoy all the decorations up there!

Thank you all for the love and prayers for our family. Thank you for remembering our wonderful son.

May I ask something? Do you mind if ask I one more thing of you who have done so much for us already? Would you pray? Not only for us, but for others and for yourselves.

You see, Andrew knew Christ as savior. Andrew was not perfect. He did not always make right choices. But a big part of his joy and laughter was due to knowing forgiveness was readily available when he messed up. He knew he did not have to walk in shame or disgrace. He had freedom and forgiveness in Christ! He could freely forgive those who had hurt him as well. He knew Christ!

He knows Him now face to face. We can rejoice in that. We can have peace and comfort through God's grace. We still hurt. We continue to need prayer and healing, but so do many others.

Please remember to pray for all who are grieving this year. Pray for those who are lost and hurting. Pray for peace for those in torment. Pray for freedom for those in addiction.

Pray for yourself. If you have never had a relationship with Christ, just talk to Him as you would a friend. Tell Him what you are thinking and feeling. Tell Him of your doubts and fears and resentments. Ask Him to show Himself to you. He will. He will answer. He will heal the broken hearted. He will cleanse our dirty hearts. He is waiting, and listening, and loving you.

As we celebrate our son's first birthday and Christmas in Heaven, please know that you can know Christ today. You can know the Creator. You can truly celebrate the Birth of Christ in a new way this year.

December 27

Special Days Sometimes Make the Pain Worse

To my friends who grieve,

On the three month mark, my husband said he didn't understand all the hubbub about that day. "90 days or 88 days. It still hurts the same to me." He says it kicks him in the gut at unexpected times, not the anniversary dates.

For some, those special dates are hard. They bring back vivid memories of painful conversations, planning funerals, waiting for autopsies. And other things we had to take care of. For others, they are just another day in a long line of grief.

I am glad we can accept that grieving is unique to each of us and that we can support, pray, and encourage one another.

For those facing anniversary dates of the loss of a loved one, I pray that you may have peace, comfort, and strength each day.

I know that our Heavenly Father will use all of this for our good and His glory. He promises that He will. And His promises are yes and amen.

Blessings to you. And to all my newly found brothers and sisters in grief and in Christ. I could not have healed so much in the past few months without knowing you all walk this path with me.

I now not only look forward to my reunion with Andrew and other family members, I look forward to a meeting of the *No Longer Waiting* parents! Oh what joy we will have sharing our stories with each other as we join our children in Heaven and they see how we lived well and supported each other here on earth while we waited.

December 27

Peter gave me a rose and a poem for Andrew's birthday On Christmas Eve. My kids love me well.

We hosted our annual Christmas Eve Open House. That night was hard for me. But I was able to hold it together until after folks left. I sobbed myself to sleep.

I am grateful that I know Andrew is in Heaven, but I miss him terribly.

December 28

My Christmas Gift

May I share what my children got me for Christmas?

My children gave me a silver bracelet with "I Love You" engraved on it.

They took some of Andrew's handwriting and had a bracelet engraved in his writing for me! What a wonderful way to remember my son! I love that they remembered their brother and showed me great love as well.

They sent a few pages from one of his school notebooks. The artist looked at all the pages and found various samples of each letter to form these words. The letters are each his writing.

The company is Scripted Jewelry. They have a Facebook page. They have other designs as well.

As my friend Patty said, "Absolutely the best Christmas present ever!! From all your kids, they just let Andrew write it. Priceless."

December 29

I read another status tonight about someone who survived a terrible car accident. "God was with him since no one should have survived this bad of an accident."

Folks, God promised His children that He would never leave us or forsake us.

God was with Andrew when he, too, was in a car wreck but did not survive! God never turned His back or left Andrew alone. God was watching over my son when he was in an accident. He was with Andrew all the time.

Statuses like the one mentioned above imply that God was not with the ones who died in an accident. Or of cancer. Or heart disease.

Please remember that God is not one to show favoritism by "being with" or "looking out for" only those who are healed or survive. He cares for all of us, even in the midst of terrible accidents or circumstances. Even in the midst of suffering.

~~~~~~~

December 30

I have had times of wondering "if I had prayed more over my kids...or done more Bible Studies with them...or had more faith...or been a better mom or better Christian...or jumped in the car at 5:47 am on August 13 and driven to Amarillo to lay hands on Andrew and anointed him...would he be alive today?"

Of course not! I could not prevent this accident. It could have been prevented, but not by me. I cannot blame myself or accept blame from the enemy. And it does no good to blame others. What happened, happened. I must learn how to live with this new normal.

It does not change who God is or what He has promised or what He has done and will do. Blessed be the Name of The Lord. He gives and takes away. Blessed is His Name.

January 2, 2014

I wish I was planning to see Andrew perform this weekend instead of planning a benefit for a memorial scholarship named for him. Thankful for all the great people helping and performing.

Lord,

Tell him I love him and miss him. Tell him that You are bringing good things out of tragedy. You promised to work all things together for good for those who love You and are called according to Your purposes. You are already doing that. I want Andrew to know how cool it is that all these groups are collaborating to honor him.

Amen

~~~~~~

January 8, 2014

God Always Gives Us More Than We Can Handle

God does give us more than we can handle. But He never gives us more than we can handle *with* Him.

He wants us to rely on Him. To trust Him. To ask Him. Ask Him for strength and peace and hope. He longs to come beside you to help you through these most difficult times.

January 11

Rejoice in Suffering

I made it through the holidays with some joy and laughter. I enjoyed my family and having friends over on Andrew's birthday/Christmas Eve. I loved having our kids' friends drop by all the time and often going to sleep to the sound of laughter and water fights in the kitchen.

Then I had a very busy week putting finishing touches on a big benefit/community arts event in our son's name. The benefit evening was a great success and lots of fun.

Now I just want to sit in my chair in my room and read or be still. I like the quiet. I don't want to go out to eat or talk to anyone or be a part of all the activities.

I think I have just now hit a time of stillness since The Accident in August: services and arrangements followed by a new semester and getting kids settled in new routines, a couple of trips to see our kids who live out of town, helping my stepmom move out if state, and holidays followed by more holidays followed by the benefit.

This is the first time of real stillness.

I started Grief Share class at church last week. I was able to encourage others and was glad I went. I have a new Bible study starting this week, and a friend is joining it for the first time. I have two appointments to workout with trainer in prep for upcoming triathlons. But when I get home, I just want to sit.

It seems like I can laugh and have fun for a bit, then I am exhausted.

I have peace and calm. Some sadness. But mainly just want to be in quiet and stillness.

It is hard to explain to the four adult children living our home or to my husband. Friends don't understand what I feel. I am not depressed. I just like quiet and stillness.

Not only so, but we also rejoice in our sufferings, because we know that suffering produces perseverance; perseverance, character; and character, hope. And hope does not disappoint us, because God has poured out his love into our hearts by the Holy Spirit, whom he has given us. Romans 5:3-5 | ESV

January 16

I can't imagine the trouble Andrew and Margaret would have gotten into since she turns 18 today. I know he would have come home and taken her out with friends.

I am grateful that they had a close friendship and enjoyed each other the past few years.

~~~~~~

January 26

Raw Honesty

For those of you interested in raw honesty, keep reading. All others, move on to another post.

The past few weeks have been a struggle. My kids have been great. No major problems here. But I have struggled. Guilt, depression, self-pity.

Many of you think you know how we are because you read my blog or see my FB posts. You see smiles and jokes. Some of that is my life. Praise God, we do have times of joy and laughter.

But... few of you have called or stopped by see for sure how I am.

Reality is rarely shown on social media. I am no different. I do not post when I have spent the morning crying or cannot sleep because of the sorrow. I greatly appreciate those who send texts or call just to say hello and "How are you?" I love the notes and emails. They help.

This grieving thing is not a quick fix. It will not be over soon or easily. I do not have sorrow the way I did the first few weeks, but I will never be the same No one who loses a child ever is.

After Bible Study on Tuesday morning, I stopped in the FBC Library to chat with Nancy. Her son is a dancer in NY. She was a home school mom. She has loved me well these past few months. She told me I should read "Room of Marvels" by James Bryan Smith. I have read some of his writing. He was in charge of the weekend event Ron and I went to six weeks after The Accident.

James Smith was very close to Rich Mullins. His two year old died just six months after Rich's death. A year or so later, his mom died. James is familiar with grief. He wrote this book during his journey of healing.

Here is an excerpt from the book. It is a book of fiction. It is not a theology book, but it gave me new insight into grace.

I took the liberty of changing the character's name for my sake. Try reading this with your name in its place.

The main character has struggled in his grief. He has finally reached the point of letting go and crying to God for help. He has relinquished control to God in desperation. He is kneeling at the foot of a blood-stained cross.

"That is not why He died for you, Kathleen. He doesn't need your service. He died for you because He loves you. He doesn't need you to do anything at all. Now you are faced with a more difficult task: to let Him love you in the midst of your shame. He did not die to coerce you into service or moral improvement. All He wants...is you." I stared in silence at the blood-stained wood.

"You must let Him love you as you are, not as you intend to be. Let Him love you as you are, without a single plea for reform. It is all about grace, Kathleen. All of life is grace. We deserve nothing; we are given everything. Until now you have only experienced the drippings of grace. You have longed for the real thing, like longing for the scent of a flower you have never been able to find, or the echo of a tune you have not yet heard, or the news from a country you have never visited. Well, you have found it. Grace is the thing you have been searching for, and it is all around you."

Lord,

Thank you for Your grace. It is what sustains the weary; it sustains me. I praise You because of who You are, not for what You have or have not done. I choose to let it all go and trust You.

Thank you for loving me in my shame, guilt, self-pity, and sorrow. Thank you for sending Your Son to die and live again so that my son can spend eternity with You. I choose to believe Your Word and to believe that Your joy is my strength. You are my healer, my refuge, my very present help in times of need and sorrow and pain.

Amen

January 28

Help Me Be Willing

This is still my prayer.

**And Mary said, "Behold, I am the servant of the Lord;
let it be to me according to your word."**

Luke 1:38 | ESV

Lord,

Help me to be willing. Especially since I cannot change what has happened. Help me accept it and to be a willing bond-slave. Thank you for your healing and joy. Thank you for your faithfulness and grace. Thank you for loving me.

Amen

~~~~~~

January 30

Thank you to the kind friend who sends cards unsigned. They seem to arrive at the time I need it most.

~~~~~~

February 1

His birthday was not bad. I knew that while we were celebrating the birth of our Savior, Andrew was seeing Him face-to-face!

Today we are hosting a party to celebrate his baby sister's birthday. This is hard! They were great friends and loved dancing together. Andrew is not here to dance with Margaret today. I miss my son.

Chapter Four

Spring

Six Months since The Accident

February 4

Two Little W-2's About Killed Me Today

Who would have thought a 1040ez with two little W-2's would knock me down. I hate adding Date of Death. Next year I will have to delete Andrew from my list of dependents. That one will be hard too. I just completed the hardest tax return I have ever done in my life. I'm going to bed.

I am praying for the parents of Eric, Julian, Clint and Amanda as they also do this hard stuff.

~~~~~~

February 12

Six months closer to the day I will see Andrew in Heaven. It is well with my soul.

~~~~~~

February 17

I know truth. The truth is found in Jesus and in God's Word. The truth is found in serving Him daily. The truth is that God is good, kind, loving, and cares greatly for me.

But I am sad. All the time. My faith is not shaken. I am not questioning God, but I feel sad.

My husband is worried about me. He travels a bunch and asks each day what I did. My answer is often "Not much." I work out a couple of times each week, go to Bible study, and that's about it. Tax season is upon us, and I work part time during tax season. I will be working some.

I don't want to do lunch or chat on the phone with friends. I want to be at home – peaceful and quiet.

I hate that Ron is worried. I want to be happy again, but that takes so much energy! Grief is hard. It is tiring. I am ready to be done with this. I want to go back to normal.

Things will never be normal again. The Accident changed that. But God is the same yesterday, today, and forever. Blessed be the name of the Lord.

February 28

Margaret had shoulder surgery in Ft. Worth. She is doing well. I am tired.

~~~~~~

March 2

Ron has been out of town twelve of the last fifteen weeks. I am so glad he is home! I love my man!

~~~~~~

March 5

Tickets are bought! I am joining Ron in Manhattan in two weeks! A few days of business then we get to travel to New Hampshire to visit friends. These friends know loss. We got to love them a few years ago when they lost a baby. I am so grateful that God put people in our lives who know loss and love Him. They give us hope that we can find peace and joy, even after the loss of a child.

~~~~~~

March 6

Dry Eyes at Market Street Today!

Major mile stone today!! I made it through a United Market Street shopping trip without tearing up!! (Andrew worked there three years during high school.)

I will miss seeing Andrew's smiling face at the checkout counter forever, but thankful to be making progress in healing.

By the way -- I make no promises that tears won't happen again. But I was excited to make it out the door this time.

**Weeping may tarry for the night,
but joy comes with the morning.**

Psalms 30:5 | ESV

March 9

I'm grateful for fresh starts and forgiveness! When we make poor choices, recognize our error, repent (true repentance includes change in behavior), and go forth in holiness, we please our Father. And we often make our friends proud.

~~~~~~~

March 14

My Thought for the Day

I can be overwhelmed by grief. Or I can choose to let a gracious God overwhelm me in my grief.

Today, I choose to be overwhelmed by God, not grief.

I am glad that so many enjoyed the album I posted on Facebook yesterday.

It amazes me how few pictures I have of Andrew without a beautiful woman on his arm.

He always hung with the most beautiful people of all- dancers, TEXAS folks, WT friends, theatre geeks, and lovers of LOTR, Firefly, Batman and Disney princesses.

I am grateful to have had him in my life.

March 25

NYC with My Husband!

I leave for NYC in 10 hours!!

Tomorrow, we are seeing "Once" then I will have dinner out and see Times Square with my husband. I will be on my own Monday. We see "Newsies" Tuesday night. Sightseeing Wednesday with Ron. We are visiting our friends Martha and Pat Thursday. Then we are heading to St. Louis Friday and home on Sunday. I am excited to have a whole week with my love!!!!!!

(FYI. We have been intentional about spending time together since The Accident. A weekend away in September and November. Date night when he is in town. We are committed to having a strong, loving marriage.)

A few days later....

Last night I learned that if my husband ever decides to leave the HVAC business, he could get a job as a NYC cabby! He drove me through Queens, Manhattan and Long Island yesterday. He can cut off other cabbies with the best of them in the middle of Midtown, the theatre district, and around Times Square. He drove on Broadway, Madison Avenue, 34th street and lots of others past the Chrysler building and Empire State Buildings.

I am amazed that he drove in these same areas pulling a 6000 lb., 16 foot trailer during the snow storms in January. He is the man.

A few days later...

Road trip took us through Manhattan. Queens. Long Island. Bronx. Yonkers. Massachusetts. Connecticut. New Hampshire. Vermont. New York State. Pennsylvania. Ohio. Indiana. Illinois. Missouri. Oklahoma. And Texas.

We saw great shows and fun sites. I watched my love sell self-contained unit ventilators, vertical air handlers, and critical environment air handling units.

I visited friends Jim and Janine, Pat and Martha and kids, Brett and Kathy, and Graham. We had great food and fun.

Now we are driving home on I-44 in MO listening to Pandora Country Love Songs and Michael Buble. I love my life.

March 27

For those who look at my life and think I have it all together: Yep, I messed up royally today. Parenting fail #1,385,642. Tomorrow is a new day.

~~~~~~

March 31

For those who have noticed that Ron and I have lost weight in the past eight months: thank you for your concern. And thank you for your prayers. We welcome them.

The weight loss is intentional. We have been trying to be careful about our diets and intentional about self-care. Not always successful, but working on it. We've had a few people notice and express concern over the past couple of weeks.

~~~~~~

April 5

I'm a grandma again!! Jacob Timothy made his entrance this morning at 1 am. 8 pounds 10 ounces!!!! He is a chunk with lots of hair.

Momma and baby are both doing well. Meredith is an awesome mom. Big brothers Colin and Elijah are very excited!

Yes, life does go on with joy!

~~~~~~

April 12

We made a surprise trip to Chattanooga to see baby Jacob! Meredith told me that she was expecting the day they arrived home last August. Such wonderful news in the midst of sorrow. This little boy will always be precious to me for that.

April 15

Some days life just sucks. Hard stuff. Lots of work. Big expenses. IRS. Exterminator. Massive amounts of laundry and housework. My house smells like fresh paint and anti-bug chemicals.

But I serve a compassionate, gracious God. He provides for my needs. I have sons who help. And one son's girlfriend who helped.

And my husband comes home tomorrow!!!

~~~~~~

April 20

I keep thinking about this passage.

Now if we have died with Christ, we believe that we will also live with him. We know that Christ, being raised from the dead, will never die again; death no longer has dominion over him. For the death he died he died to sin, once for all, but the life he lives he lives to God. So you also must consider yourselves dead to sin and alive to God in Christ Jesus.
Romans 6:8-11 | ESV

~~~~~~

April 25

For everything there is a season,
 and a time for every matter under Heaven:
a time to be born, and a time to die;
a time to plant, and a time to pluck up what is planted;
a time to kill, and a time to heal;
a time to break down, and a time to build up;
a time to weep, and a time to laugh;
a time to mourn, and a time to dance;
Ecclesiastes 3:1-4 | ESV

Today started as a "time to cry" kind of day. But counting blessings turned it to a work and clean kind of day.

Can I just say that we serve a compassionate, gracious and loving God?

May 1

As she leaves the house doing something silly:
    Me: Margaret, you are odd!
    Margaret: Better than being even! Even dumber than you!
Gotta love my daughter!! She makes me smile.

~~~~~~

May 5

Sitting in the shade after a not-so-quick run. Thinking about all the wonderful moms I know who face this coming weekend with children in Heaven. Tears are flowing.

As you celebrate Mother's Day, please say a prayer for those who were unable to conceive, for those whose babies went straight to the arms of The Father, and for us who were blessed with our child for too short a time on earth.

While we celebrate our living children with us, we never forget those living in Heaven and we look forward to our reunion.

~~~~~~

May 10

Dear American Airlines,

Thank you for canceling Ron's flight yesterday and again today. I did not want him home for Mother's Day and David's birthday party anyway. I hate you.

Sincerely,

A momma and wife who needs her husband home NOW!

~~~~~~

May 12

Thank you to all who sent messages and texts on Mother's Day. I am blessed to have such caring friends.

May 14

I never thought I could run. If I ever did anything but walk with a little jog, it would never be under 15 minute miles. Today I ran two miles with average pace of 13:45. (By run, I mean run two minutes then walk a minute then run two minutes, etc.)

With encouragement and motivation we can do all things in Christ.

Thank you, Sarah Fidlar for being Jesus with-running-shoes-on for me.

Folks, she came to my house as often as I would allow last fall to simply get me outside. She walked with me, cried with me, and loved me. When my shoulder starting hurting and I couldn't lift or swim, she walked with me encouraging me to run even 15-20 seconds as we went along. Never criticizing, always encouraging.

I love this lady!

~~~~~~

May 15

Grace

I had a meltdown while driving today. It's been months since I cried like that. I had to pull off on a side road and park for a while. When I got myself together I looked up to see what street I was on: GRACE Ave.

I was at a five-way stop with signs surrounding me that said GRACE.

But he said to me, "My grace is sufficient for you, for my power is made perfect in weakness." Therefore I will boast all the more gladly of my weaknesses, so that the power of Christ may rest upon me. For the sake of Christ, then, I am content with weaknesses, insults, hardships, persecutions, and calamities. For when I am weak, then I am strong.

2 Corinthians 12:9-10 | ESV

May 31

TEXAS

10:00 am

Tonight is opening night for TEXAS 2014 season. I am glad we are going. But I so wish Andrew were dancing again on the TEXAS stage. I miss him so much! I grateful he knew Christ and that he is dancing in Heaven. But I would love one of his hugs today.

Shower —check
Packing —check
Sobbing —check
Vomiting — check

I guess I'm ready to go.

Pray for us

11:45 pm

Thanks everyone for your prayers.

Ron and I had a great time driving. I love being in the car with him, discussing scripture, life in Christ, our kids, the world, and how blessed he is to have me for a wife.

Before the show we got to talk with the other parents of the TEXAS Angels and visit with kids from last year's show.

The show was wonderful. They did a great job. And they honored our kids well. A few new lines that referenced them and a whole new song and dance. Beautiful.

I only cried a little a couple of times during the show. But on the way out to meet the cast, the tears flowed. He was not there with his big grin and awesome hugs. He didn't have just a few folks for us to meet. Andrew was not there. But his memory is. And he is still loved.

Good night, dear friends.

June 2

When Will That Boy Stop Surprising Me?

I heard new stories about Andrew last night. This one was from a number of gals: When one of his dance buddies was having a tough few days, he would fill a gift bag with goldfish and chocolate; sprite, cheesits and chocolate; or some other salty snack, soda and chocolate. He would give it to her with a sweet smile and say, "I thought these might help. They helped my mom and sisters when they were PMS'ing."

And they loved him for it! What guy gets away with that? "Hey, you are acting weird. Must be that time of the month. Here have some chocolate. It will help." And have them love him for it!?!?!

When is that boy going to stop surprising me?

~~~~~~

June 4

The Only Things I Know Today....

Sometimes the only things I know are:

1. God is real and He loves me.
2. Jesus is Lord. And He died, was buried and rose again for me.
3. I am a mess and it's okay because of the other two.
4. My sins are forgiven. Forever and ever. Amen.

~~~~~~

June 5

I'm thinking about my son today. And thinking about something Ron said that morning. Ron said (just an few minutes after the notifying officer left): "His life was complete. It was completed the moment he died, but it was complete every moment lived."

Andrew Raymond Duncan lived life to the fullest. Every day.

June 5

Peaks and Valleys

It seems that folks assume my bad days are because of Andrew. But life is just like that - peaks and valleys. It was before 8/13/13 and will always be until death or Christ returns. God does not have peaks and valleys! He is the same yesterday, today and forever! He is all knowing, all powerful, ever present, loving King of Kings!!

If I can simply remember that in my valleys He is walking beside me and often carrying me.

~~~~~~

June 18

It Should Not Have Been Andrew

Friends have said, "It should not have been Andrew!" I say, "Then who would you have chosen?"

Recently I walked past the pictures we took the last time we were all together in December 2012. Everyone is smiling and genuinely happy. We had a great time together that weekend at Grandmother Estes's 100 birthday, celebrating Christmas, and seeing Andrew dance in Nutcracker. (My kids are all gorgeous in those pictures, by the way!)

Then there are the pictures from last month. Again we are together and genuinely happy. The whole family! The little boys are wearing Batman shirts in memory of their Uncle Andrew.

No, Andrew is not in the picture. But he is not missing. He is not lost. He is exactly where he is supposed to be. He is where he should be. He is in the presence of Christ. He is the center of God's will, doing what he was made to do: worship The Creator with his whole being, in spirit, and in truth.

Where am I today? Where are you today? Are we doing what we are supposed to do? Are we doing God's will today?

Will you worship God in spirit and truth with me today regardless of circumstances and pain?

While we wait for Christ's return, let us live well today, my friends.

June 24

Tractor therapy: Two hours on my tractor listening to awesome music which proclaims the truth regarding a loving, powerful, gracious, and compassionate God.

I think I will survive this current suffering and trial.

No. I will thrive!!

~~~~~~

June 25

This morning I did something I have never done before in my life. Even back in middle school PE. I ran an entire mile! No walking! It was slow. 13:07. And I walked most of the next two miles. But I did it!

Now that I have met this goal, I can back to sitting on the porch and reading on Monday and Wednesday mornings.

~~~~~~

June 28

I Am Not So Amazing...

Tonight we went to a beautiful wedding and got to see lots of friends.

A couple told me how amazing they think I am.

Then I told them the story of what happened to my arm, which is wrapped in bandages: I fell into a shelf of hot chickens! Major burns on my forearm. I am not so amazing.

And to prove how unamazing I am, I shared a picture of my feet from last week. I am wearing two completely different shoes! One open-toe, one closed-toe. They are two different heights.

While in Hot Springs last week, I went to a nice restaurant with Ron and then to a support group meeting at Hot Springs Baptist Church. I looked down and saw my feet!! These shoes are not slip-on! I actually buckled each one! Yep. Not very amazing. Very human. And clumsy.

July 1

How I Have Been Thinking Lately

Anyone else ever think like this? I have been thinking this way too often over the past few months and days:

"This is hard. I'm tired. I don't want to think or suffer anymore. The world is ugly and getting uglier. I am tired of people hurting the ones I love. I am tired of those I love hurting each other. I am tired of hurting.

I miss the ones who have gone before me -- Those who lived a long life and saw their grandchildren grow and play as well as those who were taken way too soon for my liking. I want to be with them and to be in Heaven with Christ.

Come, Lord Jesus! Come quickly! Or just take me out so I don't have to deal with this stuff and these people anymore!"

Have you had those same thoughts and feeling?

Rejoicing - walking in joy again and again - is a choice! I can choose depression, anger, hurting myself by rehashing things over and over in my mind, and hurting others by lashing out. I can choose isolation, anger, and self-pity over my situation and pain.

Or

I can choose to become more Christ like - study His Word, do His will, pray, worship, and listen to uplifting stuff (music and talk). I can surround myself with people who give life and joy to others instead of rejecting their efforts to love me. I can avoid negative people - gossips and those who tear others down in word and deed - and choose to be around godly people.

I can give in to the world and all the ugly stuff it has to offer me, or I can rejoice in The Lord and know He is near. I can let my own gentleness, kindness, love, and patience be evident to all.

Read in Acts about all the crappy things that happened to Paul. Then read this:

Yes, and I will rejoice, for I know that through your prayers and the help of the Spirit of Jesus Christ this will turn out for my deliverance, as it is my eager expectation and hope that I

will not be at all ashamed, but that with full courage now as always Christ will be honored in my body, whether by life or by death. For to me to live is Christ, and to die is gain. If I am to live in the flesh, that means fruitful labor for me. Yet which I shall choose I cannot tell. I am hard pressed between the two. My desire is to depart and be with Christ, for that is far better. But to remain in the flesh is more necessary on your account. Convinced of this, I know that I will remain and continue with you all, for your progress and joy in the faith, so that in me you may have ample cause to glory in Christ Jesus, because of my coming to you again.

Philippians 1:18-26 |ESV

Am I living in a way that I should be ashamed? OR am I bringing joy to others? Am I helping others have joy? Am I letting others love me and accepting the joy they offer?

Yes, to be with Christ in Heaven would be better by far, but God, in His infinite wisdom, has chosen to give me another day of life on planet earth. It will mean labor for me, but it will be fruitful labor if I choose to do the next right thing. And I can walk in His joy.

Lord,

I pray that I may glorify you today and encourage others. Help me to love others well, to choose to do the next right thing, to accept your grace and to walk in forgiveness towards others and myself.

Amen

~~~~~~

July 2

Writing helps me. It helps me to write out the good stuff. It helps me not think the yucky thoughts I have trying to take over my brain. Thinking about that which is true, noble, right, pure, lovely, admirable, excellent and praiseworthy really does change my life.

July 5

I am blessed with a man who will hold me while I sob and say he is sorry I am sad without trying to fix it.

And then he will correct me when my expressed thoughts are not in line with truth. He reminds me to accept the things I cannot change, work to change the things I can, and to pray to God for the wisdom to know the difference between the two.

~~~~~~

July 7

Early on in this journey, I saw how many of those in the Bible had their children die before them, starting with Eve.

They experienced grief, yet they still trusted God. They knew His character – His kindness, joy, mercy, grace, justice, and compassion.

And He knew how much they loved their child. He loves His Son much more than a human can: He is perfect Love. They had been together since before the foundations of the world. They are One.

But He loves us so much that He was willing to have Jesus die for us! That is hard to comprehend. This took on a whole new meaning for me when my son died. I finally understood the sacrifice the Father made in giving His Son – His only child – for us!

Do you see it?

God loves YOU so much that He, a father, freely gave His Son to die for you! Through His love and sacrifice of Christ, we can become His child. He has the love of a parent for you!

If you have lost a child, think of the love you have for you child and how much you miss him or her. How much you want to spend time, just a few more moments, with them! God desires to spend time with us even more.

What a beautiful way to help us understand His love for us!

July 9

> **During the days of Jesus' life on earth, he offered up prayers and petitions with fervent cries and tears to the one who could save him from death, and he was heard because of his reverent submission. Son though he was, he learned obedience from what he suffered and, once made perfect, he became the source of eternal salvation for all who obey him and was designated by God to be high priest in the order of Melchizedek.** Hebrews 5:7-10 | NIV

Why did God hear Jesus's prayers? Because of his reverent submission. And Jesus learned obedience from His suffering.

What are you learning in your suffering today? Seems like sometimes I am learning only to cry and complain, to sob and feel sorry for myself. Does this glorify the God I say I want to serve?

Yes, there are times for tears. God sees my tears and comforts me. But I also want to become more Christ like and to know Him more intimately. If I choose reverent submission and accept my suffering as an opportunity to learn obedience, God can and will use it to bring me closer to maturity and to make me like Him.

~~~~~~

July 10

Thank You

Friends who did so much for me these past eleven months: May I say, once again, THANK YOU for the love you have shown me and my family?

I have friends who lost children in the past year and are suffering because of the ugly things said to them, folks telling them to get over it already and move on.

You have shown us grace and love. You have allowed us to mourn. You have done and said kind things and been patient with me. You have expressed your love for Andrew and my other children as well as for Ron and me. Thank you!

And thanks to whoever sends the unsigned cards. They come at just the right time!!

July 12

12 Things I Am Thankful for on the 12th

The Accident that killed our son was on August 12. For months after The Accident, I dreaded the 12th. But I have decided to be grateful for what I have rather than constantly mourn those who have gone to Heaven before me. So now, on the 12th of each month, I will make a list of at least a dozen things I am grateful for.

We may not have tomorrow, so be grateful today!

Twelve things I am grateful for on the twelfth:

1. God so loved me that He gave His son to die for me. My sin is forgiven. And I have become the righteousness of God through Christ.
2. My amazing husband. A great provider and godly hunk. A man who makes me laugh, and holds me when I cry. He tells me his thoughts and listens to mine.
3. My seven children. They are all wonderful. I have loved watching them grow into the adults they have become.
4. I got to be Andrew's mom for 20+ years.
5. My friends who love me well.
6. Precept Bible studies that help me learn the Word.
7. Sarah, my friend and trainer. And the ability to move, train and become stronger.
8. A car in which to safely travel the country. I love road trips!!
9. My home. Lovely and big enough to hold my family, yet cozy enough to truly feel like home.
10. The opportunity to home school. I got to spend great times with my kids and see them learn cool stuff.
11. My sweet, stupid dogs.
12. Good books. I adore reading and learning new stuff.

What are you thankful for?

~~~~~~

July 15

My friend Lorie and I took a break from studying and went hang-gliding in Tennessee Tuesday. Melanie went with us to take pictures. These ladies have prayed for me. I love them. I love my life.

July 21

It looks like, once again, I will not be going straight back to Wichita Falls after the Bible study ends. Last summer, I went through Houston to see Adam and met Ron in Florida in November.

This time? I am picking up Margaret tomorrow and dropping her at Meredith's. Then I'm driving to Ohio on Wednesday and flying back to Chattanooga Thursday. I will drive home on Friday via Norman, where I will help David get settled into his apartment.

I think I need a new GPS. Mine takes me out of the way on every trip.

~~~~~~

July 23

Be Available

While in Chattanooga for the Summer Study Program, a friend became ill and was hospitalized. I stayed in town a couple of extra days to be with her. She had driven from Ohio and could not drive back alone. So I stayed, and I drove her home to Ohio.

Can just say how amazing the body of Christ is? When Linda got sick, folks at our summer study program rallied! Lots of visitors and prayers. We got her picked up and one gal stayed with her in a hotel last night. We will drive to Dayton today. My plane back to Chattanooga tomorrow is at 7 am. The ticket was paid for by folks in the study group.

As I have prayed this spring about what I should do when my kids move out this next month, I heard The Lord say, "Be Available." I said, "Ok."

When I heard Linda was in the hospital and that she had driven from Dayton to TN, my first though was, "I'm available!" I knew I could stay as long as needed and could drive her home. I am so glad that my time was available and that resources were available for hotel rooms and plane tickets.

I'm wondering what else I will be available for in the upcoming months....

Chapter Five

The First Anniversary

The End of the Firsts

July 26

And So It Begins...

And so it begins...The one year anniversary is coming up. Yesterday was the anniversary of the last time some of us saw him in TEXAS and got a group photo. Today is one year since the last time two of his siblings saw him. About twelve days after that was the last time I hugged him. A few days after that...the horrible knock on the door at 5:45 am with news that would change me and my world forever: I had become a bereaved parent - my son had been killed.

A feeling of dread has been on me for a few days, but I could not understand why. I didn't think about the anniversaries coming up so fast until last night. Then it hit like a huge boulder falling on my chest. Ron held me while we cried.

I could lay around on this rainy day and feel sorry for myself. I could retreat into sorrow and self-pity for the next month.

But I choose to rejoice that we have rain! I choose to be grateful for the waffle Margaret just made me and the silly video Adam sent me. I choose to be grateful for my loving husband. I choose to be grateful that Lyz lives nearby. I choose to be grateful that David is all moved in and ready to start OU and that Peter will be heading that direction in a couple of weeks. I choose to be grateful for Meredith's joy and her family.

I choose to be grateful for the time we had with Andrew.

I choose to think about - and pray for - others who are struggling this morning like my friend Laura and her family, my friend Keith whose mom passed this weekend, and my friend whose husband has lung cancer at age 37.

I will get up, feed the dogs, do house work, and spend time with the ones I love. I will most likely spend time calling folks who don't live nearby. I'll cry a bit. Or a lot. I'll laugh a bit. I'll eat, play, and love. I'll pray, worship, and study The Word. I may even take a road trip.

In short, I will go on living. Because that is what we do. My Heavenly Father chose to let Andrew die. I don't understand or like it, but I trust that He is good and kind and just and faithful and wise. I know He has a plan. He has me here for a purpose, and I will continue to try to live in obedience to His call.

July 30

A Subaru Would NOT Have Made Difference

I don't like the Subaru commercial "They Lived" for obvious reasons. It came on last night and brought up strong emotions.

Times like that remind me all the more that I must keep my eyes on Him, remember His truth, and control my choice of thoughts. If a commercial, show, movie, or book causes me to stumble, get angry, or have resentments or doubts...I should walk away, shut the book, close the door.

What I put IN my mind and spirit directly affects what comes OUT of me.

I encourage...no, I challenge! you all to memorize this passage. It has valuable treasures in it for us as we walk this life.

> **Rejoice in the Lord always. I will say it again: Rejoice! Let your gentleness be evident to all. The Lord is near. Do not be anxious about anything, but in every situation, by prayer and petition, with thanksgiving, present your requests to God. And the peace of God, which transcends all understanding, will guard your hearts and your minds in Christ Jesus.**
>
> **Finally, brothers and sisters, whatever is true, whatever is noble, whatever is right, whatever is pure, whatever is lovely, whatever is admirable—if anything is excellent or praiseworthy—think about such things. Whatever you have learned or received or heard from me, or seen in me—put it into practice. And the God of peace will be with you.**
>
> Philippians 4:4-9 | NIV

We must:

1. Rejoice in The Lord. He does not change, regardless of our circumstances.
2. Know that God is near. He is not in Heaven where He cannot be found. Nor in the depths that we cannot reach Him. He is here. He is near. And He cares and is listening to our cries.
3. Pray - take our thoughts, emotions, fears, and pain to Him. He is big enough to handle our honest expressions and emotions. And He is kind, loving, patient and good!
4. Accept His peace. He desires to give us His peace!!

5. Take control of our thoughts. Don't dwell on the yucky stuff. Count our blessings. And don't let our minds wander into the dark places of what if, if only, or I should have. We cannot change what has happened. We can learn from the past sometimes, but we can't change it. We can, however, impact our future by how we live and think now.

6. Put into practice what we have learned. Little by little and day by day. Do the next right thing based on what we know.

Love and peace to you all this week.

~~~~~~

July 31

In church we sang a song that has the line, "O death, where is your victory? O death, where is your sting?" So I went home to look up this passage. Good news!

I tell you this, brothers: flesh and blood cannot inherit the kingdom of God, nor does the perishable inherit the imperishable. Behold! I tell you a mystery. We shall not all sleep, but we shall all be changed, in a moment, in the twinkling of an eye, at the last trumpet. For the trumpet will sound, and the dead will be raised imperishable, and we shall be changed. For this perishable body must put on the imperishable, and this mortal body must put on immortality. When the perishable puts on the imperishable, and the mortal puts on immortality, then shall come to pass the saying that is written:

"Death is swallowed up in victory."

"O death, where is your victory? O death, where is your sting?"

The sting of death is sin, and the power of sin is the law. But thanks be to God, who gives us the victory through our Lord Jesus Christ.

Therefore, my beloved brothers, be steadfast, immovable, always abounding in the work of the Lord, knowing that in the Lord your labor is not in vain.

1 Corinthians 15:51-58 | ESV

August 1

Opening of the 2014 Season of TEXAS

Ron and I, along with the parents of the other young people killed in the car with Andrew, were invited to the Opening Night for the 2014 Season of TEXAS on May 31.

In the days leading up to our trip to Canyon, I became more and more anxious and upset. I was afraid that seeing the show without Andrew would be too hard and that I would forget what he looked like on that stage. I was anxious, afraid, sad, and angry. That morning, I was in my chair in the corner of my room sobbing to the point of vomiting.

I posted on FB that I needed prayer. I shared with the group While We're Waiting how upset I was about going to see the show my son had loved being a part of the past two summers. It was not going to be easy watching the show without Andrew on stage. The folks in this group have all lost children and they understood my thoughts and feelings. They lifted me up in prayer. They wrote encouraging comments on my post.

I shared some of what was going on in my Facebook page as well. Friends showed me love and compassion. They, too, lifted me up in prayer.

I made it through the day and actually enjoyed the evening. Yes, there were tears, but there was joy as well. I learned new stories about my son and saw that his friends were healing and living with joy! We laughed with guys and gals who knew Andrew well and got to see old friends. The evening was healing for me! Praise God!

The day after the show, I spent time reflecting on the previous week. No condemnation. I know I did the best I could. Just hope to do better next time.

What had I done right? What had I done wrong? What would I hope to do differently in the future?

Today I looked back at what I wrote. I need to remind myself of these things as the anniversary approaches.

Here are some of my reflections:

1. I got upset and anxious about the trip to Canyon because I expected it be hard. I was worried about things that might happen, but had not yet happened.

2. I did not pray or practice Philippians 4. I was anxious. I did not go to God. I did not think about things that are true and right and noble and lovely and admirable, etc. I was not choosing to be content in my circumstances. I let my mind go to ugly places.

3. I did ask others to pray, especially once I was in an emotional state where I was not able to help myself. I was transparent and honest about my feelings and fears.

4. I did the hard thing anyway. After my friends had lifted me up and loved me well, I was able to go forth with joy.

5. I would have missed a wonderful tribute to our son and his friends had I not gone. Plus I got to hear wonderful new stories about Andrew and his goofy kindness. And I got to meet more of his friends.

6. Rather than forget the image of his huge smile the last time I saw him dancing, I was reminded of dozens more memories!

7. I have wonderful friends, and I have an amazing husband who loves me well, even in my insecurities and craziness.

Lessons learned: Be a doer of the Word and not a hearer only. Ask for prayer before I am sobbing and vomiting. God often has good things for us on the other side of hard stuff.

I know I will have hard times again. Grief sometimes hits me in the gut when I am not expecting it. I will have times when Andrew's absence will clearly be evident - weddings, holidays, graduations and other family events.

I know, also, that Andrew is in the presence of Christ. I will see him again. He had a great life and brought joy to many. I know that we will continue to heal while cherishing our memories and fun stories of Andrew.

In the future, I hope I do not allow myself to get so upset about upcoming events. I have recently spent time thinking about how to handle the anniversary date. I know there will be tears and sorrow. We have the headstone to finalize and seeing it in place will be both good and hard. I have chosen not to attend some events and have chosen to participate in others. I need to learn what I can handle and what I should avoid. I want God's help and direction in making those decisions.

August 3

What Bereaved Parents Want You to Know (But May Not Say)

People of faith who have lost a child are often seen as brave and strong. We have been through something that no parent wants to experience: the death of a child.

We are not strong or brave. We endure because we must; we have no choice. We have other family members that need us. We have "good works which God prepared in advance for us to do." We have jobs and homes to care for. We cannot just give up, find a hole to crawl in, and quit living -- though we sometimes wish we could.

We are walking through life because that is what we do – we go on. We live. We breathe. We work. And we attend church and school functions because we must. We know that God called our child Home and left us here on earth for His purpose. We know we must persevere and trust Him to help us and to heal us. We do not go on because we are tough or brave or strong. Because the truth is that we are none of those things. We are most often weak, and tired, and broken.

Our reality is often different than what we show our friends, our coworkers, and the public around us.

We rarely show others the true depth of our pain. It is too personal and too raw to show others who have not experienced it themselves; we know that people cannot understand the sorrow of losing a child unless they have walked this path. And we hope and pray that none of our friends ever go through what we have experienced.

The truth is that if someone you love has buried their child, they probably won't be completely open about what they're going through because they're trying so hard to just function and hold it together.

They are trying not to "lose it" in front of you.

We know how uncomfortable our pain is to others. It is a reminder that you, too, could lose a child in an accident or to an illness. It could be your child in the wrong place/wrong time or in the wrong relationship resulting in his or her death. Our pain reminds you that you could someday bury your child.

We know that our pain also makes you feel helpless – there is nothing that you or anyone else can do to change our situation. Our child is gone. We will not see him again until our great reunion in Heaven.

For some, it reminds you that you have also lost a friend, a student or coworker. It brings up your own pain and grief when you see us cry or see the sorrow in our eyes. We don't want to cause you that pain or make you uncomfortable with our grief.

We also don't want to "lose it" because it is so hard to get control once the tears start flowing.

At first, the tears of a bereaved parent are not healing tears. They are tears of a deep, intense sorrow like none other. They are exhausting and embarrassing. We have had friends try to comfort us and tell us it will be okay. It will not be okay! Our child is dead! As time goes on, and if we do the right kinds of soul care to help us heal, the tears change to healing tears. But it takes a long time.

We are afraid, sometimes, that if the tears start, they won't stop. So we try hard not to let them start.

And the tears remind us of that horrible physical grief-pain that lasted so long. We are reminded of waking up to realize this is not some terrible nightmare. It is our reality now. We are bereaved parents.

So we hide our pain.

We smile and laugh and go on living. We thank you when you tell us again how sorry you are and how much you miss our kid. We tell you we are doing well and that God is good.

God is good. He is faithful. He is healing our broken hearts. We do have joy and peace. We do have moments of happiness and fun-filled laughter. We will be healed and go on living. But our life has changed and we will never be quite the same as we were before burying our child.

As a result, bereaved parents aren't completely honest with you. However, if we could be truly honest and vulnerable, we would tell you:

1. **Don't wait for me to call you.** Please call me every once in a while. I know you told me to call if I ever needed anything, but it's hard to call and ask when I am hurting so badly. I don't want to appear weak. Or pathetic. And I don't seem to have the strength to ask anyone to do things

with me. Sometimes just returning a text is too hard. But I need you to keep trying, to keep calling. Call with a specific plan like "can you go to lunch at 11:30 next Tuesday?" not just "let's have lunch sometime."

I *will* get better and want to go with you to that dinner, movie, or play some day. And if I say "no thanks" this time, I need you to ask again. I need you to call me just to chat, even when I may not feel like chatting. I need you to call me to help me remember that the world continues to turn and life goes on and that you want me to be a part of it.

2. **Listen. Really listen.** Please don't assume that because you read my blog or Facebook posts that you know how I feel. I don't even know how I feel sometimes! And I am not completely honest on Facebook; no one is. I may appear to be doing really well based on social media when, in reality, I am struggling. I need friends who are willing to listen to me without correction or platitudes. Listen as I talk about my kid, yet again. I will thank you for taking time to listen to me. I will appreciate your patience and caring enough to listen when I need to talk. And I will try to listen to you when you are in need.

3. **Don't assume my tears are because of grief.** Even though the loss of a child is not something we just get over, grief is not always what is bothering me. I may be having an off day because I feel ill, or because I had a disagreement with my spouse, or because we are having trouble with one of our other children. Don't assume that my issues or prayer requests are always because I buried my son. Ask me. I need you to let me have emotions and experiences that have little or nothing to do with grief. And please don't tell me it's going to be okay. Let me be honest with you about my emotions without trying to fix them.

4. **Don't ask me about how I feel.** That is a very hard question to answer honestly. Some days are good, some are bad. Some moments are good and the next may be terrible. Ask me what I have been doing lately or what plans I have for the upcoming week. Ask me what I am studying or what my kids are doing. Ask me almost anything, but please don't ask me how I feel.

5. **Be patient with me and forgive me when I am rude or short with you.** The death of a child changes one in ways you cannot imagine. And one does not get over it. Not in six months, not in a year, not ever. For some, the grief lasts a very long time. Our child is frequently on our minds. We may forget for a little while, but even small things can remind us that they are gone. If I snap at you, or ignore you, or seem unhappy, please give me some grace. It is most likely not about you at all.

6. **Forgive me if I am not interested in small talk.** Losing a child changes our perspective regarding what is important. We don't seem to care about trivial things anymore. I really do want to listen to you and care about those things that matter to you. But sometimes I just don't see the point of talking about stuff I can't do anything about. My perspective has changed; time is short. I want to care about what the Father cares about. I want to care about and think about eternal things.

7. **Forgive me if I am forgetful.** Grief often causes what is called Grief Brain. If I forget a date or a meeting, forgive me. And know that I am doing my best. If I am supposed to be at something important, you may want to send me a text reminder. I will appreciate the help.

8. **Know that I will forgive you.** Don't avoid me because you don't know what to say. I will try to give you grace when you say hurtful things, because you will. We all do. We don't know what to say around bereaved parents. That's okay. I will be glad you have taken time to be with me and that you tried.

9. **Talk about my child.** And let me talk about him. He was a huge part of my life. He still is. It helps to talk about him. And I love that you have stories to tell me that I did not know! If I begin to tear up, know that you did not cause my pain. My child's death caused my pain. I will pull it together after a few tears or I will excuse myself and find a place for a good cry. It really is healing to know that others care about and miss my child.

10. **Don't talk about my child.** There are times when I just need to talk about something else. I want to hear about your family, your children, your life. I want to talk about that new study I am doing or the trip we have planned.

How do you know whether to talk or not talk about my child? Listen for clues: if I ask you about your family, talk about that. If I am especially quiet, ask if I want to talk about him or ask me what I would like to talk about. (And know that I don't always know what I want.) When at social events, I sometimes just enjoy listening to others talk. Don't try to make me join in; let me have some room to just listen.

11. **Give me time.** Grief does not have a timetable. The loss of child is something I will be dealing with the rest of my life. I know that God is good, faithful, kind, compassionate and loving. I know that He will help me through this. But I need time. Some of us heal quickly, some take longer. Some days the burden is light; other days it is unbearable. Please ask me to participate in activities with you, but understand that when I say no,

it is not about you. It may just be the grief. It may just be too hard for me right then. But please ask again. And again.

12. **Church is particularly difficult**. We may not know why, but we tend to get emotional at church. Even those of us who never cried at church before often cry now. It is not that we are sad in church. It is just that being in worship, singing, and being in His presence bring the emotions to the surface. For us, the reality of Heaven, Hell and life after death is more pronounced. We are often overwhelmed by God's love and greatness. By His omnipotence. By His grace and love that caused Him to send His only Son to die for me. The reality of all of this is so...well, REAL!

If we cry at church, don't try to comfort us and tell us it's going to be okay or that you understand. Just let us cry. Offer a tissue and maybe a gentle hug. Allow us to worship, even through our tears. If a bereaved parent attends church alone, ask if you may sit by her. And just be near. Or better yet, offer to pick her up and let her ride with you. After service, don't make of light our messed up makeup or runny nose. Give us a few moments to pull ourselves together. Again, a gentle hug and an "I love you" or "I'm sorry you are hurting. I miss him, too," goes a long way.

13. **My kids are hurting.** They lost their brother, their friend. They may not show it, but they are hurting. They don't want to be known as "the dead kid's sister" or "the one whose brother died." They are still who they were before with the same interests and talents. They still need to be with friends and enjoy life apart from their grief. They don't want to talk about their sibling or his death and don't want you to bring it up. Except when they want you to talk about him or bring it up. Be patient with them. See items 1-12.

14. **Dads hurt as much as moms, they just don't often show it**. See items 1-12. It seemed that many of my girlfriends checked in with me that first year. They asked how I was doing. Friends called and texted me to let me know they cared. Not as many friends contacted my husband. Maybe guys just don't think it matters. It does. A few close friends do text him regularly even now to just say, "I am thinking about you. How can I pray specifically for you today?" Knowing that godly men were praying for him and knowing that he had friends to call on helped my husband heal.

15. **God is still on the throne.** Though our child has died, we still know that God is God. Or maybe because we have experienced this life-changing event, we believe more strongly in the sovereignty of God. We know we are

not in control; God is. Our faith may be tested, but we choose to believe. And because of our faith, we will be able to go on living.

I would add to this list Choose Life!

One thing I have heard myself saying to my husband recently is that I want to live until I die. I don't want grief to paralyze me. It has changed me, but I don't want it to stop me from living a full and joyful life.

The death of my son has made me realize how precious life is and how it can be gone in a moment. I want my friends to see how precious their children are. I want young people to stop making stupid choices. I want those I love to live a full and Spirit-filled life! I want you to know the Creator and to know that He loves you! Even when ugly things happen - and they will happen - God is beautiful and caring and loving and compassionate and gracious!

So choose Life! Christ said, "I am the Way, and the Truth, and the Life." Choose Christ and all that He is and all that He has to give!

Live well, my friends. Live well.

~~~~~~

August 7

Words

Words I used often last fall:

Bereavement
noun
1. a period of mourning after a loss, especially after the death of a loved one.
2. a state of intense grief, as after the loss of a loved one; desolation.

Bereaved
adjective
1. (of a person) greatly saddened at being deprived by death of a loved one.

Grief

noun
1. keen mental suffering or distress over affliction or loss; sharp sorrow; painful regret.
2. a cause or occasion of keen distress or sorrow.

Synonyms
1. anguish, heartache, woe, misery; sadness, melancholy, moroseness.

Sorrow

noun 1. distress caused by loss, affliction, disappointment, etc.; grief, sadness, or regret.
2. a cause or occasion of grief or regret, as an affliction, a misfortune, or trouble:
3. the expression of grief, sadness, disappointment, or the like: muffled sorrow.

verb (used without object)
4. to feel sorrow; grieve.

Synonyms
1. Sorrow, distress, grief, misery, woe imply bitter suffering, especially as caused by loss or misfortune. Sorrow is the most general term. Grief is keen suffering, especially for a particular reason. Distress implies anxiety, anguish, or acute suffering caused by the pressure of trouble or adversity. Misery suggests such great and unremitting pain or wretchedness of body or mind as crushes the spirit. Woe is deep or inconsolable grief or misery. 2. adversity. 4. mourn, lament.

Cry

verb (used without object), cried, cry•ing.
1. to utter inarticulate sounds, especially of lamentation, grief, or suffering, usually with tears.
2. to weep; shed tears, with or without sound.
3. to call loudly; shout; yell (sometimes followed by out).
4. to demand resolution or strongly indicate a particular disposition.
5. to give forth vocal sounds or characteristic calls, as animals; yelp; bark.
6. (of a hound or pack) to bay continuously and excitedly in following a scent.
7. (of tin) to make a noise, when bent, like the crumpling of paper.

verb (used with object), cried, cry•ing.
8. to utter or pronounce loudly; call out.

9. to announce publicly as for sale; advertise: to cry one's wares.
10. to beg or plead for; implore: to cry mercy.
11. to bring (oneself) to a specified state by weeping.
12. the act or sound of crying; any loud utterance or exclamation; a shout, scream, or wail.
13. clamor; outcry.
14. a fit of weeping: to have a good cry.
15. the utterance or call of an animal.

Synonyms
1. wail, keen, moan. 2. sob, bawl, whimper. 3. yowl, bawl, clamor, vociferate, exclaim, ejaculate, scream. Cry, shout, bellow, roar refer to kinds of loud articulate or inarticulate sounds. Cry is the general word: to cry out. To shout is to raise the voice loudly in uttering words or other articulate sounds: He shouted to his companions. Bellow refers to the loud, deep cry of a bull, moose, etc., or, somewhat in deprecation, to human utterance that suggests such a sound: The speaker bellowed his answer. Roar refers to a deep, hoarse, rumbling or vibrant cry, often of tumultuous volume

Words I find myself using often now:

Healing
adjective
1. curing or curative; prescribed or helping to heal.
2. growing sound; getting well; mending.

Noun
3. the act or process of regaining health: a new drug to accelerate healing.

Heal
verb (used with object)
1. to make healthy, whole, or sound; restore to health; free from ailment.
2. to bring to an end or conclusion, as conflicts between people or groups, usually with the strong implication of restoring former amity; settle; reconcile.
3. to free from evil; cleanse; purify: to heal the soul.

verb (used without object)
4. to effect a cure.
5. (of a wound, broken bone, etc.) to become whole or sound; mend; get well (often followed by up or over).

Synonyms
1. See cure. 2. compose, soothe. 3. purge, disinfect.

Joy
noun
1. the emotion of great delight or happiness caused by something exceptionally good or satisfying; keen pleasure; elation.
2. a source or cause of keen pleasure or delight; something or someone greatly valued or appreciated.
3. the expression or display of glad feeling; festive gaiety.
4. a state of happiness or felicity.
verb (used without object)
5. to feel joy; be glad; rejoice.

Laugh
verb (used without object)
1. to express mirth, pleasure, derision, or nervousness with an audible, vocal expulsion of air from the lungs that can range from a loud burst of sound to a series of quiet chuckles and is usually accompanied by characteristic facial and bodily movements.
2. to experience the emotion so expressed. 3. to produce a sound resembling human laughter.

Peace
1. cessation of or freedom from any strife or dissension.
2. freedom of the mind from annoyance, distraction, anxiety, an obsession, etc.; tranquility; serenity.
3. a state of tranquility or serenity.
4. a state or condition conducive to, proceeding from, or characterized by tranquility. 5. silence; stillness.

Gratitude
noun the quality or feeling of being grateful or thankful.

Thank you, Lord, for healing my broken heart and helping me to have joy, peace, and laughter. Amen

Note: Definitions from http://dictionary.reference.com/

August 8

It was one year ago today that Evelyn (Andrew's grandmother) and I drove to Canyon to see TEXAS Musical Drama. He LOVED that show and LOVED the people in it. He LOVED dancing.

I miss him every day.

Today we are one day closer to the great reunion in Heaven.

Twice in the last week I have started tearing up just as I got in bed. I was fine all day long, then weepy at bedtime.

I told Ron, "I'm sorry I started this just as we go to bed."

His response: Perhaps it's because this is a safe place for you to cry.

I am so blessed to have this man as my husband. He loves me well. And holds me when I cry.

~~~~~~

August 9

We went to the burial service for Ramon Estes today. Ron's uncle. He was a great man, a godly man. He is loved and missed. I was glad to see his kids and grandsons.

One year ago today was the last time I hugged my Andrew son. I took him to breakfast and then shopping to fill his fridge in Canyon.

A few more days and all the Firsts will be over...

Until the first day I spend in the presence of Christ. Until that first time I get to look at Him face-to-face. Until that first moment in Eternity. What a great day that will be!

But for now, I have good works which God prepared in advance for me to do.

Lord,

Thank you for letting me be my kids' mom and Ron's wife. Thanks for my life; I love it! Help me to honor my family and glorify You as I live each new day.

Amen

August 9

Shame on the Road to a Place Called Healing

There is shame on my road to Healing. May I tell you why?

Without While We're Waiting my road to Healing would have been like driving my old tractor across the deserts of the Southwest: hot, dry, and ugly at times. With knobby tires and no shock absorbers, I would have bounced all over the road and felt beaten at the end of each day. I may have gotten to the end of the journey - a place called Healing - but it would have been a long, hard trip. I might even still be in the middle of the desert right now, in fact.

Instead, I have arrived at Healing. I arrived long ago.

With my new friends from While We're Waiting, it has been a fairly smooth trip with but a few potholes and side roads along the way. Even in potholes and on side roads, friends from While We're Waiting were there to lift me up in prayer, encourage me, and show me the way to Healing. It has been like being in my SUV with comfort seats that adjust, lumbar support, and a GPS to point the way. My friends from While We're Waiting have been there to share the journey, sing with me, chat with me, and be silent with me. They even helped with the burden of driving. They spent time with me at rest stops. They made my journey more pleasant. I arrived more quickly than I would have if I had traveled alone. And they helped me arrive with fewer struggles.

So why haven't I shared While We're Waiting with the parents of the other four? There were five young people killed on August 12, 2013. Five friends. Five lives cut short. Five whose parents are grieving. What about the parents of the other four? Why have I not told them about While We're Waiting?

I was selfish. While We're Waiting was MINE! It was MY grief journey, MY safe place. I was angry that my son was with their children in that car on that night on that road. I was afraid to be honest where they could see my raw, broken heart. I did not want to share this wonderful thing with them.

A friend shared While We're Waiting with me last fall because it had helped her arrive in Healing after the death of her son. I should have shared it with the parents of the other four. I was wrong to have not invited them before now. I am sorry. I am ashamed. I should have invited them to join the Facebook group long ago. I should have told them about the parents' retreats. I am ashamed that I did not.

They are each on their own road to Healing and traveling their own ways, the parents of the other four. I pray that they have peace and joy. I pray that they each arrive at Healing.

God is gracious and He will help them to Healing whether I invite to While We're Waiting or not. God desires to heal their hearts, as He did mine, in His way and in His timing. They may not even want to join the Facebook page or participate in support group meetings. But I should have invited them. It may have made their journey a bit smoother, a bit easier, and a bit less lonely.

I should have looked outside my own grief. I should have looked to help the others on the road to Healing. I should have cared more and helped them along the way.

We became bereaved parents at the same moment, in the same Accident. Our kids were friends. I am sorry I did not love the parents of the other four better.

I've changed that, starting today. I introduced them all to While We're Waiting. And I prayed for them. I will continue to pray for them.

~~~~~~

August 10

Please pray for us and our friends Henry and Debbie Harrison, June Bush, Kimberly Starz, Victor Starz, and Gabe and Julie Diaz as we all remember our kids over the next few days. Julian, Clint, Amanda, Eric and Andrew died too soon for our liking. We miss them all.

And please pray for Timothy Johnson and the other 12 Second Warriors as they remember their friends and that horrible night almost one year ago.

The next few days may be hard for all of us, we can know healing and joy through Jesus Christ. Pray He is very present for each of us.

Thank you.

August 12

12 things I am thankful for on the 12th

1. Truth -- and that God gave it to us in written form so we can study it and understand it and live it.
2. Friends who have loved me well in the midst of my journey.
3. Evelyn, my dad's widow. She has been one of my best friends. And I miss her dearly. I think I need a road trip to Denver to spend time with her.
4. Precept Ministries and all that I have learned through their studies. Plus I have made some awesome new friends while there for summer and fall study programs!
5. Rain. I love flowers and trees and trickling streams and the smell after rain has fallen.
6. Jelly beans. Except the black ones. I don't like the black ones. That's why I like Walgreen's brand: no black ones. Black jelly beans are gross. I am not thankful for black jelly beans.
7. Rotisserie Chicken.
8. Socks. I love cute socks!
9. My kids' friends. I love having them come over. Seems like as my kids grow up and move away, so do their friends. I miss the loud noise of big parties.
10. Beautiful music. All kinds.
11. The privilege of home schooling.
12. The Comforter (John 16:7-15).

What are you thankful for?

August 13

After looking at all the pictures people have posted today...So does anyone have a picture of Andrew WITHOUT a beautiful woman in the picture??

Answer: There are a few, but they were taken *by* beautiful women.

I grateful for all the beautiful friends my son had.

August 13

365 DAYS
a poem of grief and healing

It was 365 days ago today that our world changed.

It seems like yesterday
It seems like forever

On that morning 365 days ago,

We went from sleeping peacefully
To a loud knocking at the door

From letting the cop come in
To wishing we could make it all go away

From disbelief of what he had just told us
To facing the reality of our son's death

From wanting it all to not be true
To praying that His glory and truth may be revealed

In these 365 days,

I have gone from numb and shocked
To learning we will go forth with joy and strength

From learning my son is dead
To knowing our son is alive in His presence

From asking God to help me survive
To thanking Him for helping us thrive

From wondering how can I face tomorrow
To rejoicing that we have lived well today

365 days since The Accident

365 days of grieving for him
and receiving grace from Him

365 day of missing him
and trusting Him

365 days of living without him
and knowing we cannot live without Him

365 days of our broken hearts hurting for him
and being miraculously healed by Him

365 days of remembering him
and learning more how to follow Him

365 days of choosing gratitude for the time spent with him
and choosing to go onward and to live for Him

365 days

365 days that Andrew has been in His presence

365 days that we are closer to the great reunion in Heaven

365 days

365 days that began with a death
but have taught us LIFE!

August 17

Rough weekend. Pain makes functioning hard. Physical and emotional pain. Sleeping is even harder. My shoulder is really messed up. Even after more than three months of PT and regular massage therapy. It is now officially not only rotator cuff junk, but full-blown case of a Frozen Shoulder. Surgery scheduled for September 8.

~~~~~~

August 18

Romans 8:28-39 in Action

How we look at things matters.

I am completely in awe of how over the past year our Heavenly Father has brought so much good out of something so ugly. What follows is from a Facebook post my nineteen-year-old son Peter wrote on August 12, 2014. He was looking back on the year since his big brother's death. He has gained a new perspective on life and tragedy over these twelve months. (He gave me permission to share this.)

Peter's is only one of many such stories - God has used The Accident to change lives, bring home many who were lost, and cause addicts to realize they could break free from their addiction. Families have been reunited. Parents say, "I love you" to their kids more. Young and old who thought they could never handle such a thing have become stronger through their pain at losing their friends. I praise Him for the changes I see in my son and in others.

Peter wrote:

> "On this, the anniversary of my brother's death in the TEXAS tragedy, I share how his death brought me renewed life.
>
> In the months leading up to his death, I was battling severe depression and anxiety among other things. I was, to be a frank, in a very bad, scary place. His death was like a shock jolting me awake from a horrible nightmare. Waking up to my mother's cries gave a sudden realization of the frailty of life. In the week that followed, my self-image went from worthless, broken, and annoying to loved, appreciated, and strong under the overflowing love from family and friends.

A few weeks later I was invited to join to MSU cheer squad. With the frailty and uncertainty of life fresh on my mind I decided to follow my dreams like my brother Andrew had. Cheer has instilled a confidence and diligence I had lacked for years.

Despite the great sorrow of his death, through it I gained the courage, the love, and the peace that enabled me to be who I am and where I am today. I would give the world to have my brother back, but the life and love beautifully displayed through his death have created for me a good world from a horrible one.

I love you Andrew. Thanks for everything. I'll see you soon."

This is scripture being lived out before my eyes:

And we know that in all things God works for the good of those who love him, who have been called according to his purpose. For those God foreknew he also predestined to be conformed to the likeness of his Son, that he might be the firstborn among many brothers. And those he predestined, he also called; those he called, he also justified; those he justified, he also glorified.

What, then, shall we say in response to this? If God is for us, who can be against us? He who did not spare his own Son, but gave him up for us all--how will he not also, along with him, graciously give us all things? Who will bring any charge against those whom God has chosen? It is God who justifies. Who is he that condemns? Christ Jesus, who died--more than that, who was raised to life--is at the right hand of God and is also interceding for us. Who shall separate us from the love of Christ? Shall trouble or hardship or persecution or famine or nakedness or danger or sword? As it is written:

"For your sake we face death all day long; we are considered as sheep to be slaughtered."

No, in all these things we are more than conquerors through him who loved us. For I am convinced that neither death nor life, neither angels nor demons, neither the present nor the future, nor any powers, neither height nor depth, nor anything else in all creation, will be able to separate us from the love of God that is in Christ Jesus our Lord.

Romans 8:28-39 |ESV

August 19

God Did Not Need My Son in Heaven More Than I Needed Him...

At a church social Sunday night, a kind man tried to comfort me about Andrew's death. He knew that this past week was the anniversary of The Accident and knew that those special days can be hard. He was trying to be kind.

I suppose it seemed odd to him that we can mention our children, including Andrew without tears or sorrow showing on our faces. We can go to parties and laugh and have fun even though our son is dead. (Hint: He is not dead but living in Heaven!)

God has healed my heart. And we love to laugh! Our kids - all of them - have given us great joy and great stories over the years. When talking about my kids I often smile. I love them bunches.

After asking what had happened, how Andrew had died, he said, "Well, God needed him in Heaven more than you needed him on earth."

NO! Just NO!! God is God all by Himself. He does not *need* anything! He did not *need* Andrew in Heaven!

God does want fellowship with us. He desires that all would serve Him. He loves us and wants to be with us, but He does not *need* us.

For those who think that maybe Andrew and the others died so that one more person could come to know Christ - Please know that the only person that had to die so someone could be saved is Jesus Christ, who went like a lamb to the slaughter. He willingly gave His life so that we could know God and have relationship with Him. Because of Christ's death, my son has eternal life in Heaven.

For God to kill my son so that someone else could be saved, it would have been human sacrifice, child sacrifice -- My child being sacrificed for someone else to gain salvation.

God does not want child sacrifice! I found a great article on the subject of child sacrifice[1] along with a list of scriptures[2]. (I have shared the links at the end of this essay). God does not take one child so that another person can be saved, get their life in order, or gain freedom from addiction.

God may bring good things out of ugly stuff, and He promises to do just that. His Word says that He works all things together for the good of those who love Him and are called according to His purposes. But I do not believe that God killed my son for the good of another person. (I don't know why Andrew died, other than physics and that we live in a broken, fallen world.) I believe that every death goes through His hands, His filter. He will use things that happen in this broken, fallen world for our good and His glory. But He did not take Andrew so that someone else could be saved.

Another time someone said, "God needed another angel in Heaven." Again NO!! Andrew was not an angel on earth; he did not become an angel when he went to Heaven. He did not get wings. He is not an angel.

Folks refer to the five killed in The Accident as the TEXAS Angels. I think this is sweet; they were all kind, talented young people. But it is not an accurate theological statement; they are not now angels. They are still humans, created in the image of God.

Andrew was and is a Child of the King. A man made righteous through the blood of Christ. A joint heir with Christ. A member of God's household built on the foundation of the apostles and prophets with Christ Jesus as the chief cornerstone.

Angels are created beings. OpenBible.info has a long list of verses that reference angels[3]. None of them mention a human becoming an angel or angel becoming human. If God did need another angel, he could have spoken a word and one would be created. He did not kill my son so He could have another angel.

So, please, please, please do not tell me that God killed my son so that someone else could get saved at his memorial service. Or because He needed him in Heaven. Or that He needed another angel.

When I meet you, and you feel a need to acknowledge our loss, it would be best to stick with simply saying something like, "I am so sorry. I would love to have known your son." or "That must have been painful to walk through. Is there something we can do now to help?" or simply "I am sorry."

Please do not try to comfort me with reasons why this accident happened. It happened. Period. I will not understand "Why?" here on earth. Your attempts at explaining the secrets things of God do not comfort me. They often frustrate me and make me want to correct your theology.

I know of a wonderful study published by Precept Ministries on Heaven, Hell and Life After Death[4]. If you want to truly understand want happens when one dies, get this study and work through it. It takes about 6-8 hours. It is a great resource for a small group or Sunday school class.

God's ways are not our ways. His thoughts are not our thoughts. The secret things belong to God. We will not understand all that He does on earth; however, I know He is loving, compassionate, just, wise, gracious, slow to anger, abounding in love, and full of mercy. He uses junk to make beautiful things. He can and will use The Accident for our good and His glory. He promises in His Word that He will do so.

But seeing good things come out of The Accident, does not mean that we can understand the why's of our child's death.

Notes:
1. http://dtthornton.com/2012/01/16/does-god-want-me-to-sacrifice-my-child-important-bible-study-principles/
2. http://www.openbible.info/topics/child_sacrifice
3. http://www.openbible.info/topics/angels
4. www.precept.org

~~~~~~

August 23

I am missing this guy [Andrew] beyond belief today. He always made me feel like a great mom. He brought joy into my life. I'm so glad I got to be the one he called momma.

~~~~~~

August 24

Thank you all for your kind comments yesterday. I knew you'd encourage me. I'm going to take some pain meds for my shoulder and go to sleep.

His mercies are new every morning!

Chapter Six

Healing Continues,

So Does Grief

August 25

First Day of School...

Facebook is covered with pictures of students going back to school.

My son is not going back to college this year. For the second year, he will be spending fall semester in Heaven.

Had he lived, he would be finishing his accounting degree at West Texas A&M University in Canyon, Texas, possibly with honors. He was on the honor roll. He would be graduating in December. He would then continue with classes for another year to complete his BA in dance. He was a great student. A prince of a student. A prince of a guy.

Andrew loved both accounting and dance. Accounting was not a fallback for him. He knew that every dance company and theater company needs a business manager. With his accounting degree, additional business classes and theater/dance experience, he would be perfect for the job. While working to continue in his performance career, he could earn money and help the company as the business manager. He also knew that he could only dance for so long and then would need another career. Again, he could continue to be a part of the industry with the business degree and experience.

Am I sad that he is not at WT this semester? Of course! It cuts through me in ways I cannot express. But I know he is in the presence of Christ! And his completing the degrees is no longer in the plan.

Was it ever in God's plan? I don't know. I cannot speak to that. Some parts of theology elude me. I am not sure what *was* God's Plan.

But I know that God was not surprised by what happened. He did not look down from Heaven and stare in shock at The Accident site.

> **For you created my inmost being; you knit me together in my mother's womb. I praise you because I am fearfully and wonderfully made; your works are wonderful, I know that full well. My frame was not hidden from you when I was made in the secret place, when I was woven together in the depths of the earth. Your eyes saw my unformed body; all the days ordained for me were written in your book before one of them came to be.**
>
> Psalms 139:13-16 | NIV

I choose to believe. I choose to trust God. I choose to believe and trust God because of what He wrote in His Word. I cling to His Word. God knew about The Accident before it happened. He could have stopped it, but He did not. I trust Him. I trust that He loves me, loves Andrew, and loves our whole family. I trust that He will work even this out for my good because I love Him and am called according to His purposes.

And I choose to rejoice in my boys starting OU last week - one on the rugby team; one on the cheer squad, both studying mechanic engineering. I choose to rejoice that Lyz is starting her first day teaching preschool. She is an awesome teacher. I choose to rejoice that Adam is starting a new semester of coaching gymnastics at Twistars. I choose to rejoice that Margaret is staying home this semester and taking time off from school. I choose to rejoice that Meredith is able to stay home and homeschool my grandsons. I thank God for her amazing husband Mark.

But...The pictures of others people's sons going to school today cut my heart and make me sad. The pictures of Andrew's friends heading back to class........ I choose to stay off Facebook today, the first day back to school.

~~~~~~

August 31

Friends of Andrew Raymond Duncan and friends of our family:

The headstone is finally set. The front is a traditional headstone design and the back tells his story. We prayed to honor Andrew's life and who he was with this strong black granite stone.

PS. There is a Batman symbol.

~~~~~~

September 5

Today we begin our While We're Waiting Weekend for Bereaved Parents. Ron and I are hosting at our home. Five couples who lost children plus the two couples who founded WWW. Please pray that it will not only be a weekend of healing for hurting families, but that we will glorify God in what we say and do.

The Ron and I head to Arlington Sunday night for my shoulder surgery on Monday.

September 12

12 Things I am Thankful for on the 12th

1. My husband who reminds me to take my pain meds and loves me even when pain makes me grumpy. And gives me rides when I am too loopy to drive myself.

2. Amazing medical care and great insurance that allowed me to have shoulder repair done this week.

3. That I have two arms, even if one is not working properly right now.

4. The ability to read. I love to read!

5. Literary classics

6. Friends willing to help after surgery

7. VCR and Blu-Ray movies

8. Colored pencils

9. My comfortable bed

10. Fall - I love fall decorations and the smells of fall

11. Facebook friends. Many I have not met, and may not meet until we reach Heaven. But they encourage me, pray for me, and understand my grief.

12. Peter - my 20 year old. I am so glad he is at OU and studying engineering while being on the cheer quad. He makes me proud. His birthday was yesterday.

What are you thankful for?

September 15

Why My Husband Loves Me

Today we celebrate thirty-one years of marriage. May I tell you story from about sixteen years ago?

I was having a horrible week -- yelling at our kids, impatient with everyone, being hateful to Ron, I broke the glass on the coffee table by slamming something down in it hard. It was ugly! I asked Ron why he loved me: "I am so horrible and unlovable - why would you even love me?"

His answer: "Because I said I would." It is the most romantic thing he has ever said to me!

I'm not sure I liked that answer at the time. He did not say I was beautiful or smart or kind or sexy. Because, right then, I wasn't any of those things. It would have been nice if he'd lied to me just a bit. Instead, he loved me honestly. He spoke the truth in love.

In time I realized that his answer to my question was the most wonderful thing he could ever say. He kept his promise to love me through better or worse, in sickness and in health, in richer or poorer. He did not rely on his feelings or hormones (mine or his) to determine his behavior towards me.

Ladies, that is real love: a decision and promise kept.

Over the past year my husband has loved me well. He has held me when I cried and encouraged me to get outside and ride bikes or walk when I wanted to sit and sob. He has spoken truth to me, and he has helped me see when I was listening to lies. He dealt with things no father or husband ever wants to deal with. He has carried his grief and helped me carry mine. He has helped me heal while acknowledging our shared pain.

Again, through better or worse, in sickness and in health, for richer or poorer. Ron has kept his promise to love me for thirty-one years: A promise based on a decision, not on feelings of lust or joy or admiration or need or of being in love.

We have loved each other through great times and hard times; when we had more than enough and when we did not know how we would pay the bills; when one of us was ill and when we were riding bikes and doing triathlons. Our love has not been perfect, but it is real and it is constant. And it is centered on the One who is Perfect. It has been for thirty-one years. I look forward to another thirty-one.

September 16

What Parents With a Baby in Heaven Want You to Know (But May Not Say)

This article addresses some issues which are specific to those who have lost a baby to miscarriage or stillbirth and those whose baby died shortly after birth, possibly due to premature birth or other health issues. Each baby is unique. Each loss is unique. Each person's grief is unique. But all these parents have experienced a special kind of loss.

Many of these parents do not have pictures of their baby - she was born straight into the arms of Jesus before any pictures could be taken. Their baby may not have even had a name; they never knew its gender.

Others have pictures they do not share - their child was born "asleep" and the pictures are not sweet to anyone else but his parents.

Some have only a few pictures, and they would love for you to ooh and ahh over them!

Still others have a lock of hair, footprints, and a few precious tiny outfits that were never worn.

For some, their memories are of the excitement of finding out they were expecting, followed only by the grief of knowing loss.

Some have fond memories of feeling their little one kick and move...and then stillness. Just stillness. And then the pain of loss.

Some did not even know they were expecting until they learned there would be no sweet baby to hold this time.

For some, there were the joys of a full-term baby, only to learn that their baby will not go home and learn to crawl, walk, talk or ride a bike. Because she did not live past birth.

Some got to hold their child and enjoy her for but a few hours or days. She stayed in the hospital her entire life battling to just to breathe. And then they buried her.

However long their baby lived, that life is precious to its parents. They are grieving the loss of a child. Some parents have two or three or more babies in Heaven. Each was precious. Each is missed. Each parent grieves in his unique way. They need you to understand some things about their loss, their grief, and their healing. Although not all of these apply to every parent, it is helpful for you to understand them.

If you took time to listen - to really listen - without judgement or platitudes or advice, this is what bereaved parents of infants might say to you.

1. **Though my child lived for a short time, she is real.** She lived. She lives now in Heaven. I am a parent. You may have a child who lives in Toledo; mine lives in Heaven.

2. **Please do not tell me I will have other children.** Only God knows if I will ever have another child. And by saying that, you have just brought up one of my biggest fears: that I will never have another child. In addition, you have minimized the value of this child! She is valuable to me and to her dad. And to God. And please don't ask me if we plan to "try again." I am still healing from this loss. When, and if, we decide to try again, it will be a private decision between us and God.

3. **Please don't tell me it was the will of God, or she's in a better a place, or it was for the best.** I know that the Lord gives and the Lord takes away. I know that Heaven is a beautiful place. I know that God knows what is best for me and for my child. But none of that helps me right now. And you saying it only hurts me. And it may just make me angry with you, adding to my burden because now I have to forgive you and deal with anger on top of my grief.

4. **And please don't tell me that God needed another angel in Heaven.** Statements like this do not help me. The God I serve does not need anything. He is God all by Himself. He is kind and loving and gracious and compassionate and wise. He would not take my baby because He needed another angel. He created my child. He wove her together in my womb, and He knew every one of her days before one of them came to be. I don't know why my child died. But I know that He created her and He loves her, and right now, that has to be enough.

5. **If you must speak, tell me you are sorry for our pain and that you love us.** Tell us that you will pray for us. And ask us what we need; ask how you can help us today.

6. **I may not have pictures of him, but I knew him.** I had dreams of what he would look like, how he would feel in my arms, and of caring for

him. I talked to him and thought about him as he moved in my womb. I knew him -- and I loved him. I still love him.

7. **His daddy loves him, too**. My husband is hurting. He had dreams of being a daddy to our baby. Plus he has seen his wife go through a physically difficult event. He is hurting over the loss of our child, and he is hurting because he loves me and sees me hurting. I am hurting to see him hurting. We are both hurting. We need healing. Please pray for us both.

8. **How we memorialize our baby and honor her life is our choice.** Please don't tell me it is foolish to spend all that money on burying my child. Or that I should have had a ceremony when we chose not to. This is our child, our grief, our decision. Our family is doing what we need to do to heal. If we invite you to a memorial, please come! We want you there to celebrate our child's life and to mourn with us. If we have private ceremony, please do not be offended. We needed to be alone with her just one more time. If we do not have a service, that was our decision to make.

9. **Our other children are hurting and need time to grieve.** Please be considerate of what you say to them. If you would not say it to me, don't say it to them. If you are not willing to ask me, don't ask them. They were excited about the new baby. They may have questions - answer them if you must, but we prefer that you direct them to talk us about this loss. If our children are young, they may not understand much; please don't try to explain things to them - that is our job. If our children are older, they understand more, and hurt more because they understand more.

10. **I need time to heal physically**. Even if I do not recognize it, my body needs time to heal. Not only have I been through a difficult physical event, I am exhausted from grief. I find it hard to clean, or cook or do laundry. I am tired. Please allow me to heal physically. Don't expect me back at my volunteer position at church right away or out on the jogging track. Let me have time to heal.

11. **Your offer of a meal is appreciated.** But please don't plan on staying and chatting when you drop off dinner next Tuesday. If I ask you in, please stay for just a little while. I am not up to chatting or putting on a happy face. Not yet. And don't be offended if I don't come to the door, I may be resting. Or crying. Other ways you could love us include cleaning, rides to doctor appointments, groceries and hand written cards. My family appreciates that you care enough to help us during our time of grief.

12. **Please don't tell me your horror miscarriage story!** I am sorry that you, too, know the pain of loss. But your horror story does not help

me. Maybe someday, when I have time to mourn my child and time for my heart to heal, we can find time to get together. It may be helpful to me to hear your story of loss and healing. But it will not be helpful for me to hear horror stories. Ever.

13. **I am glad for you that you are having a baby**. But your pregnancy reminds me of my loss. If I don't come to your shower, please don't take it personally. I am hurting still. I don't want to cry and take away from your joy. I am so glad you invited me, but I need more time.

14. **I rejoice with you in the birth of your happy, healthy baby**. But my arms are empty. And holding your child only makes it worse. Please don't offer for me to hold him in front of others. Could we find a time alone, in a safe place for me to meet your child? Some place where I can cry while rejoicing with you over how perfect his little toes are? I really am healing. I want to celebrate with you. I just can't do it publicly, not yet anyway.

15. **Each of us grieves in our own way**. For some, this is a huge life-altering event. They may take a long to heal from their grief. Others heal more quickly. Please let me grieve my way, even if it is different than the way you grieved - even if it is different than you expected.

Not all of these will apply to every bereaved parent. Ask me what I need. And know that I will heal. I will be happy again. Someday. With God's help.

Thank you for allowing us to grieve in the best way we know how. Thank you for loving us in our grief. Thank you for praying for us as we heal. Thank you for acknowledging that our baby lived and that we are grieving his death.

September 17

May I challenge you to memorize Psalms 103?

This is one of the Psalms I learned years ago. It brings me great comfort when I doubt who God is or what He has done for me. It talks of His compassion and mercy. His love and forgiveness. How He does not give us what we deserve but instead gives us His love!

Oh! And if anyone needs me, I'm sitting in the massage chair at Nail Retreat. They worked my legs and feet over so that they are too relaxed to move. I'm staying here the rest of the day reading.

Can someone bring me a Sonic grape slush?

Bless the LORD, O my soul, and all that is within me,
　　bless his holy name!
Bless the LORD, O my soul, and forget not all his benefits,
　who forgives all your iniquity, who heals all your diseases,
　who redeems your life from the pit,
　　who crowns you with steadfast love and mercy,
　who satisfies you with good
　　so that your youth is renewed like the eagle's.
The LORD works righteousness
　　and justice for all who are oppressed.
He made known his ways to Moses,
　　his acts to the people of Israel.
The LORD is merciful and gracious,
　　slow to anger and abounding in steadfast love.
He will not always chide,
　　nor will he keep his anger forever.
He does not deal with us according to our sins,
　　nor repay us according to our iniquities.
For as high as the heavens are above the earth,
　　so great is his steadfast love toward those who fear him;
as far as the east is from the west,
　　so far does he remove our transgressions from us.
As a father shows compassion to his children,
　　so the LORD shows compassion to those who fear him.

Psalm 103:1-13 | ESV

September 18

Do NOT Listen to the Father of Lies

For those of us who have experienced the death of a child, the enemy often tries to convince us that our child is LOST - gone forever, dead, unworthy, unsaved, and never to be found again.

He tries to convince us that "if they were not perfect, if they did not leave a box of journals filled with godly prayers and confession, if they were not leaders in their church, if they dabbled in drugs or suffered addition, if they failed in any area...then they are in fact LOST! God did not love them. He did not welcome them into His presence. They are LOST!"

Yes, the enemy will lie to us. And he is good at it. He will tell you your child is LOST. He knows what to whisper into the ears of a grieving mother. He knows how to humiliate a grieving father. He is the father of lies. He has had eons of practice.

But the Bible tells us that those who call on the Name of the Lord shall be saved. (Acts 2:21)

We cannot listen to the father of lies, for he only speaks lies and there is no truth in him. (John 8:42-44)

Instead, hold on to the truth - the truth found in His Word. Study the Word and learn what it says about eternal life and salvation by grace.

The truth is that God is merciful, loving, kind. Compassionate and gracious, slow to anger abounding in love. He does not treat us (or our children) as our sins deserve or repay us (or our children) according to our iniquities. For as far as the Heavens are above the earth, so great is His love for those who fear him. As far as the east is from the west, so far has He removed our transgressions from us. (Psalms 103).

Many of us who have buried our son or daughter must hold fast to the knowledge that our child had, in fact, made a profession of faith in some point in their life -- maybe when they were young, maybe as a teen, maybe in the moments just before death. No matter when they came to life in Christ, if they have trusted Christ, confessed Him as Lord, called on the Name of The Lord, then they are saved. They have been given the gift of eternal life. And their death does not change that.

At the point when they believed the Gospel of their salvation, they were marked in Him with a seal, the promised the Holy Spirit, a deposit guaranteeing their inheritance until the redemption of those who are God's possession. (Ephesians 1).

Our child was marked as a Child of God when they believed, even if they were not acting like it in the months or days leading up to their death. As a Child of God, the moment they died on earth, they immediately found themselves in the presence of Christ -- In the presence of a living, compassionate, gracious, merciful, and loving Christ!

Our child's salvation - his eternal life - is not dependent on him or his behavior. It is a gift of God's grace.

> but God shows his love for us in that while we were still sinners, Christ died for us. ⁹ Since, therefore, we have now been justified by his blood, much more shall we be saved by him from the wrath of God. ¹⁰ For if while we were enemies we were reconciled to God by the death of his Son, much more, now that we are reconciled, shall we be saved by his life.
>
> Romans 5:8-10 | ESV

> Because, if you confess with your mouth that Jesus is Lord and believe in your heart that God raised him from the dead, you will be saved.
> Romans 10:9 | ESV

> "For God so loved the world, that he gave his only Son, that whoever believes in him should not perish but have eternal life. For God did not send his Son into the world to condemn the world, but in order that the world might be saved through him."
> John 3:16-17 | ESV

> For the Scripture says, "Everyone who believes in him will not be put to shame." For there is no distinction between Jew and Greek; for the same Lord is Lord of all, bestowing his riches on all who call on him. For "everyone who calls on the name of the Lord will be saved."
> Romans 10:11-13 | ESV

> If we confess our sins, he is faithful and just to forgive us our sins and to cleanse us from all unrighteousness.
> 1 John 1:9 | ESV

> **The Lord is not slow to fulfill his promise as some count slowness, but is patient toward you, not wishing that any should perish, but that all should reach repentance.**
>
> 2 Peter 3:9 | ESV

> **For the wages of sin is death, but the free gift of God is eternal life in Christ Jesus our Lord.** Romans 6:23 | ESV

He does not let go of those He has chosen. Even when we try to run from Him.

> **"My sheep hear my voice, and I know them, and they follow me. I give them eternal life, and they will never perish, and no one will snatch them out of my hand. My Father, who has given them to me, is greater than all, and no one is able to snatch them out of the Father's hand. I and the Father are one."** John 10:27-30 | ESV

> **For those whom he foreknew he also predestined to be conformed to the image of his Son, in order that he might be the firstborn among many brothers. And those whom he predestined he also called, and those whom he called he also justified, and those whom he justified he also glorified.**
>
> Romans 8:29-30 | ESV

> **But in all these things we overwhelmingly conquer through Him who loved us. For I am convinced that neither death, nor life, nor angels, nor principalities, nor things present, nor things to come, nor powers, nor height, nor depth, nor any other created thing, shall be able to separate us from the love of God, which is in Christ Jesus our Lord.**
>
> Romans 8:37-39 | ESV

There are so many scriptures that teach us about eternal life for believers! Learn what the Bible says about eternal life! And hold fast to the joyful memories of your child! Remember the laughter, the smiles, and the happy times. Choose what and who you will believe today. Look forward to the Great Reunion in Heaven someday when we will see Christ face-to-face. And hang on to the hope that you will see your child again.

How then shall we live while we wait? Let us live well, my friend.

For all grieving parents, I pray today that you are able to submit to the truth of God, resist the devil and he will flee from you (James 4:7). I pray also that God will make His truth real to you today ... so real that you are unable to hear the lies of the enemy. Amen

September 19

Maybe you've heard people say, "You don't want to become so Heavenly-minded that you're of no earthly good."

But I like what Mark Buchanan says in his book, "Things Unseen"...

"Heavenly-mindedness is sanity. It is the best regimen for keeping our hearts whole, our minds clear. It allows us to enjoy earth's pleasures without debauchery. It allows us to endure life's agonies without despair. It allows us to see things from the widest possible perspective and in the truest possible proportions. If anything can give us a true scale of values -- one that enables us to sort out the disposable from the precious, the trinkets from the treasures, the surface from the substance -- Heavenly-mindedness can."

And C. S. Lewis said,

"If you read history, you will find that the Christians who did the most for the present world were just those who thought most of the next. The apostles themselves, who set on foot the conversion of the Roman Empire, the great men who built up the Middle Ages, the English evangelicals who abolished the slave trade, all left their mark on earth, precisely because their minds were occupied with Heaven. It is since Christians have largely ceased to think of the other world that they have become so ineffective in this."

I think I'll set my mind on Heaven today.

~~~~~~

September 21

Heading to bed early tonight. Not much sleep last night. And I cried all through church. I am so much more emotional at church than before Andrew died. Especially true when I am tired.

Peace out.

How to Deal With Family Who May Want You to "Get Over It"

Some of the bereaved parents I know have had difficulty dealing with family members who say hurtful things or may tell them they should "be over it by now." They feel so alone when others seem to not understand how grief affects a person.

I am grateful that I have not had to deal with much of that lately; our friends and family have been wonderful. They are patient and kind. Many of them try to understand our grief even if they cannot truly know what it is like unless they, too, have experienced the death of a child. I appreciate the love they have shown us. It has helped me heal.

Unfortunately, I know this is not the case for every bereaved parent. Friends and family can say hurtful things. They want us to get over it already. They are tired of our sadness. They truly care and want us to be happy. They simply do not understand that the death of a child changes one forever. It is like they cannot see clearly our pain or what we need time and God to heal. They cannot understand that it takes time to heal a broken heart.

We may be trusting God. Our faith may be stronger than ever. We may be praying and studying the Word more than we did before. But that does not mean we are not still hurting or that we won't burst into tears at odd moments. Part of us will grieve until we reach Heaven, and that can be difficult for others to understand. They can say hurtful things while sincerely trying to be helpful.

For those still struggling with grief and who have had others say hurtful things, maybe these words will help you in dealing with family and friends while grieving.

We all struggle. All of us bereaved parents. Whether your child died a week ago or ten years ago, grief is very real and hits you in the gut sometimes. It seems so unnatural to bury our children. And when family or friends say unkind things, even with the best of intentions, it hurts. It is easy to take offense at the words of others.

Please remember that we are not the first, nor will we be the last, to bury our child. We can learn from how others walked this path. We can try to grieve well. We have Biblical examples of how others grieved; let us learn from them.

The first parent to face the death of a child was Eve. She had two sons. And one son killed her other son. That momma was experiencing some very real pain and grief. Talk about family issues! They had issues that could lead to blaming and harmful words, but there is no indication in the Bible that this happened. When Eve gave birth to Seth, she acknowledged that God gave her another son. She knew that God is the source of life.

David sinned against God with Bathsheba. She had a son. I won't go into the whole thing, but the child died. After hearing about his son's death, David went into the house of the Lord and worshiped. He knew the Lord had taken his son, yet he worshiped Him! He continued to live and worship God.

Job's children were all killed. His response? He tore his robe, shaved his head and fell to the ground in worship! He declared, "Naked I came from my mother's womb, and naked shall I return there. The Lord gave and the Lord has taken away. Blessed be the name of the Lord." Scripture says that "through all this, Job did not sin nor did he blame God." And he had some stupid friends; they gave him terrible advice!

Please know that Our Father understands our grief; He saw His son die a terrible death. He was rejected by men and scorned prior to death. Our Father knows our pain. God knows rejection. He knows grief. He knows what it is to have folks be angry with you and treat you wrong. Yet He loves every one of those who harmed His Son and rejected Him.

There is only one healthy way to deal with our issues during our grief: We must continue to trust in our Creator and our Savior. We must ask the Holy Spirit for wisdom and guidance and comfort. We must continue to walk a path of faith and grace.

When family or friends say hurtful things, we must forgive them and extend grace knowing they just don't understand. I choose to believe that they either meant well and the words came out wrong, or that they are hurting themselves and are unable to be kind. I choose to forgive them right away and not think about it anymore. I choose to not talk about it or spread my pain to others. We must trust that God will help us in dealing with the difficult issues we may have with family and friends. He will never leave us or forsake us. His promises are amen and amen.

September 22

Suffering Is Not Just for Those of Us Who Buried Our Child

Today I am praying for a friend. She is suffering. She is grieving. Not over the loss of a child, but over the loss of dreams, her imagined life. Her marriage has suffered a blow. A blow that many marriages would not survive. But I believe hers will survive! I PRAY hers will survive!

I am amazed at how much of the truth I have thought about, studied, spoken aloud, and prayed since Andrew's death applies to her situation as well:

- God knew about this before it ever happened.
- He had every one of her days written in His book before one of them came to be.
- She must think about those things that are true and noble and right and pure and lovely and excellent and praiseworthy.
- She must not listen to the father of lies, but must consider the truth in Christ Jesus without thinking about what could have been or should have been.
- She must rejoice in the Lord knowing that He is near and that He is a loving God.
- She must walk in forgiveness and grace.
- She must welcome and receive His mercy, love, and compassion.
- She must pray for wisdom, courage, and strength.
- She needs us to pray for her, encourage her, and love her.
- Her family needs all these things as well.

I have seen so many over the past year go through trials of various kinds. The truth of God's Word is real and applicable to every type of suffering. He is the hope and solution for each of us. Once again, I find myself going to Philippians when wondering how to pray for my friend who is suffering.

And this is my prayer: that your love may abound more and more in knowledge and depth of insight, so that you may be able to discern what is best and may be pure and blameless until the day of Christ, filled with the fruit of righteousness that comes through Jesus Christ--to the glory and praise of God. Philippians 1:9-11

September 25

Ron had meetings in Memphis today. At the hotel last night he told me I get to spend the day at the zoo! He loves me well! I love the Memphis zoo! It was like when you don't tell your kids about something fun until the last minute or they'll be too excited to nap.

I walked around a bit and then he called to say one meeting got cancelled, so he spent a couple of hours with me at the Zoo!!! He joined me for lunch.

I finished the afternoon by myself - rode the tram, saw the sea lion show, talked to the camel and the giraffe keepers, and tried to stare down a silverback gorilla. I was winning until he vomited. Then he won. I left.

I walked over eight miles today!! Beautiful weather. Thank you, sweet man, for loving me well! And, the sea lions like to blow soap bubbles! So fun!

One year ago I could not make it even a few hours without crying. I will miss Andrew until I join him in Heaven, but thanks to healing available in Christ, I can have days like today, full of joy and laughter. I am thankful for a faithful God, my loving husband and friends (old and new) who have helped me come so far.

~~~~~~

September 27

This trip has been wonderful! It started with a support group meeting in Hot Springs, then the Memphis Zoo, and now we are in New Jersey. The fall colors in New England are beautiful!

I'm thinking we should sell our property and move to a condo. Then I can always travel with my husband! I need to find some teenage boys to mow the property until then. All my boys are living elsewhere now.

~~~~~~

September 28

In Saratogo Springs, NY. I was walking around town looking at all the ballet shoe statues when I heard someone yell, "Hey, Andrew! Wait for us!!" I am reminded again that he is waiting for us in Heaven, enjoying dancing before the throne of God.

September 29

In case you did not already know that my kids are awesome....Margaret saved a baby today! The baby was turning purple, choking on something. Seriously, it was purple! Margaret did the Heimlich maneuver on it and saved it! She learned how to save a choking baby from a Red Cross babysitting course. None of the adults in the restaurant knew what to do. Way to go, my baby girl!!

~~~~~~

October 1

I was thinking about Heaven. The disciples knew Moses and Elijah on the mountain. I am sure we will still have things to learn when we get there, but we will recognize other saints and call them by name. I look so forward to that Great Reunion. Until then, let us live well while we are waiting.

~~~~~~

October 2

Ron's meeting in Canada got moved up to today. So he had to drop me at the hotel (In Buffalo, NY) about 10:00 am. I have to wait for a room, so I spent a couple hours in the business center doing my Joel Bible study homework and working on www.memverse.com reviewing Philippians, Ephesians, and Psalms 1, 103, and 23.

Then I decided to go to the mall. The driver asked a question. I ended up telling him the short version of Andrew's death and long version of God's grace, peace, and comfort. He kept asking questions. He took the long way to the mall and kept asking questions. He kept driving around the mall. Many scriptures from Psalms and Philippians and Ephesians were shared. I asked if I could pray for him. "Right Here?!?!" He asked. Yep. Right here. Right now.

Thank you, Lord, for teaching me Your Word so that I can share Your truth with others. Thanks, too, for working it out that I could share Your grace with Curtis today. Show him who You are. Show him Your love. Bring him to You eternally.

Amen

October 3

Praying Scripture – Praying for Your Grieving Friends

This is about *praying* for your friends and family who are bereaved - specifically for those who have lost a child. Though the examples are include prayers for grieving parents, these Scriptures may be used to pray for anyone experiencing grief whether the loss of a child, a parent, or a close friend.

These are not platitudes for you to quote to your hurting friend. If you must say something, a simple "I am so sorry for your pain. I am praying for you" says enough. Or you could send a note with a Scripture written at the bottom and "This is my prayer for you today."

Please do not preach these passages to us. *Please don't preach to us at all.* Most of us who are grieving are hurting so much in those first few days and weeks of grief - and trying hard to just survive - that a well-meaning friend quoting Scripture to us may not be helpful. We need you to listen and to pray.

We do need to know truth. With regards to helping us know truth, as a loving friend, often times your part is to lift us up in prayer. Intercede for us using the truths found in the Word of God. Pray that God will comfort us and show us His truth through the Holy Spirit in His timing.

The reality is that we who are grieving are most likely praying as best we can, and we are seeking truth as we ask for healing from God is in the midst of our pain. The Holy Spirit is called the Comforter in the New Testament. Jesus also said that the Holy Spirit will teach us all we need to know. Please let God work in our lives. Give us time to hear from Him. Give us space to hear what He wants to say without adding noise and clutter. But please, oh please, pray for us.

Bereaved parents need prayer. When we are grieving the loss of a child, we need our friends to lift us up to the Father and intercede on our behalf. It seems that others instinctively know we need prayer - they all tell us they are praying for us. But are they really? Are *you* really praying? Do you know how to pray for the bereaved parents in your church or in your community? I didn't, not before I became a bereaved mom. I had no idea how to pray for my friends who had buried their son. My prayer went something like this:

Father, Bless Patty and Gary. Heal their broken hearts. Give them strength. Amen

While this is a valid prayer - and God knew my heart - I now know so much more how to pray for those grieving! I can pray more effectively because I have been through the death of a child. And I want to help you learn how to effectively pray for your friends who have experienced loss.

Please do not misunderstand me - I know that God heard my prayer. He knew my heart. He knew that I was doing the best I could with what I knew. There is no condemnation here at all. There is no condemnation if your prayers are just like mine were. It is just that now I am better equipped. I have learn more about praying Scripture for the bereaved - whether they grieve for a parents, a sibling, a friend or a child. We can pray the Word of God for our friends who are hurting and in need of healing!

So how do we begin?

Healing, Strength and Peace

Of course, you know your friend is hurting and needs healing, strength, and peace. Parents who have buried their child or whose baby was born straight into the arms of Heaven have broken hearts. They are wounded with a deep wound that, at first, seems like it will never heal. We need miraculous healing as only God can provide. We need restoration. We need peace.

So let's start there! Let's start with Scriptures that promise us restoration and strength and peace. Let's look at how one can obtain these things. And then let's compose a prayer using these truths.

> **And the God of all grace, who called you to his eternal glory in Christ, after you have suffered a little while, will himself restore you and make you strong, firm and steadfast.**
>
> 1 Peter 5:10 | NIV

> **The Lord is near the brokenhearted and rescues those crushed in spirit.** Psalms 34:18 | NIV

> **The Lord gives strength to his people; the Lord blesses his people with peace.** Psalms 29:11 | NIV

> **But he said to me, "My grace is sufficient for you, for my power is made perfect in weakness."**
>
> 2 Corinthians 12:9 | NIV

> **You will keep in perfect peace him whose mind is steadfast,**

because he trusts in you. Trust in the Lord forever, for the Lord, the Lord, is the Rock eternal. Isaiah 26:3-4 | NIV

He gives strength to the weary and increases the power of the weak. Even youths grow tired and weary, and young men stumble and fall; but those who hope in the Lord will renew their strength. They will soar on wings like eagles; they will run and not grow weary, they will walk and not be faint.
Isaiah 40:29-31 | NIV

Lord, Alli is hurting so much right now. She is weak and tired. She is brokenhearted and missing her little boy. I pray that you would show her that Your grace is sufficient for her in her sorrow and that You are made strong in her weakness. You are the God of grace! You have called her to Your eternal glory in Christ Jesus. The grief of not having her son with her and the family is hitting her hard today. Make Your truth real to Alli today, Oh God! Restore her; make her strong and firm and steadfast! Lord, I know that she seeks to know You and she seeks to keep her mind steadfast; she trusts You. Give her Your perfect peace today. In Jesus' Name I pray. Amen

Fear

If we have other children, we may have very real fears that something will happen to them, that they too will die or get sick or overdose or get in a car wreck. We are sometimes afraid that we will have to bury another child. After a miscarriage, the fear of not having a baby becomes very real.

We don't need to be told that we won't lose another child. Or that our others kids won't die. Or that our next pregnancy will be just fine. You don't know that to be true. We know it may not be true. But you can pray for us that we would not walk in fear of things that may or may not happen. There are so many Fear Not passages in the Bible! Here are two.

For God hath not given us the spirit of fear; but of power, and of love, and of a sound mind. 2 Timothy 1:7 | NIV

So do not fear, for I am with you; do not be dismayed, for I am your God. I will strengthen you and help you; I will uphold you with my righteous right hand.
Isaiah 41:10 | NIV

How could you pray these for your friend? I have written out a petition that I have prayed for myself many times in the past thirteen months. You could pray something similar for your friend.

Lord, Each time one of my children leaves the house, is late coming home, or heads out of town, fear grips my heart. I am afraid that I will lose another one. That I will have to bury another one of my children. Father, help me to rejoice in You. Help me to know that You are near. Help me to rejoice in the time I have with my children here on earth and to rejoice that I will spend eternity with them and with You. Strengthen me and hold me in Your righteous hand. I know Your Word tells me that You have not given me a spirit of fear, but of power, love and a sound mind! Help me to live in that truth today and every day. I choose to not be anxious about the well-being of my children; I place them in Your hands. Thank you, Lord, for giving me peace. Thank you for being with me. Thank you for guarding my heart and my mind in Christ Jesus. Amen

Trusting God

For some bereaved parents, anger at God is very real. It is hard to trust someone you are angry with. All of us must learn to walk in our new reality. And trusting that God is wise, compassionate, kind, loving, peaceful and good goes a long way to help us heal. Trusting God in general will help us to go on living. We need help trusting God in our grief. Here a just a few passages you could use while praying for your friend's trust in God to be renewed.

"But blessed is the man who trusts in the Lord, whose confidence is in him. He will be like a tree planted by the water that sends out its roots by the stream. It does not fear when heat comes; its leaves are always green. It has no worries in a year of drought and never fails to bear fruit."
Jeremiah 17:7-8 |NIV

Trust in the Lord with all your heart and lean not on your own understanding; in all your ways acknowledge him, and he will make your paths straight. Proverbs 3:5-6 |NIV

You will keep in perfect peace him whose mind is steadfast, because he trusts in you. Trust in the Lord forever, for the Lord, the Lord, is the Rock eternal. Isaiah 26:3-4 |NIV

He who trusts in The Lord will not be disappointed.
1 Peter 2:6 |NIV

Lord is good, a refuge in times of trouble. He cares for those who trust in him. Nahum 1:7 |NIV

Perhaps you could pray for your grieving friend that she would learn to trust God once again.

Assurance of Truth

The enemy often tries to tell parents that their child did not really go to Heaven, that they did not really know God. Please take time to pray for your friends that they will not listen to the lies of the enemy but will hold fast to the truth about Salvation, Eternity and Heaven. Pray that the knowledge that their child is in Heaven will be of comfort to your grieving friends. Pray that God will assure them that His truth is real. And you may want to refer your friend to the post "Do NOT Listen to the Father of Lies."

> **Jesus said to her, "I am the resurrection and the life. He who believes in me will live, even though he dies; and whoever lives and believes in me will never die. Do you believe this?"**
> John 11:25-26 | NIV

> **Therefore we are always confident and know that as long as we are at home in the body we are away from the Lord. We live by faith, not by sight.** 2 Corinthians 5:6-7 | NIV

> **And you also were included in Christ when you heard the word of truth, the gospel of your salvation. Having believed, you were marked in him with a seal, the promised Holy Spirit, who is a deposit guaranteeing our inheritance until the redemption of those who are God's possession--to the praise of his glory.** Ephesians 1:13-14 | NIV

> **Truly, truly, I say to you, whoever hears my word and believes him who sent me has eternal life. He does not come into judgment, but has passed from death to life.**
> John 5:24 | NIV

> **Yet to all who received him, to those who believed in his name, he gave the right to become children of God-- 13 children born not of natural descent, nor of human decision or a husband's will, but born of God.**
> John 1:12-13 | NIV

> **Every day of my life was recorded in Your book. Every moment was laid out before a single day passed.**
> Psalms 139:16 | NIV

And everyone who calls on the name of the Lord will be
saved.   Acts 2:21 | NIV

And God shall wipe away all tears from their eyes; and there
shall be no more death, neither sorrow, nor crying, neither
shall there be any more pain: for the former things are passed
away.   Revelations 21:4 | NIV

"Do not be afraid. I am the First and the Last. 18 I am the
Living One; I was dead, and behold I am alive for ever and
ever! And I hold the keys of death and Hades."
                                              Revelations 1:17-18 | NIV

There are so many passages about life in eternity with Christ! I will leave
you with one last prayer....

Behold! I tell you a mystery. We shall not all sleep, but we
shall all be changed, in a moment, in the twinkling of an eye,
at the last trumpet. For the trumpet will sound, and the dead
will be raised imperishable, and we shall be changed. For this
perishable body must put on the imperishable, and this
mortal body must put on immortality. When the perishable
puts on the imperishable, and the mortal puts on immortality,
then shall come to pass the saying that is written: "Death is
swallowed up in victory." "O death, where is your victory? O
death, where is your sting?"   1 Corinthians 15:51-57 | ESV

Father,

*Thank you that Andrew was a believer! Thank you for saving him through the blood
of Your Son Jesus Christ. Help me to remember the good things about his life and the
promises You gave him and us. I so look forward to that day when my faith will become
sight and I will see You face-to-face! How great that day will be when the trumpet sounds
and this mortal body will put on immortality. Help me to live a life that honors You
until that day. While I wait for Your return, help me live well. And this is my prayer for
all my friends who have experienced the death of a child: Help us to heal, to grow, to
serve, and honor You while we wait for the Great Reunion in Heaven.*

Amen

My challenge for you this month: Learn how to love those who are
grieving. And pray for someone you know that has experienced loss this
year. It may be a widow, a parent who lost a child, or a friend who lost a
sibling. Pray for those who grieve.

October 4

How Can I Love You Today?

"How can I love you today?" is a question my daughter asks me. I love this! It is so much better than "Let me know if you ever need anything!"

1. It is immediate. Today. Not just sometime.

2. It indicates understanding that I need expressions of love -- sometimes in deeds and not just words. Words are nice, but sometimes we need others to put their love into actions.

3. It acknowledges that she has responsibility and a need to show me she loves me. It is not just "the thought that counts." Especially when those you love have no idea what you are thinking.

4. It puts some responsibility on me to think about what I need and what she is able to do. I must think about the question and articulate an answer. I must take some responsibility in expressing my needs to others in ways they can understand and possibly help with.

5. It expresses her willingness to listen to me express my needs and then to act on them.

I encourage you to try this. Ask someone, "How can I love you today?"

But when you do, be ready to listen to their answer. And do what they ask of you. If you are not prepared to put your love into action, I caution you not to ask the question.

Or you can ask it in a different way:

"May I love you by praying with you about something today?"

"May I love you by helping you with something today? Maybe make some phone calls or organize meals for you? I am stuck at home today, may I love you by organizing meals for the next week or so?"

"I can't get out today, but I am thinking about. Would you let me love you by going on a walk together later this week?"

Spend time praying about how to love your neighbor this week.

Then ask her, "How can I love you today?"

October 5

Joseph and His Technicolor Dream Coat

I went to the theater last night to see Joseph and His Technicolor Dream Coat.

My youngest was the stage director for this production. It was her first paid theater job. Andrew played Benjamin in this show about five years ago. This was the first show I've seen that he was in since his death other than the opening night of TEXAS in May. (I expected to cry through TEXAS for obvious reasons and because this season was dedicated to the TEXAS Angels.)

But WOW! I did not expect last night to be so rough.

I went alone as Ron is out of town this weekend. It had been a great day and I was feeling fantastic. I have been to this theater so many times that I am comfortable going there alone. I thought I would go and just enjoy a fun night seeing the show Margaret had helped with. I had a great seat - seventh row on the aisle. I planned to move to the back of the theater for Act Two due to the song about Benjamin. But I would enjoy sitting closer for Act One. I saw lots of friends before the show and was having a great time...until the music started and the curtain went up.

The tears began flowing the moment the overture started and I heard the tunes of two particular songs, both of which they had sung at the memorial. I knew that Andrew had played Benjamin. I was prepared for the Benjamin song in the Act Two to be hard, but I forgot about another song in Act One, "One More Angel in Heaven." I was not prepared for both tunes to be part of the overture. Silly me!

When the overture played, images of him dancing and laughing ran through my mind. I smiled. And the tears flowed. I let them flow. I thought I was going to be okay with just a few quiet tears. But into Act One, the characters came out in western wear singing "One More Angel in Heaven" and I lost it. I found myself quietly sobbing. I knew my sobbing was about to get louder, so I got up and left the auditorium. I NEVER leave in the middle of a show! I think it is rude to do that. But it would have been ruder to sit there sobbing and sniffling and blowing my nose.

A few folks saw me in the lobby and asked if I was okay. They did not know me, but when I explained that I was Andrew's mom, they both said they had family in the cast and had heard about what a great guy he was. They each hugged me and said nice things.

After I pulled myself together, and after that song was finished, I went back in and sat by the rear exit. I left during the Benjamin song in Act Two as well. Once again I sobbed in the lobby, pulled myself together, and then reentered the theater. For the rest of the show, I sat in the back and let the tears quietly run down my face while I smiled, laughed, and enjoyed a great show.

It was a great show! I laughed and smiled and enjoyed myself, even with the tears ruining my makeup. I am glad I went. Really, I am. The actors were great, vocals were great, and the new sound system was great. And of course, the stage managing was awesome!

After each show, the cast comes out and greets people in the lobby. I hung around and said hi to friends, congratulated the cast, and told Margaret how proud I was of her. Many cast members who had been in the show with Andrew mentioned him to me and talked of how difficult certain scenes were the first few run-throughs. Some mentioned how surprised they were that I had made it through the show. I am glad I went.

A few things I learned or was reminded of last night:

1. I am not done grieving and may never be. Grief will hit me in the gut sometimes. Grief may hit me hard even on fantastic days after a fantastic week when I am feeling fantastic.

2. I should had thought it through more and sat in the back from the beginning.

3. I must keep more than four tissues with me at all times and I am not done wearing water-proof mascara and need to buy more.

4. Andrew is still remembered by many people. Cast members who had done the show with him mentioned him after the show. They came up, hugged me, and told me how special it was to be doing this one again.

5. I am grateful for dear friends like the man who played Joseph (and saw my sobbing in the lobby) who are willing to give me a hug while I cry (even while in costume) without asking me what's wrong or trying to make it better by talking. He just hugged me and said, "I am so sorry."

6. I am not yet ready to see shows that Andrew was in. Not yet. At least not alone.

7. I am not the only one who cried through those two songs. Or through other songs. My son was, and still is, loved

8. I should not try to do hard stuff for the first time when Ron is out of town. Or at least, I should wait to do those things when I can call him before I go to sleep and have him encourage me that I will survive.

9. ALWAYS look in a mirror before going into the grocery late at night. And I should never go grocery shopping at 11:00 pm after sobbing through a two hour show. I looked horrible! Red, puffy eyes with mascara smeared all over. The cashiers probably though I was just another crazy old woman, drunk, buying bananas and yogurt before bed.

10. Most importantly, I was reminded that God's grace is sufficient even to get me through a great show without my son. Even through sobbing. Even through laughter. Even through late night shopping trips. Even through coming home to an empty house. God's grace is now and always will be sufficient for me.

But he said to me, "My grace is sufficient for you, for my power is made perfect in weakness." Therefore I will boast all the more gladly about my weaknesses, so that Christ's power may rest on me. That is why, for Christ's sake, I delight in weaknesses, in insults, in hardships, in persecutions, in difficulties. For when I am weak, then I am strong.

2 Corinthians 12:9-10 | NIV

~~~~~~

October 6

Peter is loving cheer at OU. He is studying hard. David is doing well in his classes also. He hasn't been a student for a long time. He took five years off to serve in the USMC. I am proud of these two Sooners. Lyz is teaching preschool. Adam is coaching gymnastics. Meredith is homeschooling her boys. Margaret leaves for Tennessee in a few weeks.

This empty nest thing is not too bad when your kids launch well and you have an awesome husband to spend time with. I am grateful that life goes on. These adult children still need me. And I need them. They help me as we all heal.

Chapter Seven

Truth

Slugs and Evangelism

After I posted pictures of me at the Memphis Zoo, a friend asked me how many favorite animals I have. My answers is:

> "LOTS! My top two are Komodo Dragons (which have poisonous saliva) and Poison Dart Frogs. I'm not sure what that says about me. But I HATE slugs. I use the word HATE here. I am sure they were part of the curse. I am sure that Hell is full of shiny slug trails. And no salt. There is no salt to pour on the slugs in hell. I am not going to hell. I don't want any of my friends to go to salt-less, slug-filled hell either. So I pray that you choose Christ.
>
> 'Anyone who calls on the name of the Lord shall be saved.'"

A few friends laughed at my attempt at evangelism in this FB post. I meant it tongue-in-cheek. Then I thought about it some more.

It seems that many of our evangelical efforts are just as lame as my "Slugs are bad -- Get saved" attempt:

- Get saved so you don't have to feel guilty anymore!
- You are a terrible person and God is mad at you. Repent and serve him.
- This world sucks. Get saved so you can go to Heaven someday.
- Want a nicer car? Serve Jesus and you, too, can have prosperity!
- Your child is in Heaven? Get saved so you can see him again someday. You may be miserable until then, but you get to spend eternity with your kid!
- This can be the best day of the rest of your life! Salvation is available! (This one sounds like a pitch for a new vitamin or supplement, but really tells nothing about serving Christ.)

Many people today do not even know what some of these words mean – *Repent, Get Saved, Salvation.* They are church words that have no meaning in everyday life. We need to find a way to share the good news of Christ in a way that people who have never been to church can understand.

Yes, God is big enough to use even our lame attempts. But shouldn't we try to stop being lame?

Jesus said the kingdom of God is among you. He said He came to give us life -- abundant life. This abundant life can begin today. He said that He came to give us eternal life which also begins today. We should be living this abundant, eternal life and sharing with others how wonderful it is.

Dallas Willard puts it like this, "The kingdom of God is available to you today. Change your way of thinking." I like that. I like that the Kingdom is available to us today! Now! Not just some day in Heaven.

God wants to change our lives beginning today in an eternal way. That is good news which the world (our friends) needs to hear!

Although I am not as skilled at evangelism as some of my friends, I am willing to try. And I am working on getting better. I want to know the character of God so that I can share who He is and not just what he did for me, but also *why* He did it. I want to know Him better so I can share with people that GOD IS LOVE. He loves me! HE LOVES YOU!

That is why He sent His Son: Because HE LOVES us and wants to have a relationship with us. This is why Jesus came willingly to earth and willingly died on the cross: So that we could have relationship with the Father, not because "God was chapped and somebody had to die."

Ephesians says that through him and through faith in him we may approach God with freedom and confidence. Isn't that great news! Because of Christ - what He did on the cross and because He rose again - we can have a relationship with GOD, the CREATOR!

Unfortunately, most people are not approaching God in freedom and confidence. They are not living in the light of His Word. They are living in darkness. They are not really living at all. They are living shadow-lives.

So how do we share this good news? How do we help people step out of their dark, shadow-lives and into the light?

Here a few ways. They are simply places to start. Each of you should seek God as to how you should share Christ with your friends and with those you meet. The main thing to try, to actually open our mouths and our lives and share Christ with others.

Intervarsity has a great tool called "The Big Story." Google it. It is a neat tool to use in explaining the gospel. You should read about it. It is short and easy to understand. It is a great way to draw out on a napkin or any scrap of paper the story of the Bible and of what Christ did for us. And why we need a savior.

One acrostic about evangelism that I found uses phrases that begin with the letters in the work GOSPEL. It is a simple way to remember the basics of the Gospel:

God created us to be with him. Genesis 1-2

Our sins separate us from God. Genesis 3

Sin cannot be removed by good deeds. Genesis 4-Malachi 4

Paying the price for sin, Jesus died and rose again. Matthew-Luke

Everyone who trusts in him alone has eternal life. John

Life with Jesus starts now and lasts forever. Acts-Revelation

3. In 12-Step meetings, when they share their story of recovery, they suggest folks "Tell what it was like, what changed, and what is like now." This can be a place to start in evangelism as well. Some call it sharing your "testimony"; some simply call it "sharing your story."

1. What was your life like before you came to Christ? How did you live, think, and feel? What was going on in your daily life? In your mind? How were your relationships?
2. What changed? And what caused that change?
3. What is it like now? How are you different than before? What is your daily life like now?

I find this last method works best for me. I talk to people about what my life was like before Christ, how He came into my life and changed me, and what my life is like since choosing Christ. I share why I chose Christ and encourage them to consider Him as well.

My Story

I chose Christ not to get to Heaven, or avoid the slimy slugs in hell, but because my life on earth was hell. I was living in darkness, through a storm-filled mess of my own making. I was miserable living in my choices. Here is my story:

I heard the message of my sin and need for salvation at a church in high school. A friend had invited me to go to her youth group with her. I listened to the message and saw changes in her life. I went down to the front of the church to get saved one evening. I was baptized. I know I was saved in that I was going to Heaven. But I did not decide to actually *serve Christ* until a few years later.

I changed a few things and learned how to talk like a Christian. But there were still ugly things in my life. There were ugly things in my home. My mom drank way too much. She was abusive sometimes. I never dated in high school and was a nerd who spent lunch hour reading classics because I was afraid to go into the cafeteria. I won state-wide math contests, but had few real friends. The church where I got saved was not big on discipleship. I went to college not really knowing much about the Bible, God, or how to have healthy relationships. And I began to make bad choices.

I began partying. I was uncomfortable in most everything and had trouble making friends, even in the sorority I had joined. My sophomore year, I got stuck in a six-girl room with a gal who loved Adam Ant and another gal who loved Jesus. What a group! I was sleeping around, angry, afraid, couldn't sleep, didn't like many of the folks I hung around with. In short, I was miserable.

I had found one friend, my roommate Sally, who loved Jesus. She had joy and peace no matter what was happening, even when she got stuck with me for a roommate in the Kappa house. I saw her life, her joy, her kindness.

I wanted what she had. I did not care about Heaven. I did not care if angels or demons were real. I did not care about hell. I wanted peace! And I saw that Sally had it and that she loved Jesus. She showed us in her own life that He was the answer. Yes, she was going to Heaven when she died, but Sally was living eternal, abundant life here on earth and I wanted that!

That is real evangelism. That is what resulted in my changed life, not preaching or ideas of Heaven and hell. Not fear of what is in hell.

I began to serve Christ. I started going to church and really praying. I quit doing the ugly things in my life. I started treating people better. Sally's family owned a Christian Camp and they hired me to run their swimming program that summer. I grew so much in that short time. I began to understand who God really is.

I met Ron and we got married. Over the years, we have struggled and had our challenges. But God was with us the whole time. Divorce was never an option. We prayed together only sometimes and were not perfect in the way we raised our kids. But we know the One who is perfect. We attended church and tried to teach truth to our seven children. And through all our trials and struggles, God has helped us make it. He helped us through many moves and job changes, church issues, money problems, dealing with addiction in our families, the deaths of both our moms and dads plus a nephew, and trials too numerous to mention. He helped us live through the death of our son. Through it all we had an overarching peace, love, and joy.

Because I know His Word is Life, I have memorized a few books of the Bible and meditated on the teachings of Paul. I have read through the whole Bible many times, not because I should, but because I want to know more and more about God.

I love to worship! Oh! How I love great worship times lifting our hands and hearts to the Lord in song! He alone is worthy of our praise and adoration!

A few years ago I began studying using the Inductive Study Method taught by Precept Ministries. I learned truth from God's Word in a deeper way than I had ever learned before.

When we faced a year of trial after trial, including Andrew's death, I knew *who* God is, not just what He had done. (There was so much more that happened in the months before Andrew's death, but those are not my stories to tell.) I knew I could trust Him in all things. I could trust that God is good and kind and loving and merciful and wise and just and compassionate and powerful. I could trust Him to love me through everything. I learned that His grace really is sufficient for me.

Mostly, I knew that through all things, He would be with me and He would give me peace and joy and hope. He would give me eternal life beginning today. And I knew that He holds no grudges; forgiveness is available for everyone who asks!

I knew that, even in the death of my son and the other trials we faced, God is good. I have the joy, peace, and abundant, eternal life I saw in my friend Sally all those years ago. If you have looked back over my life from this past year, I think you can see that Ron and I have been able to walk in that peace and joy. I am grateful for a loving God, who cares for us in all things.

For those who do not yet know Christ, He is waiting. He wants you to know Him. He loves you and cares about your life today not just where you will go when you die. Peace, joy, and hope, are all available to you today in Christ. Ask God to do for you what He did for Sally so many years ago and what He continues to do for her and for me. Ask Him to come in to your life and to give you His life, His eternal Life in Christ.

If you do, let someone know about it. Find a good Bible teaching church and get involved. God can and will change your life if you let Him.

"Ask and it will be given to you; seek and you will find; knock and the door will be opened to you. For everyone who asks receives; he who seeks finds; and to him who knocks, the door will be opened."

Matthew 7:7-8 | NIV

Here I am! I stand at the door and knock. If anyone hears my voice and opens the door, I will come in and eat with him, and he with me.

Revelations 3:20 | NIV

~~~~~~

October 9

I asked Ron late one night why he never talks about it, about The Accident.

His response, "I don't like to think about my son's death. I don't want to talk about The Accident or about Andrew's death. BUT...I am always willing to listen when you want to talk about it. I love you. We will get through this together."

He has been true to his word. He has always been open to listen to me. And I have been careful to not bring it up at certain times like right before bed. Neither of us wants to go sleep thinking about that horrible day.

October 10

It's Never Too Late to Forgive...Until You Are Dead

"In the blink of an eye, Everything can change. So Forgive often and love with all your heart. You may never know when you may not have that chance again."

I have seen this type of thing on Facebook often over the past few months. But here's the deal: It is never too late to forgive someone...until you are dead!

Even after they are out of your life or dead themselves, you can still forgive those who have hurt you! Unforgiveness affects you as much or more than it affects the person against whom you are holding a grudge. It eats at your insides. It makes you angry at things which should not make you angry. It can make you a bitter old person long before you are actually old.

It is true that each of us could die at any moment. We all know that. We have experienced that in the unexpected deaths of friends and family. We read about sudden tragic deaths in the news. Just because someone dies does not mean we stop loving them, ever. I will love Andrew until I see him again in Heaven. And then my love will be perfected. So I will love him eternally. Loving him and others helps me as much as unforgiveness can hurt me.

God knew that it is not just for the other person that we love and forgive when He instructed us to do these things! Both are for our own good as well.

I know that part of what this person is saying is that we should show people that we love them. Tell them we love them and encourage them, and compliment them, and lift them up while we can. We should make amends and ask forgiveness before that person we harmed is gone. We should tell someone that we forgive them and free ourselves and them from unforgiveness and bitterness. I agree with all of that.

But I know, too, that we can choose to forgive someone even if we never see or talk to them again. We can let go of the anger, the bitterness, and the rage. We can stop thinking about the harm they did to us, what they said, or what they should have done but did not.

I encourage you to take time today. Pray and ask God to show you who you need to forgive. Ask His forgiveness for holding a grudge. And choose to walk in forgiveness. Walk in grace. Walk in love, patience, kindness, and gentleness. Encourage one another, be kind and compassionate to one another. Help others carry their burdens.

~~~~~~

October 11

I don't like all the decorations, commercials, and displays in October. I'm not scared of zombies or haunted houses. I just hate the celebration of death and gore. I prefer to celebrate and choose LIFE! I prefer to watch uplifting, fun, or enjoyable shows.

> **Finally, brothers and sisters, whatever is true, whatever is noble, whatever is right, whatever is pure, whatever is lovely, whatever is admirable—if anything is excellent or praiseworthy—think about such things.**

> Philippians 4:8 | NIV

Oh, and I'm cleaning out the fridge! I found an entire bottle of chocolate sauce that has to be used by November 9, 2014!!! I have to eat it all in the next three weeks!

~~~~~~

October 13

Someone asked me if Andrew died instantly.

I don't know. In don't care. If not, God must have had His reasons. And I believe that God was with him the whole time.

I don't get it! I don't get why people ask such questions. I guess people are just curious and our society no longer teaches boundaries and courteous conversation.

I learned years ago to answer some questions with something like, "Oh! Dear! Why would you ask such a thing?" with a very surprised look on my face. I need to practice this answer again.

October 12

Twelve Things I Am Thankful for on the 12th

My October 12th post is about my recent trip with Ron. About 18 months ago he started periodically hauling a large trailer with equipment to engineers and sales reps through the country so they could see, hear, and touch the new products. He may be gone for weeks at a time, so I try to travel with him when I can. We enjoy just being together, even driving for hours along the highway. This trip was through Arkansas and Tennessee towards upstate New York. The scenery was beautiful! Plus I got see friends, family and animals!

Here is October's list of 12 (or more) things I'm thankful for:

1. Business trips with my husband -- he loves me well. Time in the car chatting, listening to books and good music, and looking at the beautiful scenery makes for great memories. Time in the car also gives us opportunity to help each other process through our grief, discuss ideas about our future, and share our thoughts about things happening in our ever-changing life together.

2. Artist friends and getting to waste the day with them -- I got to spend Wednesday with Suzi. I met Suzi through a grief support group. I was excited to spend the day with her! I'm so glad she let me play in her studio while Ron was in his meetings in Arkadelphia. I love her art.

3. Memphis Zoo - my favorite zoo ever! We used to buy a membership to the Memphis Zoo each year so we could stop there on our road trips home to see grandparents. Ron knows it is one of my favorite places. I spent almost seven hours wandering around enjoying the antics of the various animals while he was in meetings.

4. Giraffes and elephants -- And grizzly bears. And peacocks. And tigers. And sea lions. I enjoy the variety of God's creation. And I got to feed giraffes! Poison Dart Frogs and Komodo Dragons -- These have always been two of my favorite animals. I am certain that in Heaven neither will be poisonous. But there are slugs in hell.

5. Waterfalls in Tennessee -- When we lived in Tennessee, we would go on hikes with the family. We loved finding waterfalls. On one trip we stopped at Ozone Falls, Burgess Falls, and Falls Creek Falls. We hiked, rode bikes, and played in the creeks. Our kids made a teepee out of thin, long logs at Falls Creek Falls. Such fun memories! On

our business trip we passed signs for each of these falls. And we spent the next few hours sharing memories.

6. Grandsons who like playing in Granddad's trailer -- They are a reminder that life goes on. I am thankful for them.

7. Huge Waterfalls -- I got to visit Niagara Falls with Ron. It was our last night together before he went on to Canada and I stayed in Buffalo to catch an early morning flight home. We walked a couple of miles through the town and the park to get to the Falls, and we enjoyed every step. Then we had dinner in a lovely old inn.

8. Cameras in phones -- On our trip, we took lots of pictures. At Niagara Falls we took pictures for other families, few of whom spoke English. It was so fun taking pictures of them using their phones and having them use our phones to take our pictures.

9. Hampton Inns -- Each time we book one, we know we will have a clean room with a comfortable bed. This matters when you stay in ten different hotel rooms in ten different cities across four states in ten days.

10. Hotels close to the airport -- And hotel shuttles that get me to my flight on time. I had an opportunity to sow some seeds as we drove to and from the local mall in Buffalo.

11. Great local restaurants -- Although we like eating at chains sometimes, when traveling together we enjoy trying the local fare. Our last night together we dined in an old inn close to the Falls. We cuddled while sharing a great piece of turtle cheesecake for dessert.

12. Rochester, NY - We drove along the Erie Canal for hours. It was beautiful! The trees are changing and it seemed so peaceful. We walked along the canal by our restaurant.

13. Saratoga Springs, NY - Home of The National Museum of Dance. They have twenty-four of these painted ballet slippers throughout the town. Seeing the shoes had made me think of him and how much he loved dancing.

14. Syracuse - Sidewalks were like yellow brick roads with all the golden leaves! I love all the fall colors! And I loved getting to spend time with friends there. I saw Nancy, who lost her son four years ago.

Thank you, Lord, for time with Ron, great food, fun with friends, and the opportunity to enjoy Your creation. Amen

October 21

My Last Baby Bird is Leaving the Nest

In a few days, I will be leaving Margaret in Lookout Mountain, TN. She will, most likely, never live with us again. Yet, I am not sad about this at all!

She is an amazing young woman. Her life has not been perfect; she has had to deal with some very ugly things in her 18 years. But she knows and loves the One who is Perfect. She is kind, compassionate, mature, able, smart, and fun. She will quickly make friends and she will, as always, be a good friend to those she meets. She has dealt with ugly and painful things with grace and faith. I am confident that she will continue to do so.

I have heard others say how they are so sad when their child leaves home for college or career. Perhaps because I have experienced the death of my son, I don't understand those who "grieve" when their adult child moves on to, well, to adulthood. I understand being a bit sad, but not grieving.

For years my husband has told me that their job was to grow up and not need us anymore. And it is our job to help them.

I rejoice when one of my children is ready to fly, to leave our nest. When I know they have the tools they need to be successful and to make it in the world, I am glad to see them move on to the next stage of life. And so it is with Margaret. She is ready. She has the tools. She is able to do this.

And she is moving next door to her big sister. I am really okay with that!

~~~~~~

October 25

My son Adam posted this today. It is the start of a new song.

How do I find you and where did you go. Tears of another have started to sow, I wish for a moment that you were still here. I cry in my silence as passes a year. My brother, my brother, still young when you died, a thousand ships float on the tears mother cried.

October 29

Feeling Bummed, But Encouraged

Facebook conversation from the other night:

Me: Feeling bummed. Sitting here waiting for my kids to come home. Alas, they are home. It's just that my home is no longer their home.

But our citizenship is in Heaven and we eagerly await a savior from there, the Lord Jesus Christ, who, by the power that enables him to bring everything under his control, will transform our lowly bodies so that they will be like his glorious body. Philippians 3:20-21 | NIV

My Husband: True, AND the Kingdom of Heaven is NOW among us. Immanuel, God is now with us. Christ in you (now), the hope of glory. In him we live and move and have our being (today). Today is the day of salvation (healing, restoration, transformation). Already here, AND not yet completed. If I do not participate in His Kingdom today, will I recognize or enjoy it in the next life?

Me: Yes, the kingdom is among us, but our HOME is in Heaven. I was thinking about how I felt about my kids not being in my home anymore. All of them. They are where they are supposed to be - living on their own and doing grown-up things - but some day, we will all be HOME. No more sorrow, no more pain, no more tears. Yes, we have eternal life beginning today, and I am grateful for that. We can access healing, restoration, and transformation today. I also look forward to the final transformation.

My Husband: Sometimes that "not yet" part is overwhelming. Love you.

I love this man.

November 6

Grateful Even in Death

Another bereaved mom challenged us to think of things relating to our child's death for which we are grateful.

The first thing I thought of was that I got to be Andrew's mom for more than twenty years. Today I am thinking of all the things others did for us this past fifteen months. I am still blown away when I think of all the kindnesses shown us by dear friends:

Cop who didn't want us to hear it from a stranger
Cleaning my house that day and week
Cleaning my front porch to make it comfortable for guests
Food. More food
The memorial service
Moms who sat and laughed with me and told fun stories
Flowers and plants
Kind notes
Unsigned cards coming for months
Open mic at the memorial
Notes from his cast mates and friends
Friend who offered to do his hair
The awesome video
The Gift Shop and T-shirt models
The memorial display in the lobby
Men who text Ron and check on him
Kids' friends who loved them
Church family who showed us love
BSA leaders who got the color guard together
My family and their love
So many more.

I pray that you never have to go through something like this, but if you do, I pray that you experience an outpouring of love like we have the past fifteen months.

Thank you all for loving us well.

November 10

We got robbed while in Bristol, VA. After a week in NYC with nothing bad happening, we get robbed in Southwest Virginia. While we ate dinner, someone broke out a window in the car and stole my purse and briefcase plus Ron's briefcase.

Funny how some things just don't matter anymore. I keep thinking, "Could be worse." Worse things have happened. We weren't hurt and the stuff can be replaced.

I'm grateful that my perspective has changed and is now more eternal.

I am grateful to my friend Vickie who helped drive me around to replace needed items while Ron got the window fixed the next morning. Old friends are priceless.

I am hoping the guy who stole my briefcase with my homework and Bible in it gets a bad case of hemorrhoids, because getting robbed – the paperwork, police reports, replacing stolen items, etc. - is a pain in the rear.

~~~~~~

November 12

Twelve Things I am Thankful for on the 12th

This month I am finishing the study on the book of Acts. I get to spend a week at the home campus of Precept Ministries in Chattanooga, Tennessee.

Here are my 12 things I am thankful for in November:

1. The privilege of studying God's Word and wonderful websites that are free and have tools to help me study the Word.

2. The privilege of attending the Precept Ministries summer and fall study programs. I get to spend the entire week with a hundred or so believers who are here to dig into God's Word.

3. The Precept Staff, especially Mark, the chef. Three awesome meals each day. And Teri who heads up all the "event" related stuff like

registration and housing assignments. And Cindy the sweet bookstore lady who puts up with us all week.

4. Getting to see my oldest and youngest daughters while in the area.

5. A rainy day in Queens. Last Wednesday I spent the day in a hotel working on my Acts homework. I'm not sure I would have gotten it done if it had been a sunny day. I might have gone exploring instead.

6. My Canadian friend Lorie who went hang gliding with me in July.

7. My husband's willingness to have me gone a few weeks each year for this program.

8. "Inn Rooms" at Precept. A comfortable bed and room. Plus new friends/roomies each time I come. I love meeting new sisters in Christ!

9. Kay and Jack Arthur. And their obedience to start this ministry so many years ago. I have had the privilege of dining with both these saints and their son David who now heads up the ministry. I appreciate their love for the Word.

10. The other amazing leaders who are full-time staff at Precept Ministries. They spend a great deal of time studying, writing and leading studies so that folks like me can learn from them.

11. The early church and its leaders who took the time to teach others and record its beginnings for us to read almost 2000 years later.

12. In the year or so prior to The Accident, I had completed more than a dozen Precept studies. I had immersed myself in the Word. I am so grateful for that time and those studies. When I needed truth, I knew it. When I could have questioned God, I knew Who He is and I knew His character. When I needed help, I knew my Precept friends were praying for me.

If you have never done a Precept Ministries study, I recommend you check them out. They are in-depth studies. The word proving the word. I have learned so much about God and His character through these studies. I have grown closer to my Savior as I study His truth. Many churches offer weekly classes. www.Precept.org

What are you grateful for today?

November 15

Amazing Study

I have to leave Chattanooga today. I am sad to leave. But other duties call.

This past week I have been in Chattanooga studying the second half of the Book of Acts. The story of Paul and the early church. We've looked at Paul's travels and where he wrote his epistles. So much meat in this study.

I love the Fall and Summer Study Programs. Spending a week in intense study. This is my idea of an awesome vacation!

I am on my way flying to meet Ron in San Diego. We had to disembark in DFW do to nose gear issues. Ron's response? "Don't worry. They don't need nose gear again until San Diego. That's a long way from DFW."

I love getting to do life with this man.

~~~~~~

November 19

While in Southern California for this annual business meeting, we were able to see one of Andrew's friends, perform in a great show. I cried when I hugged his neck. I am excited to see what God has in store for J.T. Saxton.

The next day we had lunch with Timothy, the lone survivor of The Accident. I am grateful he is healing and doing well. He will never be able to jump as high or dance as well as before The Accident, but he is dancing. He is now choreographing and teaching dance. He loved my son. I am grateful we were able to spend time with him.

Also, losing almost 30 pounds over the past year makes a huge difference in how long I can dance to songs like Footloose, Move like Jagger, Sweet Home Alabama, and more. We had a great time dancing this year at the AHRI Annual Meeting. Our kids would have been embarrassed had they been here.

Last year, at this same meeting, we could not dance. We left the dance early, in tears. I am grateful for healing.

November 24

How Are You? No, Really! How Are You?

Some parents I know were discussing how to respond when someone asks "How are you?" Though they are really feeling like they are in the midst of a terrible storm or walking around in a fog, many said they respond with "I'm fine" or "alright." They expressed the desire to tell people how they are really doing. But would others understand? Could others handle the truth of our grief? One mom says she refers to "putting on the clown mask." You know, a big smile despite how we are actually feeling.

I understand that with some people you may not want to tell all the things going on in your heart, all your emotions. Kind of like "don't throw pearls before swine." Our pain, grief, and experience is ours alone, it is precious to us. We do not want to risk sharing it with those who cannot appreciate it. Sometimes sharing it with others would not help them at all, just as pearls would not be healthy for pigs.

I understand the clown mask - the need to appear okay when you are not. Feeling like some of the people around us could not understand our true feelings. They would not know what to do with the information. I understand not wanting to tell people how much you are hurting and telling them you doing okay. However, I have had a different experience. I tell people I am doing well because I am ... and they don't believe me.

I cannot go into detail, but the year before Andrew's death, our family experienced a number of major issues - addiction, illness, self-destructive behavior. Each of those people had a radical change as a direct result of The Accident. God used The Accident to bring good things in so many people's lives! Seeing the good God brought about helped me heal quickly.

(I don't believe God caused Andrew's death to bring about these good things; I believe He uses junk to bring about good things. He is a good, gracious, compassionate God who does that.)

My faith and my family helped me heal. For whatever reason, my grief was very intense - deep, dark, heavy, exhausting - for only couple of months. And then it lightened.

Now I have very rare days of grief hitting me hard. It is rare that I breakdown and sob. I am more likely to smile at fun memories or share a story of something sweet or silly Andrew did. We have lots of great memories and I am humbly grateful for that.

I read posts with sayings like "grief has no time limit" and "take all the time you need to grieve" and I wish it were true. I wish I could take the time I need. I wish that if I need less time than you, you would not think I didn't care or that I am not really dealing with it! I wish it would be okay to heal quickly, even from the death of a child.

If I say, "We are doing really well. God has been our very present help in this time of trouble" Or "I am grateful to have been his momma for 20 years. That has to be enough for me" Or "I'm doing great! God's grace is sufficient" – Please believe me!

When asked how I am ... if I say one of the things listed above, which are true, I get this look - the head tilt, slight smile, small nod - and "but how are you *really* doing??" The look that says, "oh, sweetie, you poor thing. You don't really get it." Yes! Yes I do get it! I do get it! I do know the pain! I experienced it! I buried my son! I know grief!

But my grief will look different from your grief. Please let me grieve differently than you, even if it looks like less. And believe me, neither of us is doing it right or wrong, neither is more spiritual, neither loved their child more. We simply grieve in different ways, different times, different healing.

The vast majority of the time, I am really well. I laugh, I enjoy life, and I go on with things I love. Andrew will be in my thoughts every day until I get to Heaven, but God has healed the gaping wound that was there for months after The Accident. God has healed my broken heart. He had renewed the joy of my salvation. I will have moments of sadness, sorrow, and grief. But I live with joy, peace, and hope.

These are not platitudes! They are true for me and my husband. And I have seen them to be true for other bereaved parents as well.

I wish folks would believe me instead of thinking I'm stuffing it or living in denial. Part of why I want others to believe me when I say God has helped us heal is that it is true! And if God can and has healed my gaping wound, He can do it for them, too.

November 29

Sleep, a poem in one syllable words

Sleep

It helps my grief. It gives me strength. It helps clear my mind.

When I am worn out, I doubt.
I doubt God. I doubt Love. I doubt truth.
I doubt His good will.
I doubt the goals of my friends.
I doubt all that is to come.

I do not doubt these things when I am fresh.

When I am worn out, I cry more. I hurt more. I doubt more.

I cry less, hurt less and doubt less when I have had to rest.
Sleep helps me heal.
Sleep helps me know truth and think right thoughts.

But at times, I just want sleep all day and all night to make my grief go from
me.

I want to hide in my bed and act as if the hard things have not been real.
That they are not real. Not now.

I want to sleep and not feel.
To sleep and not think.
To sleep and not see the piles of his things in my home.
To sleep and not think about the truth that my son is gone.
To sleep and not deal with the hard things in my life.
To sleep and not face some choice days and the day of his birth.

This past few days I have slept.

But on the next day, I will wake up and have joy.
I will go to church with my love.
I will learn of and praise Christ.
I will see friends I have not seen in weeks.
I will go to lunch with friends.
I will do put out my crèche.

Then I will sleep.

December 5

Graduation

Andrew attended West Texas A&M University. He majored in Dance and Accounting. Two very different degrees. He planned to complete them both in four and a half years. He made excellent grades in both departments. Andrew should be graduating with his accounting degree this month. No, that's not right.

If he had lived, Andrew would be graduating this month with his accounting degree. No, that's not right either.

Before he died, Andrew was on track to finish his accounting degree this month. He planned to then complete his dance degree over the next two semesters. He might have changed his mind, or taken a year off, or gotten injured and not finished on that schedule. But that was the plan. His plan. Our plan with him. Yes, that is the right way to say it.

But that's not what happened.

~~~~~~

December 6

Graduation, Part Two

That's not what happened. I am okay with that. Because I know that God knows what He is doing. God has a plan. His plans are not my plans. His ways are not my ways. He is wiser than I. He is loving and kind. All of Andrew's days were written in God's book before one of them came to be. I know that God is compassionate and gracious, abounding in love.

I got to be my son's momma for more than twenty years. I got to watch him grow and become a young man full of life and joy. I got to see him bring joy to so many others! I am grateful for that. I thank God for that. I choose to be satisfied with that. I cannot change it. So I must accept it. Accepting it makes it easier. Knowing I serve a great and glorious God who loves me gives me comfort.

If you need comfort...If you need peace...If you are suffering...Talk to God. He is listening. He is there waiting for you to turn to Him. He loves you and wants to help you. Ask Him for help. Turn to Him today. He really is real. And living. And able.

159

Chapter Eight

Our Second Holiday Season

Without Andrew

December 9

My Thoughts on this Christmas Season

My thoughts on this Christmas season. It is a little over fifteen months since Andrew's death. Looking back and thinking about it all.....

Last year is a bit of a blur. I don't remember much of Christmas last year.

This year...

Last week, Ron and I put up all my nativity scenes before he left on another trip. I have collected them for years and have twenty plus. I'm not sure when or if a tree will go up. Probably when he gets home from his business travels, before the boys come home from college and work.

I love the nativities because they remind me that all of this - our lives, our deaths, everything we do on earth - is to be for God's glory: Jesus came to earth so that we could have eternal life beginning today. Our lives with our children and my life after Andrew's death are to be about His purpose and will.

He is compassionate, gracious, abounding in love. He sent His Son into the world not to condemn the world but to save us, that anyone who believes in Him may have relationship with the Father and live eternally. Beginning today.

The baby we celebrate grew up. He taught and walked and suffered. He, too, faced grief and sorrow. Then He willingly went to the cross, was crucified, buried and rose again. He conquered sin and death! He conquered death so that we may have eternal life and become like Him!

He is love. He loves and cares for us because we are His body.

These are truth!

This year...

I am choosing to walk in His light as He is in the light, to walk in His truth, and to walk in His life which He gave me in His death rather than in my sorrow and grief.

Remembering that our lives are but a mist that is here for a little while and then vanishes, I know a day is coming when I will be with Him in Heaven.

I choose to live for His glory now on earth - not for my feelings - while I wait for that day. I choose to not let my son's death (or anything else) keep me from living fully for God's glory today.

Is this always easy? No. Do I do it perfectly? No! Do I still have hard days? Yes. I have challenges in my life. I daily face challenges. But I believe we can choose what we think about; we can choose to concentrate on our pain and sorrow or we choose to rejoice in the Lord.

All of us, every one of us has something we could use as an excuse to wallow in sorrow or self-pity, something that could stop us from glorifying God if we let it. I choose to not let suffering stop me from glorifying my Heavenly Father. In fact, He will use our suffering for our good and His glory if we are willing.

Day by day and little by little, as we choose to follow Christ, we are transformed to be like Him. And our sorrow becomes less and less. He becomes greater and greater in our lives.

Seeing my nativity sets around me this time of year, reminds me that many women in the Bible experienced sorrow. Even Mary, the mother of Jesus, the mother of the tiny baby born in a manager grieved over her son's death.

I am not alone. I have other bereaved moms who love and encourage me. I have friends who love me. I have a husband who cares for me. And I have the love of Christ. I have life in Christ.

Father,

As we celebrate the birth of Christ who grew up and conquered death that we might live, I pray that each of us learns to walk in the truth found in His Word. In His joy. In His peace. In His eternal life beginning today.

I pray that each of us experiences His loving healing from all of our sorrows. And as we do, I pray that we can share His love and life with others. All for His glory.

Amen

Decembers 10

Seek a Balance of Solitude and Socializing

Jill Sullivan, co-founder of While We're Waiting, posts quotes from the book "Grieving at Christmastime" during the month of December. Yesterday she posted:

> "Seek a balance between time alone and time with others. Moments of solitude are helpful, but isolation isn't. Reach out to a friend when you just need to talk."

My thoughts on this quote for those grieving:

Plan for times alone. It is so busy this time of year. Plan time to be alone and allow the feelings to come, allow the tears to flow. These times of solitude will help give us strength when we are out and about. Damming up your feelings over a long period is not healthy. Let the tears flow. Feel the pain. Cry out to God. It will get better. God can heal your hurt but it takes time and effort. And it takes a bit of solitude.

And plan time with those who understand your pain. Attend a WWW meeting, or a grief support group in your area. Have dinner with a few close friends who listen when you share. Spend time with others who have experienced loss and listen to their stories. Find time to talk with a trusted friend or your spouse about your grief and your needs this holiday season. Sometimes talking with another caring person helps us understand our own needs better. Then we can make plans around those needs. It also can help us to see the bigger picture.

If you have a counselor, call and make an appointment - even if it's been a while since you've been to see them. A good counselor can give you tools to help you through the holidays. Our spouses and friends are not always equipped to help us through the hard times. Sometimes we need professional help. There is no shame in asking for that kind of help.

Perhaps now would be a good time to go back to church. Let the body of Christ love you. Enjoy the pageantry of the season. Let the traditions remind you of the happy times with your loved one. Reminisce about the good memories. Let all the nativity scenes and Christmas carols remind you of the love of God. He does love you. He wants to help you through the hard times. He wants to comfort you. Let Him.

December 11

The Bad, the Ugly, and the Good

Yesterday started out bad! By accident, one of my Nativity sets got broken. Or rather, baby Jesus got broken. He fell into the disposal. While it was on. Yes, I probably should not have that set displayed on the window sill above the sink. But I did. And baby Jesus fell in while the disposal was on. It was bad.

Then it got ugly. I got upset. I posted on FB that I was upset. I told what happened without naming names. But it hurt my daughter's feelings. I did not mean to, but I embarrassed her. She's the one who broke baby Jesus. I didn't say that in the post, but it hurt her none the less. I did not intend to be ugly, but I was. I am sorry for that.

Then it got good. Friends suggested places I could get him repaired. One friend even searched the web and found a replacement for me! It is purchased and shipped!

Then my day got even better! My big brother is circumnavigating the world in a 44 foot sailboat. Mostly alone. But the point is, he is halfway around the world. And I miss him. I haven't seen him in 15 months and I love that guy!

Well, yesterday I got a call. He is in Denver!!! I am traveling a bunch this fall with my husband as he travels for business. We've been to New York twice, San Diego to Seattle and many other places, driving everywhere.

Guess what! We are in Denver this week! So I got to have dinner with my big brother.

A day that went from bad to ugly to good to fantastic!!

December 12

Twelve Things I am Thankful for on the 12ᵗʰ

This month I have much to be grateful for. It seems I always do. In fact, my last few lists have been more than 12 things. December will be as well.

1. Traveling through new states with my husband.

2. Stopping to go tubing with him in Utah. If I was at home and knew how, I would post the video he took while we tubed down the hill of man-made snow in 50 degree weather. It was great fun!

3. Ron's laughter. I love that he has joy and I get to hear him laugh.

4. My big brother, Robert (Uncle Bob). He is amazing and interesting. Always on an adventure.

5. My step-mom, Evelyn. For years I introduced her as "my dad's wife." At some point, I began introducing her as "my mom." She is my friend and sister in Christ. She was there for me at times when my mom was not. I adore her and was thrilled to spend the last two days with her. Denver will be on my agenda this spring regardless of where Ron's travels take us.

6. The majesty of the Rocky Mountains. They are beautiful! Evelyn and I drove up to Estes Park for lunch yesterday. So much fun. And Claire's has great chicken salad if you are ever in Estes Park for lunch.

7. Hotel business centers - where I can catch up on blog posts and work on www.memverse.com to help me with my scripture memory.

8. Jill Sullivan, co-founder of While We're Waiting. There was an issue on the FB group yesterday. A gal I adore got her feeling hurt. That happens when dealing with grieving parents. I am not placing fault; however, a man commented in a way that could be misunderstood. Then my friend commented, then he commented, then she commented, then...you get the picture. It was ugly. Jill handled it with grace and honesty. My friend is still hurting. I wish I could make it better for her. I love her. And I love that Jill is following the leading of the Holy Spirit in moderating the WWW FB group.

9. American Airlines - they are the only airline that flies into our town. I am glad I get to fly in and out of Wichita Falls instead of driving 2-3 hours to DFW. I'll be flying home Monday.

10. The Word of God. Powerful and alive. I am working on memorizing 1 John 1. I don't like to memorize just one verse. It's too easy to take out of context that way. So I memorize chapters. Or large parts of chapters.

11. The love of Christ and the ability to share it with a lost and broken world.

12. My daughter who is house-sitting while I travel. She takes great care of our home and our dogs. She spoils the dogs, actually. Essential Oil rubdowns, special treats, playing ball numerous times each day.

13. The EMT's on Lookout Mountain who cared for Margaret when she passed out at work last week. One of them asked her some questions to figure out who she was and where she lived. He figured out that her brother-in-law was one of his good friends, whipped out his own cell phone, and called Mark to let him know what happened. Her big sister was there within five minutes. She rode in the ambulance with Margaret. I can't imagine how scary the whole thing would have been for her if her sister was not there with her.

14. My daughter Meredith who took such great care of Margaret and called or texted me through the whole thing so I knew what was going on. I would have been panicky if not for her updates.

15. The image of Margaret laying on a backboard with a C-collar while still dressed in her Elf costume. And the fact that she was laughing about. "Mom, I looked at myself in the ceiling of the ambulance and thought "I just look silly." I love that she has such a great outlook on life and rolls with the punches.

16. Friends who loved me, encouraged me and even found a replacement for me when one of my nativity sets got damaged.

Be blessed today. And take time to count your blessings.

What are you grateful for today?

December 15

Nutcracker

He was the Dancing Bear
He was the Rat King
He was the Arabian Prince
He was the Snow King

He was giddy
He was proud
He was excited
He was wonderful

His first performance in The Nutcracker
The second weekend of December 2012
Just before his 20th birthday
With a dance company in Amarillo

We were proud for him
His father and me and all his siblings
The last time we were all together in one place
We loved watching him dance

The lifts!
The spins!
The jumps!
The joy!

Never again will he dance the Nutcracker
Never again will he be the Dancing Bear or Rat King or Arabian Prince or
    Snow King
Never again will he put on tights or ballet shoes or wear stage makeup
Never again will he enter stage left with his silly grin showing that he
    absolutely loves being a dancer, loves being on stage, loves performing

The Accident changed all of that

Now he dances for the King of Kings
He dances for the Prince of Peace
He dances for the Lord of Lords
He dances for the Great I Am

He dances with Arabians
And Israelites
And Somalis
And Spanish

He dances with Africans
And Asians
And Brazilians
And Cherokee

He dances with men from every tribe and tongue
From every race
From every color
From every nation

He dances with saints who walked with Moses
And Joseph
And David
And Matthew

He dances with men and women who walked with Martin Luther
And John Wesley
And Corrie Ten Boom
And Dallas Willard

He dances with his Granddad Bailey
And his Grandma Duncan
And his unborn niece or nephew
And the children of many of my friends

He dances for an Audience of One
The Three in One
The Holy One
The One who was and is and is to come

He dances in worship
He dances in truth
He dances in Heaven
He dances in eternity

He dances in the presence of the Perfect One
Of the Compassionate One
Of the Holy One
Of the One who knew no sin but became sin so that we could become the
  Righteousness of God

He still dances
He still lives
He still has joy
He still grins

Some day we will join him
Some day we will stand before the throne
Some day we will be face to face with God
Some day our joy will be complete

Until then I am grateful that I got to see him dance the Nutcracker
Until then I have peace in grief
Until then I have healing and joy and love
Until then I will live today.

**For everything there is a season,
and a time for every matter under Heaven:
a time to be born, and a time to die;
a time to plant, and a time to pluck up what is planted;
a time to kill, and a time to heal;
a time to break down, and a time to build up;
a time to weep, and a time to laugh;
a time to mourn, and a time to dance;
a time to cast away stones, and a time to gather stones together;
a time to embrace, and a time to refrain from embracing;
a time to seek, and a time to lose;
a time to keep, and a time to cast away;
a time to tear, and a time to sew;
a time to keep silence, and a time to speak;
a time to love, and a time to hate;
a time for war, and a time for peace.**

Ecclesiastes 3:1-8 | ESV

December 19

How Reasonable Is It To Expect Family and Pastoral Staff to Be Supportive?

A question was posed by a gal on While We're Waiting. The answers were profound. When my friend posted this question, lots of moms and dads commented.

How reasonable is it to expect family and Pastoral staff to be supportive after the death of a child?

If you have a friend who lost a child, please read the following comments in answer to the question. These comments were written from the heart by moms and dads who have experienced the loss of a child – often this loss is compounded by feeling alone in the months and years after the funeral.

Our church families do not know that we still hurt, still need love, still need compassion and still need someone – anyone - to mention our child's name and ask how we are doing. Many expressed that their pastors never called or checked on them after the service. Even those of us who have been active in our churches for years experienced this. Many families change churches after the loss of a child due to the apparent uncaring of the staff. I do not believe the staff does not care. I believe they simply do not understand the depth of the loss of a child and, thus, do not know that they families need continued ministry.

Perhaps reading these raw, honest responses to the question will help you understand better that parents who have lost a child are changed forever. We need love, we need compassion, and we need support.

Ask how to help. Send a card on the child's birthday. Mention them when you see us. Quietly and privately say something like, "I know the holidays are hard without Johnny. Please know that we remember him and pray for you" when you see us out and about.

You may even want to print this out and give it your pastoral staff.

The men and women who commented below are not in deep despair; they live lives full of joy and peace. You may see them volunteering at church, active in Bible Studies, participating in worship. They do not appear to be despondent, because they are not. We go on with our lives. We raise our other children. We go to work and church and coffee dates. We are not mentally ill. But we are hurting still. We will miss our child until the day Christ returns. (They gave me permission to use their answers.)

QUESTION:

How reasonable is it to expect family and Pastoral staff to be supportive? One thing that has been hard is that we have no "family" support. I am an only child. My husband's family have not been supportive since shortly after our son's service. The small church we were in for many years, was helpful at first but not after about six months. We found another church that has been very healing though. Praise the Lord.

Answers:

Ann - Finding support after the loss of a child is difficult. Many do not know what to say. The staff of the church we had been in for several years did little after that initial week. Our pastor did an awesome job at the service, but after that, nothing. We found that our friends in that church and elsewhere were our biggest support. It may be unreasonable to expect those who have not gone through it to understand. I have a few friends who lost children before I did, so our local homeschool group was familiar with this type of loss and does an awesome job of loving us. As for family, all of our parents are gone. I am glad they did not experience the loss. Only one of my husband's brothers and my brother really keep in touch. They try, but just don't understand.

Barb - It was surprising to me that we are being pressured to do more for the other family members, and they all act uninterested in our lives. It has helped to accept it for what it is and learn boundaries.

Cathy - Yep, I can relate to that! My mom called and told me my sister was grieving and having a hard time with MY son's death and I needed to call her and console her!! That is true of everyone. Paul wrote to the Ephesians, "Everyone looks out for his own interests and not those of others." Selfishness has been around since the dawn of time. It will continue until Jesus returns. Learn to say, "No" without explanation or excuse and without getting angry. We do not have to explain our actions. Those who love us will understand; those who don't won't.

David - I'm sure it's because they don't understand how you feel. I know it's a feeling unexplainable to those who haven't been there! I am glad that most of family doesn't understand. It means they have not felt this pain.

Elise - I try to lean on friends who have been there. Family tries but most of them have no idea and say hurtful things like...it's time to move on or I'm not blaming his death for me falling off the wagon but I'm just not as strong as you. Or my favorite is when they call trying to make you cry then when you feel just ready to punch them they apologize for crying and start explaining how they grieve. Anyway. It's been five years and people do care they just don't know what to say so they ignore you. Or say "it's so sad but at least he is with Jesus on his birthday." To which they expect you to be like "wow I forgot that now I'm super happy let's get a cake and balloons."

Frank - Our church was the same way. Our son's name was never mentioned again and not one staff member ever asked how we were after that initial week. Our son's name was taken down in the nursery that next week, too. We changed churches...our pastor lost his son a year ago. It's totally different.

Gretchen - It's funny that you bring this up. My son and I were talking about this earlier today. Neither my husband's family nor mine have been particularly helpful or supportive. Any time I talk about it with my sister about my daughter, she asks me to change the subject because it is too painful for her. Maybe it's my personality or something but it doesn't bother me. It just is. I always think "thank you God that I am the emotionally sturdy one."

Helen - I was also speaking with a friend tonight whose husband died two days after they found out she was pregnant, almost four years ago. We were talking about "grief cool points." When it first happened EVERYBODY wanted to be her friend. She had people coming out of the woodwork with Facebook friend requests, inviting her to dinner, asking to watch her girls for her.....Now, she was telling me everyone is like "oh, you're still dealing with that?"

Irene - My support has come from the same place that my support came from before my daughter's accident. My Savior that loves me so much more than I deserve. My sweet husband. My other kids. My friends that I meet at Waffle House (it's a southern thang) for breakfast once a week for over eight years. My friends that helped me not end up in a psychiatric hospital after the adoption of a daughter with reactive/attachment disorder. My small group leaders at my church. And....THIS GROUP!!!! While I have never imagined myself in a group like this and the initiation fee of a broken heart is really steep I am honored to be a part of a group that tries to walk out this mission field of grief with faith, joy and thanksgiving.

Jack - People who say they will always be there and if you need anything "I'm just a phone call away." Well it's not true. I feel so alone 24\7. My mom has nothing to do with me. I have my dad and my husband and they are there for me but it's different for men than it is for women. We carried these babies gave birth to them and got to raise them for so long. Then God took them back I am angry and have a lot of questions. Seventeen years just wasn't enough time.

Karen - It does kind of bother me that the youth pastor at my church has not once asked how my teens are doing. I have been praying that someone would call and invite my 17year old and my 15 year old out for coffee to just talk. Or take them to the mall. Or do anything to help them. Unfortunately the person in their lives who did it all the time was the same one who died.

Lance - I totally agree with the "grief cool points." Everyone and their dog wants to be a part of your loss the first few months. Then...they all disappear.

Michael - I kindly emailed my pastor and told him that the one thing churches get wrong is death. Especially the death of a child. He was totally supportive. I truly think people just don't know.

Nancy - If nothing else, this has opened my eyes to a new career journey. I really think I am going to look into grief counseling. It seems so hard to find someone that has truly been there. Hoping I can help others get through this ugly beautiful journey.

Olivia - I am blessed that my pastor's wife (who is also a very dear friend) is always very supportive and loving and remembers hard days for me. So even though I may not get that from anyone else in my church on a consistent basis that is, she is always in my corner. She sends me cards, she brought flowers on Monday (the 5th year date of passing) and she lets me know she remembers our boy. Outside our immediate family, one of my sisters-in-law is the one who is the most sympathetic and does not try to make it about her. It's amazing how some family members who were not that close to my son turn everything around to be about them...even the passing of MY son. My mother passed a year and a half ago and now my dad lives with us which is extremely challenging. I had to remind him of the significance of the date Monday and even he made it more about him than me. Sigh.

Peter - In our church my son has been the first child loss in many, many years. People seem to equate my loss with that of other types of losses - seniors, older parents. Of course, in this group we know how very different losing a child is than a grandparent or a senior parent.

Rhonda - I called one of the female youth leaders and asked them to take my daughter out for coffee. She did - twice.. It made her feel loved and appreciated for the moment., but the relationship didn't continue.

Steve - I really don't think church staff (for the most part) knows what to do. Also, it is not a personal loss for them even though they sympathize and feel badly for the family. They cannot possibly be what we feel we need for very long. It's just the way it is. But if only one or two friends "get it" and continue to be whatever support to you they are able...it can be enough. I can so relate to you and so many of you who have shared on this thread. My daughter's youth pastor never even checked in on her and she had been an active participant in his youth group for over three years. So sad...I find comfort here because we understand one another! Thank you!

Tara - My vicar hasn't mentioned our daughter or asked how my husband and I are since the funeral (one year ago) and we are in the choir. Only one couple at our church shows interest. Most of my family members say nothing and friends are the same. It's a lonely road and made me question my faith many times - but there's nothing left without it - is there?

Vance - Thanks to each of you for your prayers, comments, advice and understanding. Now I see how common it is for our "family and clergy" to leave us in the middle of the stream. Fortunately, we have found a church that cares now, we have this group, some wonderful friends who have become like family, good books, Grief Share, and JESUS most of all.

Wanda - My husband went to speak to our pastor (at the time) around the 2nd anniversary. The pastor said, "I didn't know you were still dealing with that." I remember telling my husband that we were like the three guys in the furnace that came out not smelling like smoke. This pastor had no clue and he'd seen us put on smiles and keep going to church so he thought we were okay. He'd also seen my husband be strong for me whenever I let the tears flow in church. Pastors and church staff are just ordinary people. If they haven't walked this road they have no idea how to guide us down it and no idea of how to help us.

My Answer:

I would like to educate pastors and church staff on how to help us.

But the issue is:
> each of our kids was unique
> theirs lives were unique
> their deaths were unique
> their siblings and their needs are unique
> our families are unique
> our grief journeys are unique
> what we find comforting and helpful is unique

The only thing that is the same for each of us is God. He is the same yesterday, today and forever. He is. His love, compassion, and grace carry us through.

One of the many things that came out of this for me is the desire to help new members of this club and their families heal. I keep an eye out on Facebook for news of child loss, send friend requests and then a message about While We're Waiting. That's how I met a few others in this group.

Those of us who are believers and who have experienced this loss know what it is like. We understand. We can support those going through this journey. We are the body of Christ, joined and held together by each supporting ligament, growing and building itself up in love as each part does its work.

We cannot expect clergy to do everything. The church is meant to be a living, active body, working together for the health of the whole body. This means that you and I must do our part. We must be supportive of others who are grieving.

Yes, the loss of our child has changed us. And perhaps God wants to use those changes to help others who are hurting.

December 20

Give Them a Call

Do you know anyone who lost a love one this year? A widow? A friend who lost their parents? Parents who lost a baby or adult child? A young person who lost a sibling? Why not give them a call and invite them to ride with you to your church's Christmas Eve service?

Grieving people often find it hard to attend church, especially alone, as it is an emotional place to be. The holidays can be extra hard. Having a friend pick you up and walk into church with you makes it feel like a safe place to be.

Pack some extra tissues in your purse or pocket as tears will likely flow once the carols start. But pick up the phone and call. Don't assume that someone else will do it. Don't assume that family is in town. Don't assume they already have plans. If any of these is true and they say "no thank you," you still made them feel loved by your offer.

Do you have plans for Christmas afternoon? Why not invite another family over for an afternoon of watching football or playing games? You know you have lots of leftovers. And there is always room for a few more folks in the living room.

For a grieving family, the time after all the presents are opened and the turkey is sliced can be hard. The quiet. The stillness. It makes us acutely aware that our loved one is not here.

Maybe you can help that family start a new tradition! A tradition of noisy games and leftovers with friends! Order pizza if you don't have leftovers! Invite them over. Even if they say "No thank you. Not this year" you showed them you care. Maybe even leave it with, "We will be here if you change your minds. Come on over. We'd love to see you."

December 21

Joy

Most days, most times I have joy. Lots and lots of joy. My life is wonderful. My kids are great. My husband is loving and kind. We have a beautiful home and caring friends. I am happy and laugh a lot. It is hard to convey that my life really is good without sounding like I'm bragging.

I write about grief and helping those grieving. Writing my thoughts helps me get them out. I pray it helps others know how to help the grieving, but it only gives you a small glimpse of a small part of my life. And grief is becoming a smaller part of my life daily as I walk this path, as I walk with Christ.

If you saw my Facebook daily, you would see pictures of my adult children and grandchildren, Ron and me traveling, and the beauty we've seen in our travels. You'd see jokes and songs and stories. You'd see how our friends love us so well and encourage us. In short, you would see God's faithfulness bring lived out in my daily life. You would see my joy!

God is good and so is my life. Even as I walk this grief journey, my life is good.

On this Sunday before Christmas I am full of joy. I am grateful for Jesus. I am excited to go to our home church with my husband for only the second time in more than two months. I am so glad we are both home from our travels. I am thankful for friends, teachers, and a pastor who shares the Word in truth.

It's the season for JOY!

December 24

New Friends on Christmas Eve

Yesterday I was driving my husband to work in the industrial part of town when we saw two sketchy looking young people walking their bikes. Ron noticed they are "self-contained, through cyclist" meaning they carry all their gear on their bikes.

As I drove him to work, I thought about those folks out on a cold day.

I stopped to check on them on my way home. One of the bikes was having trouble. They had ridden across the country from Pennsylvania and were on the way home.

Long story short -- I invited them to come and camp at our place. They called a bit later and accepted the offer. I took them to get the bike fixed, bought some groceries, and brought them home, dreadlocks and all.

Ashley and Steve are great folks and we had a bunch of fun yesterday.

They will be camping here for a few days, spending Christmas with us, and going to our church service this afternoon and joining us for our open house tonight.

Yep, they could rob us or kill us. But they won't. And if they do, there are worse things that have happened to me. And I survived.

I have two new friends and a house full of fun today.

Happy Christmas Eve

and

Happy Birthday Andrew

I reached out to two people that needed some love and a warm place to stay. In the name of our Lord and Savior Jesus Christ and in honor of my son.

December 24

Happy Birthday 22ⁿᵈ Andrew

Clockwise:
Andrew age 18. The Wichita Theatre Marquee the day after The Accident.
Andrew Age 19. All seven children at a family photo shoot in fall 2010.
From top to bottom: David, Lyz, Andrew, Margaret, Adam, Meredith, Peter.

Clockwise: Andrew age 2. Andrew Age 12. Andrew in Nutcracker December 2012. Peter, Margaret and Andrew at the Home School Prom May 2012.

Family December 2012
Back row Standing: Lyz, David, Margaret. Front Row: Mark holding Elijah, Meredith holding Colin, Kathleen, Ron, Adam, Peter, Andrew

Family May 2014
Margaret (Maggie), David holding Colin, Mark holding Elijah, Meredith holding Jacob, Adam, Kathleen, Ron, Lyz, Peter
The little boys are all wearing Batman shirts in memory of their Uncle Andrew.

December 28

My Living Children

This morning someone criticized me for thinking and talking about Andrew too much. Her words were, "Cherish those you have around you rather than focusing on the one you have lost."

She is young and has no children of her own. She has not experienced parenthood or the loss of a child.

But are her words something I should consider?

Recently, I have thought about him often and have posted his pictures and name almost daily on Facebook. But that is mainly because I in the heavy lifting part of the Annual Andrew Raymond Duncan Memorial Arts Benefit. This benefit is next weekend, so we are doing lots of publicity. Most posts that have his name in them are directly related to the Benefit. I am the chair person and have lots of work to do in the last few weeks.

Normally, his name is not in my daily post nor is his picture. Nor do I talk about him in casual conversation. Andrew's birthday is Christmas Eve, so I do think more about him this time of year.

Do I cherish my other children? Do I show them love and care? Has my grief overwhelmed my life?

I have a wonderful life! I have six terrific living kids and three beautiful grandsons. I have two spoiled puppies and lots of caring friends. I enjoy all of them!

A typical day starts with stretches (due to a bum shoulder), checking email and Facebook, and taking care of household business. I do some housework and run errands. Then I spend time in the afternoon on my Bible study.

If I am traveling with Ron, my day often starts with packing up and checking out of the hotel before going to the next appointment.

A couple of days each week I try to exercise - running with my friend, biking, yoga, walking at the Y, or swimming. Though exercise has fallen aside since I had shoulder surgery in September, I enjoy physical exercise.

I usually spend time each day talking with at least one of my kids on the phone or checking in with my stepmom who lives in Denver. Checking in on friends who are hurting either via phone or on-line takes part of the day as does blogging.

I have found myself in a position of ministry to hurting people.

It is rare that I mention Andrew as my day goes on, though I do think of him. I post about grief, in part, to help others and, in part, because it helps me. Typing my thoughts helps me clear them.

When with friends from church or elsewhere, they are usually the ones who bring him, not me. They ask how we are doing or share a fun story. If I am with people who did not know him or don't know about The Accident, I don't mention either.

I laugh. A lot. I smile, joke, and tell stories. If we meet, you will most likely find me smiling. I have many friends and enjoy spending time with them. I love hang gliding, exploring, good food, biking, triathlons, and sightseeing. I enjoy life!

Has grief overwhelmed me? Rarely. Do I cherish my living children and show them love and care? Maybe not as much as they would like, but I do love them and show them in many ways. Do I value life and the joy to be had in Christ? Absolutely!

So, should I consider what this young lady said? Yes. We should always consider criticism offered in love. And sometimes, after careful consideration, we should dismiss it.

**Search me, God, and know my heart;
test me and know my anxious thoughts.
See if there is any offensive way in me,
and lead me in the way everlasting.**

Psalms 139:23-24 | NIV

December 31

Andrew Raymond Duncan Memorial Arts Benefit

The last few weeks I have been working hard on the Annual Andrew Raymond Duncan Memorial Arts Benefit. I'm glad we are doing it. Lots of great things are happening. Community arts organizations that never work together are cooperating for this. It's a good thing.

But I am tired of seeing his picture and name. I'm tired of saying, "Yes, that's my son." TV and news interviews. Tired of hearing "I'm sorry" and "he was a great guy." Tired of saying, "We are doing well. Friends and family have helped us through this past year."

I am so ready for Saturday. The fat lady will sing and it will be over. Sunday morning I'm going to rejoice.

Yep, I'm tired. And a bit grumpy. Good night my friends. And thanks for listening. It'll all be good when the sun comes up.

~~~~~~

January 1, 2015

Thank you to my friends who commented on the above post and prayed for me.

Two live theaters in town, on the same street even, who rarely worked together. This year, the event starts at one theater, we ride the trolley to the other theater for dinner and act one, then ride back up the street for act two.

They sat down monthly to work on this. One director from each theater. Performers from twelve arts organizations on one stage! Andrew was a part of all of them except one. And his little sister was in that one.

It is exciting to see! Many of his friends will be performing.

Andrew's memorial service in August was the first time these organizations worked together on a big project. Now we have a big community-wide event to raise money for scholarships and local arts.

I am thankful that this good thing came out of something so ugly. But it is a bunch of hard work.

I am praying for peace and strength over the next few days. Artsy people often have drama. So I'm praying the only drama is on the stage.

And I'm praying my water-proof mascara holds out.

~~~~~~

January 4, 2015

Last night was the second annual Andrew Raymond Duncan Memorial Arts Benefit.

It was a great evening of entertainment with performances by artists representing a dozen arts organizations from North Texas. Food was great. Shows were great. Auction was great. Five college students will be awarded scholarships again next fall in our son's name. Five arts organizations will benefit financially and from the publicity. Over all a huge success.

But I am worn out. It was bunch of work. I am going to stay away from people today.

Father,

Thank you for allowing me to be Andrew's momma. Thank you for allowing us to honor his life with this event. May we also honor You as we go forth in joy.

Amen

January 9

I'm Tired

I'm tired.

Lots of traveling last fall

Holidays

Andrew's birthday

More holidays with my boys home

The ARD Memorial Arts Benefit

Maggie home for a week

Cleaning up and putting away Christmas decorations

I love all these things. But I am tired.

I wrote a few blogs before Christmas.

Scheduled them to post over the next month or so.

I'm glad. Because I am tired.

And when I am tired, I can't think of good things to say or write.

I just want to sit in my chair and read a good book.

It's been very cold these last few days.

So I've been sitting by the fire reading.

I read other blogs. I read my Bible. I read good novels.

But I probably won't write for a while.

Or maybe I will.

Chapter Nine

Continuing in Gratitude

January 12

Twelve Things I am Thankful for on the 12ᵗʰ

The activities of the last six weeks have been both wonderful and hard. I have enjoyed parts, but they have also reminded me of what I have lost.

As often happens when we are worn out, I have felt a bit down the last few days. When I am down, I begin to doubt. The solution for me when battling discouragement is always the same: prayer and looking again at the truth found in the Bible.

Many years ago I began memorizing scripture. I like to study whole chapters because it's too easy to take a verse or two out of context. I like looking at the verses around the one I am studying. I started with one verse, and then wanted to learn the ones around it, and so on, and so on. That is how I began memorizing chapters.

Memorizing chapters may sound scary. It takes lots of time and repetition, but anyone can do this. If you are a believer in Jesus Christ, you have the Holy Spirit in you to help you learn the Word of God. Start with a familiar passage like Psalms 23. Read the chapter out loud twice each day. Every day. Out loud. In a few weeks, you will have it down! I also use a free website to help me learn and review passages. www.memverse.com

To help me battle discouragement, I have been reviewing passages I had memorized, reminding myself of the wonderful things God has done for me and who He is.

This month, I am grateful for the Word of God. I have chosen passages from some of the chapters I have memorized to be thankful for and to meditate on. All of these are from the NIV.

Genesis 1:1
In the beginning God created the Heavens and the earth.

Psalms 1:6
For the Lord watches over the way of the righteous, but the way of wicked will perish.

Psalms 23:6
Surely goodness and love will follow me all the days of my life, and I will dwell in the house of the Lord forever.

Psalms 103:8-10

He made known his ways to Moses, his deeds to the people of Israel: The Lord is compassionate and gracious, slow to anger, abounding in love. He will not always accuse, nor will he harbor his anger forever; he does not treat us as our sins deserve or repay us according to our iniquities.

Psalms 139:13-16

For you created my inmost being; you knit me together in my mother's womb. I praise you because I am fearfully and wonderfully made; your works are wonderful, I know that full well. My frame was not hidden from you when I was made in the secret place. When I was woven together in the depths of the earth, your eyes saw my unformed body. All the days ordained for me were written in your book before one of them came to be.

Isaiah 53:6

We all, like sheep, have gone astray, each of us has turned to his own way; and the Lord has laid on him the iniquity of us all.

Ephesians 1:4

For he chose us in him before the creation of the world to be holy and blameless in his sight.

Ephesians 2:4-5

But because of his great love for us, God, who is rich in mercy, made us alive with Christ even when we were dead in transgressions--it is by grace you have been saved.

Ephesians 3:12

In him and through faith in him we may approach God with freedom and confidence.

Philippians 1:4

In all my prayers for all of you, I always pray with joy because of your partnership in the gospel from the first day until now, being confident of this, that he who began a good work in you will carry it on to completion until the day of Christ Jesus.

Ephesians 4:15-16

Instead, speaking the truth in love, we will in all things grow up into him who is the Head, that is, Christ. From him the whole body, joined and held together by every supporting ligament, grows and builds itself up in love, as each part does its work.

Ephesians 5:8
For you were once darkness, but now you are light in the Lord.

Philippians 2:12
Therefore, my dear friends, as you have always obeyed--not only in my presence, but now much more in my absence--continue to work out your salvation with fear and trembling, for it is God who works in you to will and to act according to his good purpose.

Philippians 3:10-11
I want to know Christ and the power of his resurrection and the fellowship of sharing in his sufferings, becoming like him in his death, and so, somehow, to attain to the resurrection from the dead.

James 1:12
Blessed is the man who perseveres under trial, because when he has stood the test, he will receive the crown of life that God has promised to those who love him.

James 4:7-8
Submit yourselves, then, to God. Resist the devil, and he will flee from you. Come near to God and he will come near to you.

1 John 1:5-7
This is the message we have heard from him and declare to you: God is light; in him there is no darkness at all. If we claim to have fellowship with him yet walk in the darkness, we lie and do not live by the truth. But if we walk in the light, as he is in the light, we have fellowship with one another, and the blood of Jesus, his Son, purifies us from all sin.

What are some of your favorite verses?

What are you grateful for today?

January 13

Did YOU Notice?

To my dear friends who have lost children,

Please do not get upset when others do not seem to care. It is not worth the pain you are causing yourself by getting angry when another family member or a friend is unable to comfort you in the ways you would like. Sometimes the comfort we need can only come from our loving Heavenly Father.

Please know that I understand you are hurting. I understand your pain. I have been there. Really, I understand. I know what it is like to want to shout in the middle of the store, "How can you go on with life as usual? Don't you all know my son is dead????" I know the disappointment of having a dear friend not ever say his name or mention that he is gone. I know the pain of someone bringing him up at a time I would rather not talk about it. I know the pain of family members who never contact you.

I also know that I did not understand how to help grieving families before we lost our son. Sometimes, I do not even know what I need or want from others. I cannot expect others to know what I need or want or how to help us. But I know that God knows. He knows what we need and He alone is faithful. He alone is always there for us, always able to comfort us, always loving us, and always listening to our cries.

Did you notice that family struggling with a child with mental health issues before your child began to deal with depression or addiction? Did you think about the costs - money, time, energy - of dealing with teen with an eating disorder before your son became bulimic? Before your child took her own life, did you notice others who suffered (and survived) the suicide of a loved one?

Did you notice the woman whose mom had breast cancer before your child was diagnosed? Did you think about trips to the nearest big city for yet another doctor's opinion? The chemo treatments, the PET scans, the CT scans, the MRI's and the waiting for results? When your friend had a child with cancer, did you think to take meals or offer rides for their other children? Before your child died from cancer, did you reach out to others who had lost a child to cancer?

Did you notice the passing of another anniversary date for that family who buried their son before you buried yours? Before your daughter was in an accident, did you love other families whose child was killed in an accident?

Did you call me on October 12 or January 12 to tell me you cared? When you saw me on April 12, did you mention Andrew or ask how we were doing? On the 9 month or one year anniversary did you call or text or email to tell me you were praying for me?

If you never did these things for others, then why do you expect others to do them for you? Before you understood, you did not understand. How can you expect others to understand? Why do you get upset when a milestone passes without a word from family or friends? Why are you angry when it seems that no one remembers your child but you?

I know I did not notice those who dealt with a sick parent until I was helping my in-laws. I did not think much about our friends whose daughter is Schizophrenic until one of my own kids dealt with severe depression. I did not notice the passing of anniversaries for those who had lost children. My own sister-in-law and brother-in-law buried their son a few years before we buried Andrew. After the funeral I never sent a card or called. They lived in another state; we were not close. I never checked on them. I was too busy raising my own children. I am sorry for that. I wish I could go back and change that.

I have close friends who buried their children before we lost Andrew. I did ask how they were periodically. I often asked if I could help with their kids and was willing to listen when they wanted to talk about their grief. I drove hours out of my way to spend a weekend with them and show them love. But their struggles were not forefront in my mind; I had my own life to deal with. I did not know how to help or even that they needed help. Thankfully, when we lost Andrew, each of those families went out of their way to come visit us and love us. They called and emailed and prayed. Those who had walked through it knew how to help. And they did help.

So in everything, do to others what you would have them do to you, for this sums up the Law and the Prophets.

Matthew 7:12 (NIV)

Jesus did not tell us, "Expect others to do for us what we want them to do." He did not teach that we can expect others to notice us or care about us. He taught that we are to care for others.

If you are suffering, I am sorry. Really, I am. I so wish I could take away your pain. But only God can heal your broken heart.

Sadly, that is what we should expect in this broken and fallen world - suffering and pain and sickness and death. And we can only expect truly good from the Father.

I have friends who say, "expectations are only resentments waiting to happen." When we place expectations on others, we are setting ourselves up for disappointments which can lead to unforgiveness and bitterness.

For me to get upset or angry because others do not notice Andrew's birthday or the anniversary of The Accident is only setting myself for problems and disappointment. I cannot expect or demand that others notice my pain. I cannot expect them to notice passing milestones or remember sweet stories of our son.

I notice. I remember. Ron notices. Ron remembers. His siblings know. His siblings remember. Some of our friends notice. Many of his friends remember.

And most importantly, God knows. God notices. God remembers. God cares and God loves you. And God loves your child. *That has to be enough.* That always has to be enough. Because He is the only One we can truly rely on.

We cannot ever expect others to do for us what only God can do. He is our comfort. He is our fortress. He is our healer. He is our redeemer. He is the one who cares for us. He is faithful and compassionate and merciful and abounding in love.

When something happens and you are feeling anger or hurt, talk to Him. Tell Him about it. Leave your anger at the foot of the cross. It really is the only way to heal without bitterness.

I love you my friend. I pray for you.

Much love,

Kathleen

January 14

Connect the Dots

WordPress Daily Prompt: Open your nearest book to page 82. Take the third full sentence on the page, and work it into a post somehow.

Last night I decided to start a Read through the Bible in a Year program. I know, I know - I'm a couple of weeks late starting. But is ever too late to start reading the Bible in a year?

One year I did not start my Read through the Bible in a Year program until November 10. But I got it done. Yep, I read all 66 books by Christmas. It took hours each day. I learn a lot and really enjoyed reading it just to read it.

This year, I'm starting in January. So my Bible is on my night stand. It is the closest book. Page 82. Exodus. Interesting. I'm starting a study on Exodus with our women at church next Tuesday.

Third full sentence: Moses answered him, "Because the people come to me to seek God's will."

Oh! Wouldn't it be wonderful to be known as one who knew God so closely that others came to you seeking God's will!

No, I don't want to have other people looking to me for answers or expecting me to speak for God. He gave each believer the Holy Spirit for that. All believers have the Holy Spirit in them to teach them all they need to know and to guide them.

But to be known as one who knows God! That is my desire: to know Him and have Him shine through me, my words, and my life in such a way that people would say, "Kathleen knows God!"

Psalms 103 says that God "made known his ways to Moses and His deeds to the people of Israel." The people saw only what He did - the miracles, the gifts, the wonders - but they only saw the external deeds. They did not understand His ways, the reasons for His actions.

Moses, however, understood God's ways. He knew God's character, why He did what He did. Moses understood that God is awesome, compassionate, Judge, Creator, Healer, Redeemer, Lord. God made known His ways to Moses.

I want to know His ways. I want to understand who He is and just what He can do for me or what He already did for me.

If we know His ways, then when trials come we will trust Him. We will rely on His goodness and mercy and love. When good thing come, we will know that every good and perfect thing is from the Father and can remain humble. If I know His ways, then when faced with decisions, I can turn to Him for guidance.

Father,

Help me to know Your ways. Teach me and lead me in the way everlasting. Guide me. Prompt me to search out Your truth. Open my eyes to understand in daily bible reading and studies. As I work on memorizing your written word, help me to understand it, and in understanding it, help me to know You more fully.

Amen

The LORD works righteousness
   and justice for all the oppressed.
He made known his ways to Moses,
   his deeds to the people of Israel:
The LORD is compassionate and gracious,
   slow to anger, abounding in love.
He will not always accuse,
   nor will he harbor his anger forever;
he does not treat us as our sins deserve
   or repay us according to our iniquities.
For as high as the Heavens are above the earth,
   so great is his love for those who fear him;
as far as the east is from the west,
   so far has he removed our transgressions from us.

Psalms 103:6-12 | NIV

January 18

Selfishness

As we were going to bed, a wise man told me last night, "Selfishness while suffering prolongs the healing process. And makes it harder to heal."

He is right. Now I'm having to examine my own selfish tendencies.

As most believers know, it is a daily battle against the flesh to joyfully and humbly obey His will at the cost of my own desires. I'm going to have to work on this.

I hate it when he is right.

Thinking about selfishness - if we wallow in selfishness to the expense of our spouse and other children, we are wrong.

If, however, we are selfish for short periods and take time to feel the pain, cherish the memories, and even wish for a different outcome, we may be simply being honest. And being honest enough to acknowledge our pain, our selfish desires, and our dark thoughts is often the beginning of true healing. We must then take these dark thoughts to the cross. Share them with Christ and let Him help us with them.

This is how we will heal. Denying our thoughts, desires, and pain does not result in healing but in more pain.

~~~~~~

January 25

June of 2013, a tornado hit the Moore area of Oklahoma. I headed up a Texas state-wide 4-H project that summer to gather school supplies for the victims of that tornado. We had a large trailer full of supplies to be delivered August 13. That morning I woke to find my son had died in a car wreck the night before. Other folks delivered the supplies. I have thought often of the families who lost children in the tornado.

Today I met one of them through While We're Waiting. Isn't it beautiful how God brings people together?

Chapter Ten

Grieving Families Need Healing

January 30

What **NOT** to Say to a Grieving Family

When we see someone hurting, we all want to say something, anything, to make it better. The truth is, for a grieving family, you cannot make it better with your words. And some things you might say can actually make a grieving parent feel worse.

Only God can heal the brokenness felt by a parent who has buried their child.

Here is a list of things not to say to a grieving family. If you do say one of these things, know that we will forgive you. We know you are trying to help and love us. We are thankful for that. We try to walk in grace and forgiveness. However, if you can, take time to think before you speak. And please try not to say these things to a grieving mother or father.

1. **I know what you're going through**. Unless you have walked in their shoes, you cannot know all that another person is facing. You cannot know their fears, pain, and struggles.

Unless you have lost a child, you cannot know what a bereaved parent is going through. It sometimes feels as if you are minimizing my pain when you compare what I am going through with your own loss. The loss of a pet, friend, job, or parent does not compare to the loss of a child. Please don't try to compare them. Instead, try saying, "I am sorry you are going through this."

2. **I understand your pain.** Unless you have lost a child, you cannot possibly understand the pain of bereaved parents. Even if you have experienced a deep loss yourself, your loss was different than mine. Each of us is unique. Our children were unique. Their deaths were unique. And our grief is unique. A better thing to say might be, "I understand that you are hurting. I am sorry."

3. **How are you doing? Or How are you feeling?** Only ask this if you have the time to really listen. And please don't try to get us to *really* tell you how we are unless we are close friends. Only ask if we are in a private place. If we open up to tell you how we are really doing, it may get ugly. Grief can be ugly. Tears and snot and stuff. Honestly sharing how I am may not be easy for you or me. Please know that this road is hard. It is harder than you could ever imagine. We have good moments and bad moments.

We will survive, but talking about the hard stuff is…well…hard. Maybe you could ask, "How is your week going" or "What do you have planned this weekend?"

4. **God always picks his best flowers first.** Statements like this are theologically wrong at best; at worst, they are hurtful. You have just told a grieving momma that God picked her son to be killed by that truck or to die of that rare cancer because their child was such a good flower. This is not helpful.

I had a friend tell me just two months after The Accident, "You may not be ready to hear this, but God killed your son." No, I was not ready to hear that. I don't think I will ever be ready to hear that.

There is scriptural foundation to say that God chose and knew their child and that He controls the number of our days, but to tell a grieving parent that God picked their child to die because they were so wonderful is completely unhelpful.

Again, try sticking with, "I am sorry you are going through this."

5. **God must have needed another angel in Heaven.** God does not need anything. He is God all by himself. He did not take my son because He needed an angel. If God needed another angel, he could have spoken a word and one would be created. He would not allow a child to die just so He could have another angel.

Angels are created beings, very different from humans who were formed in the image of God. www.openbible.info has a list of scripture passages on angels. Check it out. Or look at the concordance in your Bible and look up passages on angels. None of them mention a human becoming an angel or angel becoming human. When a person dies, he or she is still a person, not an angel.

Folks often refer to the five killed in The Accident as the TEXAS Angels. I am okay with this; all five were kind, beautiful, and talented young people. To call them angels is more of a reference to their character, not a theological statement. Others talk of their child "earning their wings." Again, not a theological statement, but it is easier for some than saying, "my child died."

It's okay to refer to our children as angels, but please don't tell a grieving parent that God took their child because he needed an angel. Perhaps you could stick with, "I am sorry. It must be so hard to lose a child."

6. **She's in a better place.** Yes, Heaven is a wonderful place; however, knowing Heaven is wonderful does not make us hurt any less. Knowing truth does not take away the pain or sorrow. Platitudes do not fix our grief. We miss our son. We always will. Knowing he is in Heaven does not change that for parents. It might be best to validate our feelings and express your condolences. Again, try sticking with, "I am sorry you are going through this."

7. **At least you can have another child.** You do not know that. No one knows that. Only God knows if they can have more children.

A friend told me after a miscarriage, "When people say things like that, they have just brought up one of my worst fears: that I may not be able to have another child. It brings up my pain and fear."

Even if we do have more children or adopt, those children will never replace the one that died. That child is special to us. He was loved and wanted. This kind of statement diminishes his importance. Please acknowledge our loss and our pain. Acknowledge that this child was special to us and can never be replaced. A better thing to say to a momma who has lost a baby is, "I am sorry for your pain. I am sorry you are going through this."

8. **It's a good thing you have other children.** Yes, my other children are a blessing. They love me and I love them. They helped me heal. But none of them was Andrew. They are each unique. Having other children does not fill the void left by the death of our son. It is better to acknowledge our loss. Acknowledge that we will miss our son. A better thing to say would be, "I am sorry for your pain."

9. **If you had just had more faith, this might not have happened, or your child might have been healed, or whatever.** There are many instances in the Bible of Jesus healing people who had great faith and of Jesus healing those who had no faith. And there are those who had great faith but still suffered. Jesus suffered. Paul Suffered. David Suffered. Moses suffered. My child did not die because of my lack of faith.

This statement feels like you are judging my faith, like you are saying it is my fault my child is dead. And that is very hurtful. Please do not ever say this to a family who has just buried a loved one. Sometimes it's best to just say, "I am sorry for your pain. I am sorry you are going through this."

10. **God must be trying to teach you something.** The truth is that God is always teaching us, but saying this to a grieving parent is hurtful. This statement is saying that God killed my child to teach me something. Do you want to serve a god that would kill your child to teach you something? I don't.

Yes, God will use this. I will grow and learn. God will use all things in my life for my good and His glory. But, sometimes it's best to just say, "I am sorry for your pain. I am sorry you are going through this."

11. **God will never give you more than you can handle.** God often gives us more than we can handle. He does this so that we rely on Him. He promises to never leave us or forsake. He promises to always be with us. He promises to love us. But He never promises to give us only what we can handle.

He will walk with grieving parents and He will help them through this horrible grief, but the death of a child is absolutely more than any of us can handle without His help. Perhaps this would be better -- "I am sorry you are going through this. I pray that God will give you comfort."

12. **You're so strong. I could never be as strong as you.** To some, this implies that we are facing the death of our child because of our strength. As if, well... if we were not so strong then we would not be going through this. Like it is *my fault* for being so strong.

This statement also makes it difficult for us to be weak. It may feel like others are expecting us to be strong all the time. As if they expect us to be super-human or super Christians. Please let us be weak. Let us be human. Let us grieve.

If you had asked me a day before The Accident what would I do if my child was killed, I would have told you that I would curl up in corner and want to die myself. However, I have gained strength through Christ as I have walked this path. He has strengthened me through His Spirit in my inner being so that Christ can dwell in my heart through faith. And my faith is the gift of God; it is not my own doing.

Some days I am still weak. I still grieve. I still cry. I still have bad days. I am grateful that God gives us strength to walk the road He has set before us. Rather than telling a parent how strong she is, try saying, "I am sorry you are going through this."

What should you say?

The morning after The Accident, our dear friend Jeff appeared at our door. He arrived within an hour of us learning of our son's death and posting it on social media. (That was the only way we knew to let Andrew's friends know what happened.) Jeff had clearly been crying. He came in, wrapped his arms around Ron and me and said, "There are no words. I am sorry. I love you."

This is exactly what you should say to a grieving parent:

**There are no words.
I am sorry.
I love you.**

Finally, brothers, rejoice. Aim for restoration, comfort one another, agree with one another, live in peace; and the God of love and peace will be with you.

2 Corinthians 13:11 | ESV

February 1

Supporting a Teen or Young Adult Who Has Lost a Sibling

"It does bother me that the youth pastor at my church has not once asked how my teens are doing. I have been praying that someone would call and invite my teenaged sons out for a Sonic date. Or just to talk. Or for a bike ride. Or do anything with them. Unfortunately the person who took my sons to Bahama Bucks all the time was the same one who died."

"I called one of the college interns at our church and asked them to take my daughter out for coffee. They went out a few times. And it helped her feel better. She felt loved. But it didn't continue. As if after a few coffee dates, her pain would be gone."

These two quotes made me sad. Very sad.

I have six adult children who lost their brother. They were ages seventeen to twenty-nine when The Accident happened. They each handled their grief differently. They each had friends who loved them well. Some in the church and some not.

Meredith is married and has her own family. She has a strong faith and an amazing husband. She lives in another state. She handled Andrew's death with strength, faith, and the help of her husband. Their church loved them well.

Margaret is our youngest. She was close to Andrew, they were friends. A fellow theater gal who had lost her own brother four years earlier and who knew Andrew (She was Cinderella to his Prince Charming) loved Margaret well. And though there is a ten year difference in their ages, Margaret went to lunch with Terrace, they went to parties together, and hung out at Terrace's apartment. Terrace's mom, Nancy, loved Margaret well and helped her understand my grief. That family continues to show her love. Our youth pastor and his wife (who had lost a little brother) did an awesome job of loving Margaret. She even spent some nights at their house, watching movies and cuddling their dog. I am grateful for these people.

Now Margaret lives near Meredith. Their church continues to love them both well.

Peter was attending a different church than we were. He spent time at the youth pastor's home. Friends rallied around him, inviting him to just hang with them as they went about life. One night, some friends invited him to cheer practice. He ended up on the cheer squad for the local university. He now cheers for the University of Oklahoma. This summer, he was in Norman for a cheer event, just a month or so before he would move to Norman to attend school away from home for the first time. He called to tell me he had met another guy on the squad whose mother had died last year. He was so excited to have met someone who understood his grief! That matters - having someone understand your grief.

My oldest son David has lost lots of friends; he is a Marine who has seen two tours in Afghanistan. But seeing his little brother's worn-out ballet shoes on the floor of his empty apartment knocked him to the floor. My older brother saw how he was hurting and invited David to join him on his sailboat. David spent 104 days sailing the South Pacific with Uncle Bob. I will never know for sure, but I think some of the rising sea levels last fall were caused by the tears David shed while at the wheel of that 44 foot boat. I am forever grateful for Uncle Bob taking my son on that sailing trip.

Lyz lived with us until March. She had just moved here a few weeks before The Accident. Some folks from various walks of life reached out to her. Many of her brother's friends from theater began including her in activities. I am grateful for those who invited her to parties and offered rides.

Adam lives in Michigan. I know his friends reached out to him as well. A few moms of his gymnast kids friended me on Facebook and let me know how he was doing. These moms had lost kids. They knew he would need help. I am grateful they offered a hug and listening ear. One of them works for an airline and has offered to get him home free whenever he needs to come see me and get hugs from his momma.

We made counseling available to all our children. We offered to help them find a counselor near them. Some took us up on the offer. Others did not.

For some of us, church family helped in amazing ways. For others, it was friends and people in the community. I wish the people in the church knew how to help a grieving family, but I am convinced that unless you have experienced a profound loss in your own life, you will not be able to understand the depth of our pain. You cannot know what it is like to lose your child unless you have been there, just as I cannot know what it is like to lose a sibling.

But from watching my own young adults, I can know some of what they need.

- Siblings need time away from their grieving parents. They need to talk with someone other than family.

- They need someone who will listen - young people often do their best thinking with their lips moving, as they talk their ideas and feeling out, they begin to understand them better. And they begin to handle them better.

- They need time to be a young adult or teen - not someone whose brother just died, but an individual. With laughter and silly jokes and friends who don't mind it when they break down in tears in the midst of the laughter and jokes.

- They need someone who will make them feel special - not in the "Your brother is dead so I feel sorry for you" special, but the "You are unique and I love you" kind of special.

- They need to be included in normal, everyday life. To be reminded that life goes on even in the face of tragedy. To be asked to the party or football game or out to dinner. And they need people who understand when they decline the invitation and ask again next week.

- They need to have people in their lives who speak truth to them and help them understand that bad things happen but God is still good, compassionate, gracious and loving.

- They need to be encouraged to pursue their relationship with the Father and know that He will never leave them and that He understands their pain.

- They need help understanding that they cannot take away their parents pain by hiding their own.

- They need to know that their family will get through this and that there are people who will walk through it with them.

You may not know exactly what to do to help a grieving friend, but we can all work harder at showing love and compassion. We can listen to that friend talk without comparing our loss to theirs. We can make a phone call, send a card, send a text, and invite them to lunch. We can say, "I am sorry." We can say, "this sucks." We can share a memory of the person who died - a story or a picture. We can learn to love one another with the love of Christ.

February 2

How Did He Die?

Was he sick?
Was it suicide?
Was it a heart attack?
Overdose?
Did he die instantly?
Who found him?
Did he have a stroke?
Did they try CPR?
Who was he with?
Did they do an autopsy?
Have you read the report?
Where was he?
What is the cause of death?
Is there a history of drugs or alcohol?

Do any of those things matter? Really? Do they matter? He is dead. Another family is grieving. They are making plans to bury their son.

I, too, have questions. But I know the answers don't matter. It is not my place to ask those questions. The answers are not for me to know.

What matters is that the parents are hurting. They loved their son. They thought he was wonderful! They loved every bit of him! They had dreams! They loved hearing him play music and laugh! Oh, how they loved his laugh!

Now they are planning a funeral.

I must pray for them and love them from a distance because they don't know me. But some day, if they want to meet and talk, I am available to listen. And share what I have learned these eighteen months of grief and healing and growing in grace.

Until then... I will pray. My prayer today is:

Lord,

Thank you for a sweet dream of Andrew this morning. As I wake up in tears missing my son, I pray for Annette and David as they awake to a nightmare of missing their son and planning things no parent wants to plan. Continue to comfort and guide them today and in the days and weeks to come. Make traveling easy for family coming in and help friends and loved ones express love in kind ways. Give everyone Your peace as they grieve for Jay.

Father, help them to look to your Son as the author and finisher of their faith. Wrap your loving arms around the whole family. And around our community. And, Lord, for so many young people hurting over this, having to face the death of another young friend, I pray that they would turn to You. So many questions. So many tears. Help us older and wiser folks to speak Your truths in trying to comfort.

We need you, Father. Be real and evident to each of us today.

Amen

And if you must ask a question, try asking, "Could you tell me about your son? What was he like?" Or "May I tell you about one of my favorite memories of your amazing son?"

Love these hurting parents well, my friends. Love them well.

~~~~~~

February 4

I hear people say, "It's my grief! I will grieve how I want to."

But there are times when we need to put others first. We must hold in our own grief and our emotions to help others. To do this nonstop is unhealthy. To pretend is not good. But to momentarily push aside my own feelings to help others is a beautiful thing. Then, once the task is complete, once I have helped where the Holy Spirit directed, I find a time and place to feel, sob, and cry out to the Father.

> **Do nothing out of selfish ambition or vain conceit. Rather, in humility value others above yourselves, not looking to your own interests but each of you to the interests of the others. In your relationships with one another, have the same mindset as Christ Jesus: Who, being in very nature God, did not consider equality with God something to be used to his own advantage rather, he made himself nothing by taking the very nature of a servant, being made in human likeness. And being found in appearance as a man, he humbled himself by becoming obedient to death—even death on a cross!**

Philippians 2:3-8 | NIV

February 5

Isaiah 61

God's Word promises us a crown of beauty instead of ashes, the oil of gladness instead of mourning, and a garment of praise instead of the spirit of despair.

With the help of the Holy Spirit, I can walk in this daily. I don't always do it, but when I do, it is glorious! The joy! The peace! The laughter and hope to be found in Christ!

For those experiencing one of the many kinds of grief today, turn to Him! Pray. Ask God to be real in your life. Ask Him for the oil of gladness instead of mourning and a garment of praise for the spirit of heaviness.

Pray and ask God to help you in whatever kind of grief you face today.

The Spirit of the Sovereign Lord is on me, because the Lord has anointed me to preach good news to the poor. He has sent me to bind up the brokenhearted, to proclaim freedom for the captives and release from darkness for the prisoners, to proclaim the year of the Lord's favor and the day of vengeance of our God, to comfort all who mourn, and provide for those who grieve in Zion--to bestow on them a crown of beauty instead of ashes, the oil of gladness instead of mourning, and a garment of praise instead of a spirit of despair. They will be called oaks of righteousness, a planting of the Lord for the display of his splendor.

Isaiah 61:1-3 | NIV

February 7

Tears in Church

It has been almost eighteen months since The Accident. Today is exactly eighteen months since the last time I watched him perform. Tomorrow marks eighteen months since the last time I hugged my son or spoke with him. The last time I saw his smile and heard his laugh. Until I see him in Heaven.

Grief is hard. But as times go by, and if we do the next right thing, it becomes easier to deal with. We can heal from the intense grief of losing a child with the help of God.

Church services are still hard. Songs mentioning Heaven always bring tears as do songs about the goodness of God. I believe God is good and kind and loving. I cling to that truth! Still, singing about such things causes tears.

Some Sundays only a few tears escape and run down my cheek. Other Sundays, they come in a flood. It is rare that I make it through a service without tears.

I don't know why.

Perhaps it is just that my emotions are still tender. Perhaps they always will be, like a wound that heals but leaves a sensitive scar.

I have learned to accept that the tears will come. I keep tissues with me. I sit with people who are not uncomfortable with my tears.

My tears don't mean I am sad. They mean I remember. I always will remember.

Record my misery; list my tears on your scroll – are they not in your record? Then my enemies will turn back when I call for help. By this I will know that God is with me.

Psalms 56:8-9 | NIV

February 8

Tears in Church, Part Two

The last four days I have been weepy. Silly thing have brought me to tears. Small things. Memories. Songs. Writing this post. Sometimes it feels good to have a cry. Other times it's exhausting. These past few days the tears have been good. Cleansing even.

We sat in the back at church yesterday because I knew I would cry. We have been traveling. When we go back to our home church after a long trip, I always cry more.

Last month, the last day before we left on this trip, I cried during service. A few folks said something. One gal lovingly asked if she could give me a hug. "You look like you could use one." I love her for that. My friends are so kind! Comments like, "I'm sorry" and "I can't imagine how you feel. Please know we care" really do mean a bunch to me.

If you were to stand on the platform and watch me during the song part of worship, you would see me smiling, joyfully praising God. And you might see tears at the same time. I love to worship in song, to lift my hands in praise, worship, and surrender. Joy shines on my face even while the tears flow.

It felt strange sitting in back. I suppose it doesn't matter if people see me cry. Next time it's back up front for me! Let them see my tears. Let them know I still grieve, still suffer! But let them also know that there is peace to be found in the midst of suffering if we are in Christ!!

Yes, my son died. Yes, it hurts. But yes, Jesus is still Lord and God is still on the throne! Yes, I can still worship my Lord and Savior and experience the joy of freedom in Christ even with tears streaming down my cheeks!

I know my Redeemer lives! I know my son is with Christ! I know this life is but a vapor and we shall meet Him face to face one day.

I pray that my tears shout these truths to all who see me as I worship each Sunday morning. Tears and joy and all. If you don't have a church home, please find a bible-teaching fellowship and join them next weekend.

February 9

Nothing Will Be Able to Separate You from the Love of God

In the midst of grief and trials, I have experienced closeness with the love of God. My husband and I are closer than we had ever been before the trials. Some of our adult children have made major changes in their lives for the better. We have seen the Lord move in ways we could not have imagined. We have seen amazing things come out of ugly situations. Through it all we have known the love of Christ! We have felt His love, His compassion, His grace.

If you are struggling with trials or one of many kinds of grief, He is available to help you as well. Nothing will be able to separate you from the love of God in Christ Jesus if you choose Him as your Lord.

> **No, in all these things we are more than conquerors through him who loved us. For I am sure that neither death nor life, nor angels nor rulers, nor things present nor things to come, nor powers, nor height nor depth, nor anything else in all creation, will be able to separate us from the love of God in Christ Jesus our Lord.**

> Romans 8:37-39 | ESV

~~~~~~

February 10

Some days I just feel like a complete failure. I think I need a nap. Or chocolate. Or jelly beans. Or a margarita.

Thinking about my mistakes as a mom. Unfortunately my kids have had to pay for some of my failures.

I am grateful for their forgiveness and the forgiveness of Christ.

February 11

I Am Humbled

Yesterday I woke to read a comment on my article "Do NOT listen to the father of lies." I am humbled and amazed by what was said:

"Dear Kathleen,

I was always under the impression that in America there is no more faith in the Lord (evidenced by poor attendance in traditional churches, Hollywood movies etc..,) but through your writings I have come to know that so many people still know and love and follow the Lord. I was prejudiced and I am shamed many times over.

Thank you for sharing and writing."

Believers, we must stand for biblical truth. We must live it out, speak of it, and show it to a hurting world. Compassion, faith, grace, and truth spoken in love are needed in our world today.

Choose you this day whom you will serve. And make it known to the world by your love; show it in words and deeds.

Put on then, as God's chosen ones, holy and beloved, compassionate hearts, kindness, humility, meekness, and patience, bearing with one another and, if one has a complaint against another, forgiving each other; as the Lord has forgiven you, so you also must forgive. And above all these put on love, which binds everything together in perfect harmony. And let the peace of Christ rule in your hearts, to which indeed you were called in one body.

Colossians 3:12-14 | ESV

February 12

Twelve Things I am Thankful for on the 12th

This month, I am thankful for love.

The love of....The Creator, my Heavenly Father who loved me so much that he sent his Son to die for me.

The love of....My Lord and Savior Jesus Christ who knew no sin but became sin that I might become the righteousness of God.

The love of....The Holy Spirit, the Comforter and Teacher. How I have needed Him these past two years of suffering!!

The love of....My husband Ron who has loved me well for 31+ years.

The love of....My children who forgive my failures and bring me great joy.

The love of....My sweet step-mom Evelyn who has been a mom to me even when I did not want her in my life. And who forgave me for rejecting her in those awkward teen years. And my daddy. I miss him.

The love of....My mom who did not know what true love is until late in life. She did the best she could. And I choose to remember the good things about her.

The love of....My grandparents, whom I also miss.

The love of....My darling in-laws who showed me what marriage can be and how to love each other despite our human frailties.

The love of....My 12-Step friends who accept me. And who have taught me much.

The love of....My homeschool friends and theater/dance friends who have done so much for me and my children, before The Accident and afterward.

The love of....The body of Christ. Imperfect as we all are, the body has shown us love and kindness.

May you have much love in your life.

How priceless is your unfailing love, O God!
People take refuge in the shadow of your wings.
Psalms 36:7 | NIV

Chapter Eleven

Recovery

February 15

Recovery

Recovery will not mean a once-and-for-all conclusion to your grief, especially with any loss regarding a child. It's a twofold process: (1) regaining your ability to function as you once did, and (2) resolving and integrating your loss into your life.

In a sense, you will never recover completely, because you'll never be exactly the same as you were before the loss. Your loss changes you. As someone once asked in a counseling session, 'If I can't be the way I was before, and I never recover completely, what is all this about recovery? I'm confused. What does it mean? How can you recover, but not fully?'

Recovery means you get your capabilities and attributes back so that you can use them. It means that you reach a point where you're no longer fighting your loss, but accepting it. Acceptance doesn't mean you would have chosen it or even that you like it, but you've learned to live with it as a part of your life. Recovery doesn't mean you don't mourn occasionally and watch out for holidays and special dates. It means you learn to go on with your life.

Recovery means reinvesting in life. A newfound source of joy is possible. But you could very well feel uncomfortable with whatever is new. You may think that experiencing the joys of life again is somehow wrong. Besides, if you begin to hope or trust again, you could experience another loss.

I've talked to some people who never want another child or who distance themselves from their remaining children to protect themselves. But there still is life, and in the midst of sorrow there can be joy.

The Lord is the source of our joy. The Psalmist stated that He 'clothes us with joy.' God extends to each of us the invitation to reinvest in life.

~H. Norman Wright, Missing the Child You Love

Hello, I'm Kathleen. I'm a recovering mom-in-grief.

My 12-Step Friends

Did I ever tell you that a group of bikers (not cyclist) from a local 12-step program offered to raise funds to help pay for things such as transporting Andrew's body back to Wichita Falls, the casket, funeral, and headstone?

A man in leather riding gear, covered in tattoos, was sitting by me on our front porch just two days after The Accident. He leaned over and gently said to me, "I hope I don't offend you, but do we need to do a fund-raiser to pay for all of this?" I loved him for that! I loved that these friends were thinking of how they could help us, how they could love us.

Those who know me well know I am not the Harley type. I'm not even sure how I met some of these bikers, but they loved my family well in the days and weeks after The Accident.

My older sister mentioned how, at the memorial service, she saw bikers in leather sitting next to Boy Scouts in uniform. Yes. These are our friends. On days I visited Cowboy Church with David, they would come up and hug me. I was grateful for their friendship.

A few months after The Accident, I found myself wanting to hide bottles of wine in my house so I could drink whenever I wanted to. I did not do it. But I wanted to.

I am not against alcohol in general, but the reason I wanted to drink was to numb the pain, change the way I felt, take away to horror of what happened if for only a few hours. None of these are healthy reasons to drink. So I attended a few AA meetings.

Again, these people loved me well and welcomed me, after harassing me a bit just for fun. Listening to their stories helped me understand that we do not all think the same way, but the answer to our problems is the same: A Power greater than ourselves who can restore us to sanity. I know that Higher Power to be Jesus Christ.

Today as I drive to a workout session, I am thanking God for all these friends. I am in tears as I remember their kindness. I know if I ever truly have a drinking problem they will help me.

And if I ever decide to buy a Harley Davidson, well, they will probably clear the roads in fear. No, they will ride beside me and teach me. They leave no one behind.

February 18

Alone on 2/14 and Glad of It

This year I spent Valentine's Day alone in a hotel. And I could not have been happier!

I worked on my Bible studies of Daniel and Exodus.

I am part of a Tuesday morning study at my church. I try to be a few weeks ahead in the homework so I have plenty of time to prepare.

Also, I am hosting a nine day study of Daniel in April. Ladies from around the country will be coming to my home for this study. We will spend five to six hours each day discussing lessons and watching lectures on this book! I am so looking forward to this! I have lots of homework to do to be prepared.

I got quite a bit of work done Valentines night. But that is not why I was glad to be alone in a hotel room in Chattanooga.

My darling husband abandoned me that evening to take two beautiful women to a play. They saw "Little Women" in Ringgold, GA.

Our oldest daughter is married with three wonderful little boys. Our youngest daughter just started Covenant College. They both live on Lookout Mountain. They went on a daddy/daughter date with my valentine. And I was thrilled!

You see, Ron and I spend lots of time alone together. Empty Nest and all that. We have been traveling together quite a lot the past six months and will be together most of the next two weeks before I head home. I know my husband loves me. I don't need flowers and a special date on a specific day (appointed by national retailers) because he shows me that he loves me daily. And he doesn't get to have alone time with his oldest and youngest girls very often - living sixteen hours away makes impromptu dates a bit difficult.

I love that my husband of 31+ years has his priorities right. Sometimes the right thing to do is leave your wife alone in a hotel to go out for a date with two beautiful young women.

February 19

Today

Today I choose to trust You.

Today I choose to not be anxious about anything.

Today is in Your hands.

Today I will remember that You are close to broken-hearted.

Today I will praise You because I am fearfully and wonderfully made.

Today I will think on those things that are true and noble and right and pure and lovely and admirable and excellent and praiseworthy.

Today I will strive toward being holy as You are holy.

Today I will rejoice because You are near.

Today I will live for today.

Today I choose to not worry about tomorrow.

Today I choose to forgive myself for past failures.

Today I will not live in the what if's.

Today I will try do the best I can with Your help.

Today I will trust You with my adult children. They are Yours.

Today I will be grateful for all I have.

Today I will not resent what was has been taken from me.

Today I will not be concerned about what may or might or should happen.

Today. Not yesterday or tomorrow.

Yesterday is gone. Tomorrow is in Your hands.

Today is all I have. Help me make the most of it.

February 25

Chris Tomlin

Four years ago we attended a Chris Tomlin concert with our kids. Andrew (eighteen at the time) was unhappy to have to sit with his parents.

He started the evening grumpy, standing with his hands folded across his chest. (If you have a teenager, you get the picture.)

As the music started, he began to move side to side a bit, shifting his weight from one foot to the other. His hands went to his pockets. Then back to his chest. Then back to his pockets as if he was trying to maintain control of them.

Then he began to sing. He was moving a bit more. Then his hands came out of his pockets and were at about waist level, palms up.

By the end of the first song, he was dancing and singing with his hands raised in worship.

The rest of the concert involved prayer, praise, singing, and lots of worship!

Thank you, Lord, for the wonderful memory of my son worshipping You. Thank you for yet another confirmation that he knew You. That he knows You now!

Amen

~~~~~~

February 26

Throw Back Thursday

When I see TBT group shots of my kids' friends on social media, I search in hopes of seeing his face. A new picture that I had not seen. A glimpse of his smile I had not viewed before.

I miss my son.

February 27

Recovery, Again

A few weeks ago I posted a quote regarding recovery. The quote below reminded me of that post.

> "When you take the step that lands you in recovery, something happens; the numbness fades and your emotions come flooding in. It is both wonderful and horrible at the same time. You are strong. You made it here alive and you can deal with all of this, have faith, trust the process."
>
> Katie Maslin

"Recovery" does involve feeling lots of emotions - and many of those emotions are painful. But I believe that we can get through them and recover with the help of Christ. I also believe that as we walk into recovery, the joyful memories and emotions will come as well.

The one thing I would add to this quote is that our faith must be in the One True God. He is the only One who can heal the broken-hearted.

For my friends who are walking through grief, I am praying today that we each take yet another step towards recovery.

~~~~~~

February 28

I had lunch today with two While We're Waiting moms. I had not met them until today. As I travel with Ron, I often have free time during the day. I posted on the WWW page that "I'm in southern Florida and who wants to eat with me." One gal picked me up at the hotel and we met the other gal at a local lunch place. We shared our stories and cried. And laughed. I am glad to have two new friends.

Tomorrow I am driving across the state to see a dear friend I haven't seen in 10 years! I'm glad I have lots of old friends, too.

February 28

Serenity

Continuing the theme of Recovery. Here is the full version of *The Serenity Prayer*. This prayer is said at many 12-Step meetings in its shortened form. I love the long form. This world is not as I would have it, but I am trusting my Father. I pray this prayer for you all today. And for myself.

The Full Original Copy of the Serenity Prayer

by Reinhold Niebuhr (1892-1971)

God,
Give us grace to accept with serenity the things that cannot be changed,
Courage to change the things which should be changed,
and the Wisdom to distinguish the one from the other.

Living one day at a time,
Enjoying one moment at a time,
Accepting hardship as a pathway to peace,
Taking, as Jesus did, This sinful world as it is,
Not as I would have it,
Trusting that You will make all things right,
If I surrender to Your will,
So that I may be reasonably happy in this life,
And supremely happy with You forever in the next.
Amen.

March 1

Repentance

Why? Oh Why does God wake me up at 3:30 am? I usually can just quote in my head one of the Bible chapters I have memorized and go back to sleep. I'm usually asleep before I get halfway through a chapter.

But last Thursday at 3:30 in the morning...a whole sermon came from thinking about three chapters: Psalms 51 (a Psalms of repentance), Jonah 2 (Jonah's prayer), and Romans 8 (part of Paul's letter to the church at Rome).

First I considered Psalms 51. David wrote this after being confronted about His sin against Bathsheba and against God. He wrote this prayer to ask God for forgiveness. Just look at what David wrote in this Psalms. Look it up. Read it. He had messed up! And he cried out to God knowing he would be forgiven even of adultery and causing a man to be killed!

I mentally recited Psalms 51. Twice! And thought on it. Hoping to get sleepy. But I was still wide awake. So I read Jonah's prayer found in Jonah Chapter 2.

When reading this, keep in mind that Jonah was inside a large fish as he prayed. He was still suffering, still in a predicament, and not yet saved from trouble! He had done wrong and had found himself in a bad place: drowning at sea because of his own disobedience. He called out to God and God sent a big fish to take him where he should have gone in the first place. In the belly of the fish, Jonah cried out again to God ending with the statement, "But I with the voice of thanksgiving will sacrifice to you; what I have vowed I will pay. Salvation belongs to the Lord!"

After reciting Psalms 51 and reading Jonah 2, realizing that sleep was not happening, I moved on to Romans 8.

This chapter talks about there being no condemnation for those who are in Christ Jesus, our adoption as sons, being heirs of God and joint heirs with Christ, and much more. I love this chapter! It took me months memorize it, but it is so full of truth I need to hear and meditate on. Especially after thinking about all the ways I had messed up as a believer, as a wife, and as a mom. I need to be reminded that God does not condemn me, He has adopted me, and He loves me. Nothing can change that.

After reciting the three chapters, I began to pray my own prayer of repentance. Some of my repentance concerned my attitude about the poor and hurting in my community. I don't want to have the attitude towards my community that Jonah had towards his. I want to love those who are not like me, care for orphans and widows in their distress, feed the hungry, clothe the naked, and love the unlovable.

There were many other things I talked with God about that morning, but that is just between Him and me.

After praying and crying out to God, I was reminded again of verse one of Romans 8. There is no condemnation for me as I am in Christ Jesus. I thought about my adoption into His family and how nothing can separate me from the love of God that is in Christ Jesus my Lord. And I laid there softly crying in gratitude. I am so grateful for God's redemptive work, for His forgiveness and His love.

Have mercy on me, O God, according to your unfailing love; according to your great compassion blot out my transgressions. Wash away all my iniquity and cleanse me from my sin.

For I know my transgressions, and my sin is always before me. Against you, you only, have I sinned and done what is evil in your sight; so you are right in your verdict and justified when you judge.

Surely I was sinful at birth, sinful from the time my mother conceived me. Yet you desired faithfulness even in the womb; you taught me wisdom in that secret place.

Cleanse me with hyssop, and I will be clean; wash me, and I will be whiter than snow. Let me hear joy and gladness; let the bones you have crushed rejoice. Hide your face from my sins and blot out all my iniquity.

Psalms 51:1-9 | NIV

March 4

Please Mention Andrew

A month or so ago I went to lunch with a dear friend I had not seen since The Accident. She loves me and loves my kids. She is one of my dearest friends even though we live far apart and only see each other every couple of years. I know she would do anything for me and I for her.

And yet, she said nothing about Andrew until brought him up. "I wanted to say something but was afraid it would upset you," she said in love. I know she loves me.

My response to her? "I LOVE you for that! But I love to talk about Andrew and all my kids. I will be glad to tell you what happened. Thank you for loving me and caring. Please feel free to ask me about it and mention him."

Then I probably talked about him too much. But she let me go on and on and on because she loves me! We had a wonderful supper together filled with joy and laughter and fond memories. I look forward to seeing her when she comes to town again.

My point - even those who love us very much and care deeply may not mention our pain, our loss, our child for fear of upsetting us, hurting us, or causing tears to flow. They do not intend to offend so they don't ask about things related to our child or his death. They never want to hurt us! Never! They only intend love and compassion.

I have friends who have gotten offended when someone did not mention their loss. I chose not to be offended as she meant the best. Why would I ever be offended by someone who does something meaning to love me?? It really is the thought that counts sometimes. If I think someone means well I'm less likely to be hurt by them.

I will not be angry or bitter when others don't know what to say or do. I choose to not be easily hurt by those who try to do the right thing but miss the mark. After all, they *are* trying. That counts for something. Doesn't it?

We all have much to learn. Let's help each other along the way! And let's give each other lots of grace when we flub it up.

March 5

A Bit of Truth

I spent the morning working on my shoulder. After a hard workout followed by a deep-tissue session with the massage therapist followed by a great "counseling" session, I considered going home, getting on comfy clothes, curling up in front of a roaring fire and reading the rest of Les Mis.

Instead I am going to get a root canal. Yes, I know how to have a good time!

Here is a bit of what my friend and I talked about at lunch:

"Just because someone calls you a chair doesn't mean you are one."*

"Just because someone calls you a rug doesn't mean you should let people walk over you."

"Just because someone you care about won't take responsibility for their own recovery doesn't mean it becomes your responsibility."

Have I mentioned lately how much I love my 12-step friends? They speak truth to me in ways I can hear it.

Here are a few more my readers added:

"You don't have to attend every fight you are invited to."

"When the audience leaves, the show usually stops."

"It takes two hands to clap."

"It's okay to be right when no one else knows it."

---

*Others may say we ugly things about us. Their saying it does not make those things true. Don't buy into the lies others say about you.

March 6

Fears and Anxiety from the Past

I have been experiencing something that seems to be common among grieving people: fears and anxiety that had bothered me long ago, but which I had conquered, have come back to haunt me.

I am writing about this because I have heard from others experiencing intense grief that this is not unusual, but it can be a bit concerning. Perhaps my sharing will help make you feel more normal. Or maybe this article will help you understand a friend who is grieving and seems to have "fallen back" into old fears or habits.

Issues such as fears, sleeplessness, overeating, depression, aches and pains, and many others may reappear for people stricken by grief - even after years of recovery or being free from such things. Being tired, worn down and emotionally spent makes us vulnerable to mental and physical health issues.

After The Accident, I began to fear crowds and not want to be alone in groups of people. I was fearful of entering new places by myself.

These are issues that had been problems for me in the early years of our marriage. No need to go into why, but due to things that happened in my childhood I hated walking into a new place alone such as a new church or a social event. I experienced panic attacks in large crowds like an airport tram or a service counter where people crushed in to place their orders. Ron was aware of this and was very sensitive towards me, always telling me when he would be back if he stepped away from me while traveling, telling me when he left the house, making sure I was comfortable when at a crowded event, etc. He knows the story of why this was an issue for me. He loves me well.

With prayer, good counseling, and learned coping techniques, I overcame these issues. In fact, it had been more than twenty-five years since experiencing them. So much so that I had forgotten all about them!

For years I have traveled alone doing Home School for High School seminars around the country. I have been to many events unescorted. Having a husband who travels meant I did some things alone. And I was very okay with that. But since The Accident, I have experienced fear and anxiety again. This is not something I face daily or even regularly.

I have had lots of time while traveling the past year that I did things on my own.

- I flew into Chicago alone and had no problems in the airport or on the subway. In fact, I have flown to meet Ron six or seven times in the past year.
- I wandered through a trade show full of people alone. No anxiety!
- I wandered the Memphis Zoo all day alone and had a blast!
- I have attended plays, concerts, and arts events unescorted while he was gone and thoroughly enjoyed myself.
- I have participated in the Precept Ministries summer and fall study programs, traveling there alone.

No need to give more examples, but believe me when I say this is not something my friends should worry about. I'm not going crazy and I am not usually afraid or anxious. And it rarely happens in my hometown. But it does creep up sometimes.

A Panic Attack

For example: Going to Tennessee alone a couple of weeks ago I was fine. But going through the Orlando airport with Ron on the way home, I was very uncomfortable. Rational Me knew I was not in danger, but I began to have symptoms of a panic attack. The ticket counters were crazy crowded! Then Ron got through security ahead of me. He finished first and went around the corner. When I got through I could not see him and panic started.

I recognized it, took a deep breath, and did some quick self-talk: "He will wait for you. You have your ticket and know where to go. He is probably around the corner putting his shoes on. If you don't find him, use your phone." And of course, I reminded myself that in more than thirty-one years, he has never left me in an airport. If he did today, it would be a first!

My symptoms began to lessen. I kept taking deep breaths and walked through the crowd. And there he was, around the corner putting his shoes on - just as Rational Me had expected.

Ron noticed I was clearly uncomfortable going through security - hot, flushed, and sweaty. He asked if I was okay. I told him I was just a bit warm. No need to go into it all right then. After I found him past security, he noticed how hot I seemed and offered to get me lighter shirt from his carry-on for me to borrow. I thanked him as we rode the train to our terminal. I was dealing with panic and did not want to explain right then.

Once in the terminal, away from the overcrowded ticket counter, stuffy security area, and packed train I told him what had happened. I told him that I have begun to experience the fears and anxiety that plagued me in our early years together. He was loving and kind and understanding. He encouraged me. He did not make a big deal of it or offer platitudes. He didn't say, "you dealt with that years ago." He did not tell me this is silly or irrational or stupid.

He recognized this as a very real issue for me and gently placed a hand on my shoulder, helped me find a place to sit, got me something to eat and a cool drink (making sure I could see him as he went to the counter), and sat down to chat with me as if it had never happened. He loved me well.

I was soon feeling better: no more sweats, not flushed, heart rate slowed, and breathing became normal. The rest of the trip went beautifully despite crowds and weather delays all around.

I had had a small panic attack, recognized what was happening, used coping techniques, and asked for help. I have recognized that the issues of fear and anxiety have crept back up in my life since The Accident. And sometimes recognizing what is going on is more than half the battle. Understanding what is happening, we can often figure out how to deal with it.

Grief affects us.

Going through a tragedy like losing a loved one wears us down. Grief is exhausting! And when exhausted, issues that we had dealt with (and maybe even conquered) in the past may creep up again. It can be scary. You may feel like you are losing you mind. Or like you are taking steps backward.

If I feel like I am not doing well, I start feeling bad because I am not doing well, which makes me feels worse leading to more self-condemnation, thus starting a downward cycle ... unless I make choice to stop. I can make a choice for recovery.

After I began to experience these issues, I asked myself and God what was going on. I spent some time thinking about why I had become fearful, examining the times I had begun to panic. I prayed for guidance and wisdom. "Oh! I am tired and worn out from grieving this past year." I realized that I was not going crazy.

While talking with other bereaved parents I found out this kind of thing is common; it's not something to get upset about. But I also learned that I could and should do something about it.

Tools I use

I know fear of crowds and anxiety may be an issue for me periodically, so I take steps to help prevent fear or anxiety:

For hotels,

- I verify the schedule for the week so I know what to expect.
- I make sure I have healthy snack stuff and good reading material on hand. Stephen King books would not be a good idea for me!
- I make a list of folks I might meet for lunch or call to chat with while Ron is in his meetings.
- I check area maps to look for places I would be comfortable exploring or hanging out while Ron works.
- I try to get plenty of rest and a bit of exercise.
- I get outside for a while every day.
- I make sure I have some cash on hand.

For airports,

- I make sure my phone is fully charged.
- I hold my own ticket.
- I make sure I know what flight and which gate.
- I slow down to carefully read signs and am sure of where I am going.
- I am not shy about asking the folks at the counter for directions or help.
- I don't pack carry-on bags too heavy so they are easy to manage.
- I find the restroom before boarding in case we have delays in take-off.

For social and arts events,

- I invite a friend to go with me.
- I carefully choose which events to attend. Some theater shows that Andrew was in are still too hard for me.
- I sit in the back of the theater in case I need to leave. During Joseph, I stayed in the lobby for the two songs they sang at Andrew's memorial service.
- I arrive just before the curtain rises so I don't have to stand alone in a crowd.
- I wear comfortable, familiar clothing. This is not a good time to try out new fashions.
- I asked a friend who directs the Community Orchestra if I could attend the dress rehearsal for the free Christmas concert as I knew

it would be standing room only and did not have someone to go with. She was thrilled I wanted to come.

And on the rare occasions when fear or anxiety hit, I use the techniques I learned year ago: deep breathing, self-talk, thinking through the event, asking for help, etc. They still work.

Seek Help

The one thing I had not done until the Orlando airport was to tell Ron I was dealing with this again. I know he would have encouraged me, helped me, prayed for me, and loved me. I suppose I was a bit embarrassed. After all, I had overcome this years ago! This is not Ron's issue; he was not the cause of any of it. The things that caused this in the first place happened long before I met him. I didn't want to appear weak or crazy to him. Silly me! He loves me! He wants to know what is going on in my head. He wants to help when he can. He wants me to be transparent and truthful. I should have been months ago.

I don't know how long I will have to deal with this. But I know I can deal with it with the help of the Holy Spirit and with the love of my soul mate.

If, after the loss of a loved one, you have experienced rekindled fears or anxieties or other issues that you thought you had been rid of years ago, I encourage you to be truthful with those close to you. Let them know what is going on and how they might help. Don't hide it!

But don't give in to it either! Choose recovery! Get professional help if you need it, There is no shame in asking for help. There may be shame in pride and hiding secrets, but there is no shame in asking for help.

Take steps towards recovery, knowing that recovery takes time and effort. But recovery can happen if we do the right things, are patient, and seek help.

I am glad that I have tools to manage my issues and the love of my husband to help me. I am also grateful for the love of the Creator who sent His only Son to earth so that I can live an abundant, peaceful, and joy-filled life!

The Creator loves you, too, and will help you walk through whatever trials you are facing.

And maybe we can meet in a crowded place for dinner sometime to share how God brought us through yet another trial.

March 7

Responsibility

I am not responsible for:

- Anyone else's happiness.
- Anyone else's recovery.
- Anyone else's behavior, choices, or mental health.
- Anyone else's financial well-being, living conditions, or eating habits.
- Anyone else's spiritual condition.

I AM responsible for:

- My happiness
- My recovery
- My behavior
- My choices
- My mental health
- My financial well-being
- My living conditions
- My eating habits
- My spiritual condition

I am responsible for how I treat others and for my reaction to how they treat me.

And I am responsible for asking for help when I need it need.

In dealing with friends and family who are hurting due to their own choices, sometimes I just have to say over and over again:

Not my monkey. Not my circus.
Not my monkey. Not my circus.
Not my monkey. Not my circus.
Not my monkey. Not my circus.

God, Grant me the serenity to accept the things I cannot change, the courage to change the things I can, and the wisdom to know the difference. Amen

March 9

Steps towards Recovery

Yes, I'm posting about Recovery. Again. Some of you may disagree with me.

Please note: When talking about recovery from grief, I am not saying that this can or should happen quickly. Read through the first year! I struggled. I sobbed. I grieved! Read the quote on recovery I posted last month to understand what I mean by recovery from grief. Recovery takes time and work. It will not happen overnight. But when you are ready, with God's help, recovery can happen.

I believe that recovery is a choice. I believe that we can:

1. Choose to recover and take steps towards healing OR
2. Choose to stay in our addiction, depression, grief, or whatever -- without taking steps towards recovery.

In regards to recovery - I am not saying that your grief, addiction, depression or other issue was something you chose in the first place. Not at all. I know grief was not a choice for me! It was forced on me by a tragic accident. Sometimes we are faced with the need of recovery by no fault or choice of our own. I am saying that we can choose to stay there in our grief, depression, addiction or other issue, wallow in it, cause others pain while we languish in it, and eventually die there.

Or we can begin to take steps towards recovery.

Each person's recovery journey is unique just as each person's experiences and issues are unique. Regardless of the issue, the first steps to recovery are the same.

Here are the first three steps of recovery as written in "The Big Book" of AA:

1. We admitted we were powerless over alcohol—that our lives had become unmanageable.
2. Came to believe that a Power greater than ourselves could restore us to sanity.
3. Made a decision to turn our will and our lives over to the care of God *as we understood Him.*

I am not an alcoholic; however, recovery is not just for alcoholics and addicts. I found myself in need of recovery, so I looked at the 12 Steps. I have many friends who have been helped out of their addictions, mental health issues, and other problems by a 12-Step recovery program. I thought the steps could help me recover from the intense grief that followed the death of my son as well as from other issues in my life.

Step One

Regarding my grief, Step One was admitting that I had no power over my son's death; there was nothing I could do about it. It was done. He was gone. This realization and admission came within moments of hearing the news. I also came to point where I could admit that grief was not something I controlled; it hits when I least expect it! When grief overwhelmed me, I admitted the second part of Step One: that my life had become unmanageable.

I saw that grief could become overwhelming if I gave in to it completely, making my life unmanageable. Grief could overwhelm me. And it did many times in those first few days, weeks, and months. When grief became overwhelming, I had to admit my condition. I had to admit that I was not managing things well. I was suffering and not functioning. I had to recognize this and admit it. This was fairly easy for me. I knew I needed help to survive this tragedy.

Step Two

Then I had to choose to take Step Two - believing that a Power greater than me (God) could restore me to sanity. Or in my case, that only God could restore my broken heart and help me recover from the loss of my son.

I repeat: I came to believe that God could restore me to sanity. In order to be restored to sanity, I had to know I had lost sanity. I was thinking wrong thoughts, not functioning, and in need of recovery. I knew God could help me. I believed that He could help me recover. I believed that He could heal me in my grief. I believed that I did not have to stay in this pain or allow grief to control my life.

I could not listen to those who say, "It will never get better. You will always feel this way. It will hurt this much until you die." Or "This is just the way it is. You will sob at wrong moments. You family will just have to deal with it." Or "It's okay for you to not function, that's part of grief. You are now a mom who lost a son, the world will have to accept your new normal behavior."

I believed that God could and would restore me to sanity if I would let Him. I have watched friends go through the death of a child. Our many friends who had gone through this before us encouraged us, prayed for us, and shared their journey with us. These couples helped me to know that the pain would lessen and I would be able to heal. Step Two was easy for me as I had seen God work in the lives of other bereaved parents.

Step Three

I then had to take Step Three. I made a decision to turn my will and my life over to the care of God. I turned my pain and grief over to God. (The God of my understanding is the God of the Bible: the Father, His Son Jesus Christ, and the Holy Spirit.) There is freedom in turning it all over to God. In my grief, I was constantly turning things over to God. I was searching the Word and reading and studying and praying. You can, I hope, see my faith in my blog the past eighteen months.

Working through these first three steps in recovering from grief happened fairly quickly. The other nine...I am still working through those. And I am working these three in other areas of my life.

Recovery in other areas

I am not only recovering from the death of my son, I am working through other issues as well. I have had a number of alcoholics and addicts in my life. Their addictions have affected me in ways I cannot explain. Some are working a great program - going to meetings, working the steps with a sponsor, reading the materials, sponsoring others, etc. - and have been sober for years. Others are not. I work the steps as an "Al-anon" as well as being a bereaved parent. Realizing that I have no control over the choices and addictions of others, and that the issues surrounding addiction had made my life unmanageable, I came to believe that God could restore me to sanity even with Andrew's death and people I love struggling with addiction and mental illness. I daily made a decision to turn my life and will regarding these issues over to God.

I have a strong faith and have spent years studying the Bible, learning who God is, and memorizing scripture. I have a relationship with Christ. I know that God is good, compassionate, gracious, loving, and kind. I know He wants to help me, lead me, and care for me.

But turning my will and life over to Him? All of my will? That can be difficult. It will take lots of prayer and making right choices. I seem to want to pick it all up and carry it myself.

I have found that this is a daily challenge for me right now. I have to daily wake up, thank Him for another day on planet earth, and tell Him that I am His today - my life and my will are His and I need Him. I ask Him to lead me, guide me, and show me His will. I ask Him to help me to obey His will for me. This exercise helps me remember the truth. At night I thank Him for another day and ask Him to help me sleep.

I am sure that I will be working through all 12 Steps over the next few (or many) months. I may share some of my journey. I cannot share parts as they involve others whose stories are not mine to tell. Therefore much of my recovery story will be shared as it relates to grief. The steps are the same. My Higher Power is the same. The things I must do to fully recover are the same. Because ultimately recovery is not about what we are recovering from or the other people in our lives. Recovery is about dealing with my own life, my thoughts, my behaviors, my choices, and my issues as well as my mental, physical and spiritual health.

If you find yourself in need of recovery, may I encourage you to visit a 12-Step Program specifically geared toward your issue? It may help.

~~~~~~

March 10

I hear many bereaved moms complain that their spouse just doesn't grieve the way they do. Really? Oh sweet friend, have you noticed that you don't grieve the same way he does?

Ron once told me that he didn't want to talk about The Accident or Andrew's death. "But I don't mind that you do. I'll listen," he said. He meant it. And I love him for that.

But I also was careful not to talk about it as much after that. And when I stopped talking about it so much, I stopped thinking about it as much. I purposely tried to think about fun things, good memories, and that's what I bring up when mentioning Andrew.

Just like every other part of our marriage, there must be give and take, understanding, and less selfishness for us to walk hand in hand. Our lives have been changed, our marriage has been changed, and our walk has been changed. Hopefully for the better.

Not only can I expect Ron to let me grieve my way, but I will heal more completely if I let him help me and I help him.

Adoption

As I lay mentally reciting Romans 8 at 4:30 one morning, I was praying for friends who had flown to China to get their son the day before. They were matched with him more than two years prior but paperwork was taking forever! The time had finally arrived when they got to sign all the forms and bring their son home.

I thought about what Paul wrote concerning adoption. I lay there praying for my friends and thinking about how their situation illustrates what Paul wrote. I wrote them a note about it. Here are some of my thoughts.

"Dear Jeff and MaryAnn

I lay in bed early this morning praying for your family. I thought about your son and how long you have all waited for this time to come. In Romans chapter 8:18-25, Paul talks of our adoption as sons.

I was reminded of how Caleb was yours more than two years ago! He had been adopted in your hearts and minds. In your whole being he was and is your son. Both you and he were waiting with eager longing for the revealing of his adoption, for his body and life to be brought to your home, for him to be redeemed into your earthly home. He, of course, is too young to understand what all that means, what a glorious thing it is to be your son! But he will learn! And his fellow heirs will teach him. They have been interceding for him since his adoption. They, too, have loved him since he became their brother. He has been your son that whole time. Just not living in the same place, not yet seeing you face to face. Only the final paperwork was left to be done.

Your journey is a beautiful shadow of our own adoption as sons of God! Thank you for waiting patiently. Thank you for being used to show me a glimpse of what this passage is about. May all of you be blessed today and showered with His grace, peace, and love."

You may want to read Romans 8 to understand more about this adoption in Christ. It is available to all. It is available to you. Just ask for it!

Chapter Twelve

Life Continues,

And the Headstone

March 12

Twelve Things I Am Grateful for on the 12th

Today I am grateful for....

1. Lap 1
2. Lap 2
3. Lap 3
4. Lap 5
5. Lap 8
6. Lap 11
7. Lap 18
8. Lap 22
9. Lap 25
10. Lap 33
11. Lap 38
12. Lap 45

About a year ago I injured my shoulder. Three years prior to that, I had gotten off the couch and started working out. I went from overweight couch potato to overweight, slow triathlete.

I had cared for my wonderful mother-in-law during the last weeks of her life as she battled pancreatic cancer. It was one of the hardest things I have ever done. And it was one of the most wonderful things I have ever done. After the funeral and helping clean-out and sell her home within three weeks of her death, I was exhausted in every way. I was concerned that I would fall into depression, so I started working out for my mental health. About two months after Rita went to be with Jesus, I finished my first triathlon wearing number 44, her Post Office Box number.

Over the next two years, I completed a dozen or so triathlons, usually coming in last place. I loved that I could complete an event that involved swim, bike, and run! I worked out a couple of days per week. Workouts included weight training, yoga, swimming, biking, and walk/jogging. I am not in great shape, but I am healthy. After The Accident, I did only two more triathlons. I continued to work out a few times per month, but not like I had been.

Then last March I injured my shoulder; it involved a small tear in the muscle. Before my shoulder injury, I could easily swim a mile (35 laps) in about 40 minutes. Swimming has always been my strongest portion of a triathlon. But per doctor's orders I could not swim at all after the injury. From May through December the only activities I could do were walk and lots of Physical Therapy. I had surgery in September followed by more PT.

I cannot express how frustrating my down time was. Not working out regularly resulted in me getting as weak as when I first started.

With my doctor's okay, I tried swimming in January but could only go two laps before the pain was too much to go on. I cried. My shoulder simply had not healed enough for me to swim.

Since early January I have been working a couple of days each week with a trainer when not traveling with Ron - just simple weight lifting and a bit of cardio. Yesterday morning I worked out for an hour and then I decided to try swimming again.

I went slow and steady. It took me a full hour. My plan when I got in the water was to swim only five laps. Just five laps to see if I could go that far without pain. Even if I only kicked for two laps. But I felt good so continued swimming. Going for 10 laps. Then I thought, "I can do 15." Then "maybe half of a mile." Then on to 22. And so on. I decided to stop when I did because I was afraid I would be too sore tomorrow.

I swam 45 laps!!! That is 2250 yards. 6750 feet! That's almost 1.3 miles! I have never swum that far in my life!

Yet another lesson on recovery: Recovery takes time, hard work, encouragement, and help. Sometimes from a professional.

Now I need to find a bike riding buddy who is willing to go slow and start with short distances.

~~~~~~~

March 15

Conversation between Ron and our youngest daughter:
Ron: I fixed your car
Maggie: What was wrong with it?
Ron: It was out of gas.

I love it when he fixes our cars like that.

March 16

Seeing Les Miserable

I went to see Les Mis Thursday night. Alone. Well, kind of alone. I drove by myself. I wanted to go see it after seeing the cast perform at the ARD Memorial Arts Benefit. However, I did not want to go because of so many memories.

Andrew played Thenardier at the same community theater when he was 16. It was his first big lead role. He loved that show! He was amazing! I knew it would be hard to see the show performed without my son. A friend encouraged me to go and even reserved my ticket for me. She sat by me and held my hand through a couple of the songs. I'm glad I went.

I cried. Not right away. "Bring Him Home" did it. And the tears flowed the rest of the night. Thank you cast and crew for your hard work and for sharing your talents with our community. And thank you for helping me heal, though many of you do not even know me.

Here's a message I so would like to share with the world: My son lived! He was real and he was loved. My son still lives. He is still real and he is still loved.

You see, grief is painful, takes time, and involves hard work. Recovery from grief takes doing the next right thing over and over. The next right thing for you. This is true whether your child was preborn and you don't know the cause of death; was five and died from cancer; was twenty and died in a car wreck; or was 48 and shot herself.

If you know someone who experienced the death of a child and you have not, please don't judge, offer platitudes, or give advice. Simply listen and love. If you need help learning what that looks like, ask someone who is further down that road or search the web for articles on helping grieving parents.

If you don't want to be around grief, don't be. If you don't want to read posts about it, don't read them, hide them, or unfriend those people on FB. Please do not tell them they are too ...whatever. Don't tell them to get over it already. If you need help on what to say and what not to say to a grieving mom or dad, Google it! If in doubt about whether to say something, keep your mouth shut and fingers away from the keyboard.

March 17

Miscellaneous Thoughts Today

For those who don't know it, grief sucks. It hits when you least expect it. You can't fix what caused it. Time alone does not make it easier or better.

But good friends who love me, encourage me, and remember my goofy Andrew do help make it easier and better. When you mention him or post pictures, it lets us know he was and is still loved and missed. Thank you. You guys know who you are. I couldn't have made it through without you.

It took us a year to get the headstone designed and set. Ron and I went together to see it once it was set. I expected to be sad. But it turned out just like we planned and I love that it gives a glimpse into who he was. It made me happy to see my son's life and joy honored.

It is not a sad place for me at all. He is not there! It's just a monument to his life placed over his mortal body. It also doesn't give me any comfort for the same reason, so I don't go visit his grave.

I charge you in the presence of God and of Christ Jesus, who is to judge the living and the dead, and by his appearing and his kingdom: preach the word; be ready in season and out of season; reprove, rebuke, and exhort, with complete patience and teaching. For the time is coming when people will not endure sound teaching, but having itching ears they will accumulate for themselves teachers to suit their own passions, and will turn away from listening to the truth and wander off into myths. As for you, always be sober-minded, endure suffering, do the work of an evangelist, fulfill your ministry.

For I am already being poured out as a drink offering, and the time of my departure has come. I have fought the good fight, I have finished the race, I have kept the faith. Henceforth there is laid up for me the crown of righteousness, which the Lord, the righteous judge, will award to me on that Day, and not only to me but also to all who have loved his appearing.

2 Timothy 4:-8 | ESV

March 18

Spring!

I'm writing this sitting on my porch swing. It is a beautiful evening! I spent much of the day working on our property. I have an old Kubota tractor that I love to mow with. With just over fifteen acres I need the five-foot mowing deck. Mowing is peaceful. Some days I listen to music. Fall of 2013, I spent my mowing time talking to God. Today I just was. I mowed and thought and looked around at the beauty of our property.

I posted a picture from the porch looking out to our tank. (For you non-Texans, that's a pond.) We are in the middle of a five year drought. But our tank stays full most of the year, drying up only in late August the past few years. When the drought ends, we will stock it with small fish.

If you look to the left of the tank, you can see a large nest in a tree just over the tank. We have had a pair of hawks nesting there for at least eight years. It is fun to hear the babies calling for dinner. I haven't seen them yet this year, but I hope they come home soon. In a week or two, leaves will hide the nest.

To the right are The Three Trees. A hammock hangs down there and is a favorite place for reading. My children spent many hours doing their school work in that hammock. A tire swing hangs from one of those trees as well. There is also a tall hanging swing. Nearby is an old dead mesquite tree that fell over when we had floods in 2007. It is a great place to climb and for taking family pictures.

On the other side of the creek, which runs along the tree line, we have five acres which the boys turned into a paintball battleground. They have foxholes, bunkers, and a two-story fort back there. We've had many days when they pulled the picnic table to The Three Trees to have a place for snacks, drinks, and ammo. I've loved looking out my front window to see a few dozen homeschool kids in common heading to the woods to play.

You can't see The Fort in this picture. It is a three-level play fort with slide, gravel pit, climbing ropes and more. The top is eighteen feet up! My boys built the whole thing. My grandchildren love it. We also have a fire pit around back where teens have spent many cool evenings talking and singing and telling stories.

I am grateful for all the wonderful times we have had here. Yes. I am blessed.

March 19

Fake It!

"Sometimes smiling is an act of defiance against what's pressing down hard. Sometimes smiling is an act of sheer bravery.'

Sometimes smiling in brokenness is how we remember: We are the Resurrection People and there is more happening than what seems and this is how to practice faith."

~Ann Voskamp

The quote above reminded me of the motto "Fake it 'til you make it." Smiling in the midst of brokenness, or faking it until we are making it, can help us as we recover from intense grief.

Sometimes we smile when we don't feel like it. Sometimes we have to *act* like we are okay because we have forgotten what "okay" feels like, what it looks like, or how it behaves. Suffering and grief has become the norm and it may seem that we will never feel "normal" again. can be okay again, that I can talk about things other than loss, that God can and will heal my heart. As I act like I am okay, over time that behavior once again becomes normal, familiar, and comfortable.

And then one day - after time has passed and I have been doing healthy things as part of my work towards recovery - I wake up to realize that I am okay, not just acting like it anymore. I am beginning to experience recovery as defined by H. Norman Wright! (See February 15)

Additionally, acting like I am okay allows others to be okay around me without worrying if I am going to breakdown down yet again. It allows them to breathe and not be walking on eggshells around me all the time worrying that something they say will cause me more pain or bring on another sob session. It allows us to enjoy being together in this adventure without the focus being on me.

It is a gift of serenity and peace from me to them. A gift they cannot demand but which I can freely offer. And we all know that folks say dumb things when they are trying so hard not to hurt us and show us love in their imperfect ways. Acting like I am okay allows them to stop trying so hard and to get back to simply being my friend.

Then our conversations can be about something other than death, funerals, grief, missing my kid and how I am. We can talk about their lives, and I can love them rather than being so needy. I can rejoice with them, hear stories about what is going on with their family, and listen when they hurt without making it about me or my grief. And in loving others I heal even more. I begin to truly experience recovery from my grief and pain.

I am not talking about stuffing my pain or denying my feelings. That can be harmful and delay recovery. I am talking about acting okay around others and taking time to be real with God at a more appropriate time.

If you are suffering or grieving, perhaps you can act okay for a little while today. And then tomorrow act okay for a little longer. Maybe try acting okay at church, or work, or school. Or at dinner with friends. You may find that it feels nice to act okay. And then you may find yourself beginning to *be okay*!

Fake it. Until you make it.

~~~~~~~

March 19

Two years ago this weekend I did a triathlon in Denton, TX. In this event I rode 24-27 MPH going out and 8-10 MPH coming back. Strong wind. In the run, I had horrible shin splints and almost quit. But I did not quit; I limped to the finish line.

And I won a silver medal!

I was last out of 386 athletes. I finished way behind the other athletes, but since there were only two in my age bracket, I got a silver medal.

There are advantages of being an old triathlete. I hope to do a couple of events this year. If I continue until I am 60, I'll win most events (for my age bracket) by default.

I choose not to quit in my life race either. No matter how hard or painful it gets. I face pain, suffering, and heartache. But I will not quit. And I will also face joy, laughter, healing, and peace.

Finish the race. Finish it well, my friends.

March 20

My friend Kathy came to visit me yesterday. She was in OKC and came through Wichita Falls on her way home to St. Louis. Yes, my version of geography is rubbing off on my friends!

As we ran some errands together, I asked her if she minded swinging by the cemetery with me so I could place the coin on the headstone. She looked funny at me and said, "That's weird. I had a vision of us going to the grave on my way here. But thought about how you said you don't go there often. I wasn't sure how to bring it up."

I am praising God for good friends who are listening to the Holy Spirit and are willing to swing by my son's grave with me while out running around town.

The reason I wanted to go by the cemetery? I took one of the 50th Season commemorative coins Kris Miller, executive director of TEXAS, gave us to place on Andrew's headstone. I did it for those of you who come through town and stop there on your way to Canyon.

Congrats to all who made it in the cast and crew of the Texas the Musical 50th Season.

We went shopping after that. Graham, Chandler, Marshall, Peter, David, Adam, Margaret, Elijah, and Colin will all be getting Easter basket packages in the mail soon.

Kathy and I had fun together.

March 23

The Headstone – Front Side

There are not many places where families can post pictures of their child's grave marker and have others comment on how lovely it is. The While We're Waiting page is one such place. A gal recently asked "How do you decide what to put on a headstone?" Dozens posted comments and pictures showing the diversity in our choices for headstones and markers. I hated looking at those pictures. And I loved looking at those pictures.

It took us just over a year to get our son's headstone set.

We had discussed the need to decide on a design many times during that year, but we wanted to get it just right. After all, it would be written in stone.

We wanted to honor Andrew and design it such that anyone who sees it would understand some of who he was while here on earth.

We chose black granite. It looks strong and masculine. Powerful! The base is rough and unpolished, like Andrew sometimes was. But most of it is polished and smooth. Oh! How smooth he could be when presenting his arguments for some project he wanted to take on!

And when he delivered a pick-up line, he was smooth! That boy loved his pick-up lines. They rarely worked, though -- Perhaps because so many of the women he danced with or went to school with saw him as a true friend, not just another guy trying to get a date. Maybe it was because he never used his pick-up lines to ask out the gals he actually wanted to go out with. To those he was kind and considerate, and a bit shy. To Andrew, the pick-up lines were funny, a joke, and a way to bring a smile to those around him.

Andrew's siblings had said they wanted "FOREVER OUR PRINCE" on the front of the headstone. They had asked the local community theater to put this on the marquee the week he died.

Andrew had played Prince Charming in community theater productions of Sleeping Beauty, Snow White, and Cinderella. He made a wonderful Prince Charming. Snow White was one of his first roles when he was just about 12. A few years later his big brother Adam played a dragon/boy (Prince Charming's friend) in Sleeping Beauty. In that show, during rehearsals, Sleeping Beauty actually threatened to slap him if he really tried to kiss her in the Kissing Scene. He and the actress had a bit of middle school history. They made up later, but never kissed. At least, not that I know of. Cinderella was produced his senior year of high school. At six feet tall, Andrew looked dashing as the prince. Years of dance had made him graceful as well. He loved the role of Prince Charming.

Andrew did not just play a prince on stage.

He was a prince of a student -- honor roll at both Midwestern State University and West Texas A&M University. He majored in both dance and accounting and made great grades in both areas of study. He would have finished his BBA this past December and his BA in dance a year later. Instructors from WT sent kind notes after his death telling us how much they enjoyed having him in their classes.

He was a prince of brother -- his siblings all had their challenges and conflicts growing up, but they all agreed that he was a great brother. He loved them and they loved him. Family dinners were full of stories and laughter. Three of the brothers had taken a road-trip to visit their oldest sister his last Christmas. The boys had lots of fun adventures together, and Margaret and Andrew looked amazing when they hit the dance floor together at parties and weddings.

He was a prince of a dancer -- though clumsy off stage, he loved to dance! And he was being paid to dance with Lone Star Dance Company in Amarillo. Yes, Andrew fell sometimes. All dancers do. But he pushed himself to try harder, leap farther, jump higher, and to do lifts beyond what his experience. It was a joy to watch him dance.

He was a prince of a son -- I adored my son. Andrew had a way about him that made me feel like a good mom. He was quick to blow up, but quick to repent as well. We had lots of deep conversations about what was going on in his life, his fears, dreams, hopes, and friendships. I loved hearing my Prince Andrew tell stories. He made me laugh. A lot. I smile when I think of him. I am grateful to God for allowing me to be him mom. I miss his hugs and hearing him stomp through the house.

On the front of the headstone, we have his full name: Andrew Raymond Duncan. His middle name is after his paternal great grandfather Ramon Estes. Ramon Estes was a godly man, kind and compassionate. He loved music! Even in his 80's he would go to "the old folks home" to do "singing's." I know he and Andrew are worshiping together now.

We knew we wanted a passage of scripture on the stone. Andrew was a follower of Jesus Christ and we wanted to reflect that in the design of the stone. His little sister Margaret suggested Psalms 16:11|NIV: **"You make known to me the path of life; in your presence there is fullness of joy; at your right hand are pleasures evermore."** Andrew brought joy to many people in his short life. A huge part of his joy came from knowing Christ. The rest came from just being Andrew - fun, smart, kind, and a bit goofy. He is experiencing the ultimate joy now in Heaven.

Back of the Headstone

The back of the headstone tells more of the story of who Andrew was.

Many people put the last name at the top of a headstone. Andrew never went by "Duncan." (He did go by "Dance Drew" at TEXAS. And his Uncle Bob called him "Ronnie Bob." But that is a whole different story.) And since his full name is on the front, we put just his first name at the top "ANDREW."

The cross design is from a dog tag Andrew had hanging from his rear-view mirror from the time he first learned to drive. Even when he had to change cars with one of his brothers for some reason, he took that cross dog tag and hung it from his mirror. I bought duplicates of the necklace and gave one to each of his siblings after his death. The original still hangs from the mirror of the car Andrew drove. Margaret now drives that car.

While trying to design the headstone, I made little cutouts of these symbols to arrange. Our oldest son David walked by and saw what I was doing. He reached down and moved the cross to the top. "The cross has to be at the top, Momma. It's obvious," he said and walked off. He was right.

Going clockwise from the cross -

Batman needs no introduction. Andrew loved Batman! When we first talked to the other kids about what to put on his headstone, "Forever Our Prince" and Batman were the two things they insisted on.

In the pictures of our family taken in May 2014, you can see his nephews wearing Batman t-shirts, and they got Batman bathrobes for Christmas this past year. Some day they will understand the significance of Batman. At rehearsal for the first production after The Accident, Andrew's dance teachers from WT wore Batman in his honor. I love them for that. I could list dozens of times his friends have worn Batman clothing and sent me pictures with a note of how much they cared for Andrew and still think of him. I love them for those pictures and notes.

Next is the **Boy Scout Eagle symbol**. All of our boys are Eagle Scouts. Andrew worked hard to achieve that honor. He was proud of being an Eagle Scout. I am glad to have four Eagle Mom pins. In the days after The Accident, his Scout leader had a new uniform made with all the correct badges and pins. He built a shadow box frame for that uniform. It was on display at the memorial service. Scouts from around town led a Color Guard ceremony during the memorial service. It was touching to see dozens of Scouts line the theater aisles and to hear Scouts of all ages throughout the audience recite the Scout Oath.

The bottom shows the logo from the show **TEXAS**. Andrew was in the show summers of 2012 and 2013. He loved being in that show. He was on his way home from the annual cast party when The Accident happened killing five cast members. Including the show's logo on the headstone is also a tribute to the others involved in The Accident and to the 12 Second Warriors.

Next is the **West Texas A&M University** logo. He attended WTA&MU summer of 2012 through his death. And loved it! Andrew was majoring in both dance and accounting, working on two separate degrees. He made excellent grades in both areas of study. He loved both accounting and dance. And he loved his classmates and instructors at WTA&MU.

The **drama masks** represent Andrew's love for live theater. He started acting at about the age of twelve in "It's a Wonderful Life." He was in more than 24 community theater shows during high school and worked for three summers as a professional actor/dancer. When not on stage, he was often working backstage for productions at our two community theaters. Some of the shows he was in include Sleeping Beauty, Snow White, Cinderella, Cats, South Pacific, Guys and Dolls, Narnia, Beauty and The Beast, Little Women, Les Mis, Pirates of Penzance, Joseph and his Technicolor Dream Coat, A Christmas Carol and many more I can't remember. He was in some youth shows, but because of his height and talents, Andrew starred in many shows with adults as well. He sang with the Community Orchestra and Community Singers. He was a part of Opera Breve at Midwestern State University while in high school. I am grateful that I have hours of video of my son singing and dancing and bringing joy to audiences of all ages.

The very bottom has the quote **"Hey! I'm in the show!."** Whether only chorus or leading man, Andrew was glad to be on stage. When he explained his role in TEXAS the first year, he said, "I am carrying a flag. The Mexican

Flag. I am in the back row. The best guys dance "partner dances" and are in the front row. I am in the back. But, HEY! I'M IN THE SHOW! And hundreds of people who auditioned for dance rolls are not. I can get better and move up if I work hard." The second year, he was in the center of the front row for the opening number. He did all partner dances that summer. He had worked hard, had great instructors and had become a talented dancer. He was still thrilled to be in the show.

All of these symbols surround the word **DANCE** because that was his passion. Andrew began taking dance lessons at age sixteen because of his passion for music theater. He was a great actor and had a terrific voice; however, dance was his weakness. He knew he had to improve his dance skills to make it in musical theater. Once Andrew began taking dance lessons, he fell in love with dance and took every class he could fit into his busy schedule. Gals loved to dance with him - on stage and off. He owned a tuxedo and rarely was there a high school dance in our town that Andrew did not have a date to. As a homeschool guy, Andrew got asked to dances at just about every public high school around. What high school girl doesn't want to go to a dance with a guy who will spin her around the floor, make people laugh, and looks good in a tux?

We were pleased with the way the back of the headstone turned out. It tells the story of our son's life. His was a life centered around dance under the cover of the cross of Christ. It still is. Now Andrew dances for an audience of One. Someday I will join him in worshiping at the throne.

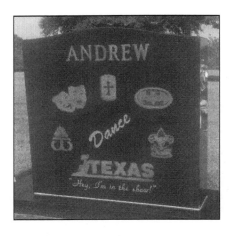

Chapter Thirteen

I Have Other Children

And Other Issues

March 23

Police at the Door

A strange thing happened Sunday night.

Apparently someone from next door called the police about some kids trespassing on their property. But the call contained the wrong address. Cop came to my door by mistake.

I am thankful I was on the phone with Ron when saw the police walking toward my door. I called him back after the cop left.

The last time a cop came to our door was at 5:45 am a little over 19 months ago to tell us Andrew had been killed.

Took me a while to get my heart to stop racing after I shut the door, called Ron back, and hung up the phone.

But in the moment just after I realized who was coming to my door...before I opened it...thoughts of why, who might be hurt or dead this time, what might have happened ran through my mind....I also had a weird peace. Kind of like I thought, "I have survived bad news before and will be okay no matter why he is here. With Christ I can face this."

Some of the changes brought on by this suffering are good. I pray more, react less, and have peace even in potentially bad situations.

When I don't know how to pray or what to think, or am scared or lonely, the Holy Spirit is leading me and interceding for me.

I know that God works even ugly things for my good and He has called me to be transformed to the image of his Son. I know that even if the police officer had been bearing bad news, it would not separate me from the love of God in Christ Jesus my Lord. I hold on to these truths more than I did before. These help me have peace, even when a cop knocks on my door after dark.

March 25

Why I Don't Write a Lot About My Other Children

My blog began after the death of Andrew. It was a way to let family and friends know how we were doing in the months after The Accident. It morphed into an outlet for my thoughts on grief, God, and healing. Many of my followers have experienced loss and I pray that my words encourage them as they walk through healing and recovery.

I have shared much about who Andrew was, but I have six other children still living. Why don't I ever write much about them?

In a nutshell: Because they are alive. I believe that we should respect the privacy of others and not share their story - it is theirs to tell.

You see, I believe their lives are their stories to tell. I don't post about them by name or picture unless I ask them first (other than on their birthday when I like to post a birthday story about them). I rarely share details about their lives unless they have made it public. For example, Peter can be seen on national TV broadcasts cheering for OU, so I am comfortable telling you he is attending OU and is on the cheer squad. Who he is or isn't dating, what he likes or dislikes, etc. are not for me to tell.

I do sometimes tell of something they have done for me or said to me that blessed me. I am a momma who likes to brag on her kids. And I have permission from our daughter to post any pictures of her sons.

So, though I love my other adult children, when I write about them it will be to share my thoughts, my struggles, my joys, and my views. And I will try to respect their privacy as I do.

~~~~~~~

March 26

Live in harmony with one another. Do not be haughty, but associate with the lowly. Never be wise in your own sight.
Romans 12:16 |ESV

I failed at this yesterday. But will try to do better today.

March 31

Reflections on My Weekend

1. Road trips can be fun no matter the reason or destination if you are with the one you love.

2. Attitude matters. We had fun because we looked at it as adventure.

3. God knows what I need. We had been trying to sell my suburban for two months. If it had sold, we would not have had a vehicle to tow the Harley home with.

4. Even after 37 hours in a car, no shower and road trip food, we can choose to overlook stuff, be kind, and enjoy the ride.

5. I do not want to live in my car. Ever. Not that I was considering it, but it has now been eliminated as an option.

6. When taking an emergency road trip, pack more than one each sleeping bag, blanket, air mattress, and pillow. Just in case you end up sleeping in the car.

7. I'll do just about anything for my adult kids if they need my help...provided it really is helpful for them and they are making wise choices and doing the next right thing. If not, my answer will be, "I hope that works out for you."

8. I love my husband and his quirky sense of humor. Me (as we make a bed in the back of the SUV): "If anyone breaks in you will have to protect us. I forgot to pack my weapon." Ron: "Don't worry. I'll squeal real loud."

9. God provides. Shortly after the above exchange, the hotel security guard knocked on the window. "Just wanted to say good night. Don't worry. Sorry there is no room in the inn. Sleep well. I'll walk by every 30-45 minutes and keep an eye on you. You're safe here." He could have made us leave.

10. Always check on hotel rooms before getting to an area of national park with no cell coverage.

11. If you can't find a hotel room, cuddling with the one you love in the back of an SUV for a few hours can be the next best thing.

12. When your parents are taking an emergency road trip to help you, be sure you get lots of sleep: you're doing the driving on the way home. David seemed to know this naturally and did a great job Sunday.

Yep. Emergency road trips can be an adventure. I love my son. I love my husband. I love my life.

April 2

Myth: Kind words will help them heal.

No! Truth will help us heal. Truth spoken in love. Church leaders need to know the truth about Heaven, hell, and life after death. So they don't say hurtful stuff. And the kindest words are often "I'm sorry" followed by nothing else.

Myth: Time heals all wounds. Given time, the family will get back to normal.

Time spent doing the right things, including grieving, and time spent with God will help us help heal. But we need help from friends and family. And we will never be the same as before our loss.

Myth: They will never heal. This is a wound that just cannot heal.

With Christ we can heal. Healing often leaves a scar, a reminder of the wound. But healing can happen.

~~~~~~~

April 4

Hard Week

Yucky stuff has happened this week. Horrible stuff. Stuff involving my other kids. Stuff I can't share because it is not my story. I hurt when my kids hurt. I wish I could fix it. I can't. God can.

God is still on the throne.

I have been watching for weeks to see if the hawks will come back to our yard again this year. I saw them this afternoon! They are home from their winter travels and will soon have babies. I enjoy knowing they are home.

Father,

Thank you for sending the hawks back again this year. I enjoy them. They remind me of Grandmother Estes and Grandma Duncan who loved birds. They remind me that Your eye is in the sparrow (or hawk). Thank you for loving me and for grace.

Amen

April 5

Ten Years

Ten years ago on Easter morning I woke to a phone call. It was my sweet stepmom. She called to tell me my daddy was gone. My daddy had died during the night. He was and is at peace.

I miss him. I wish he had known how great my kids turned out. I wish he could have seen the boys get their Eagle badges. I wish he could have held my grandchildren. I wish I could call him when I need a laugh or a hug. Sometimes a girl needs her dad to say, "I know it hurts. I love you."

Someday I will join him in Heaven because of the Cross and Resurrection. Death has been overcome.

Funny story: A few minutes after that phone call, I came out of my room with tear-stained face and asked one of my boys to get me a suitcase out of the attic. I went back into my room to get dressed and pack to go be with my stepmom.

When Ron went into the living room a little while later, the kids were waiting for him. Their message: "Whatever you did, dad, Fix It!" All they knew was mom is crying and packing. Must be dad's fault.

We quickly sat them down and told them Granddad Bailey had died. I'm not sure but I think they were relieved. Then they were sad.

Even in his death my daddy made me smile. And gave me a great story. He loved to tell stories! I am sure he and Andrew are telling stories in Heaven.

~~~~~~

April 6

Peter made the cheer squad at the University of Oklahoma! He will be cheering for the Sooners again next year! (They have to tryout each year.) And majoring in engineering, as is our oldest son.

Other OU grads from my family: all four of my grandparents, my mom, and my dad. Ron studied engineering and I studied accounting. My sons are fourth-generation Sooners. Boomer Sooner!

April 7

Sweep, then Mop

A number of years ago, we had friends stationed here with Air Force when he received orders for overseas deployment. She had schizophrenia. I volunteered to keep an eye on her while he was gone. I dearly loved Tina.

One day I went to visit her on base. The house was a wreck. She was hearing voices again. Long story short: she had run out of meds five days before. I helped her get to the doctor and get more meds. I also helped her clean the house. She got out a mop and started on the floors. I could see a ring of mud around the walls and rugs. I stopped her. "Tina, sweetie, we need to sweep first then mop. Otherwise you will just be moving wet dirt around."

Her response, "Oh! No one has ever taught me how to clean! Sweep .... Then mop! That's the ticket!" She did a great job cleaning.

I checked on her almost weekly. Others helped as well. I was glad when her husband came home. It was a long seven months. We lost contact after they moved. I have wondered what happened with her. I pray she is well. I fear she is not.

"Sweep, then mop" has become a mantra for my husband and me. Sometimes it's the simple things that matter. Do the first right thing. Then do the next right thing. That is the way to recovery. Step by step.

We can help others by doing and teaching these simple things. Don't assume others know the basics, be willing to model and teach and work with those needing your help.

Today on FB my husband posted, "Process is essential. Sweep...then mop." He and his friends mentioned a few more examples:

- Pillage then burn.
- Think then speak.
- Train then transform.
- Tear down then rebuild.
- Determine wind direction then pee.
- Wax on, wax off.
- Rehearse then perform.
- Measure then cut.

April 8

Truth

One of my sons posted this yesterday:

> "There are always three sides to any story:
> yours, mine, and the truth. "

~~~~~~

April 9

My thoughts today: Anger is not sin. It's okay to be hurt, angry, upset.

How we act towards others and what we do with our anger determines right or wrong. If I lash out or am hateful to those around me in my anger, that is sin. If I pout, take revenge, or hang on to bitterness that is wrong.

If I cry, yell, call out to nature, or God or in my car alone... Nothing wrong with that. We are human. We feel. We hurt. We have thoughts. We deal with it.

Grief has changed me.

Be angry and do not sin;
do not let the sun go down on your anger,
and give no opportunity to the devil.

Ephesians 4:26-27 | ESV

~~~~~~

April 10

When I told my big brother I was expecting, he said we should name the baby Ronald Robert after him and Ron. We'd just moved to Tennessee. Since Tennessee babies need two names, we could call him Ronnie Bob.

We named the baby Andrew Raymond. Uncle Bob suggested Andy Ray was almost as good, but he always called him Ronnie Bob.

I miss Ronnie Bob.

April 11

Daniel Study

I may not post much this week. I am studying Daniel. With six ladies from around the country. Using Precept Ministries studies.

Parts I & II. Eighteen lessons. Discussions plus video lectures. That is eighteen weeks' worth of lessons in eight days. Three on Saturday and three on Sunday. Then two each day for six days.

Slumber party at my house. Good food. Spiritual and physical food.

End times. Integrity. Wisdom. Principles. Convictions.

Observation. Interpretation. Application.

Word of God + sisters in Christ = great week.

~~~~~~~

April 16

Friendship

Tonight the ladies and I sat on the front porch enjoying the beautiful weather. We talked and shared and laughed. Discussion of biblical prophecy can be intense. I'm not sure I agree with everything the other gals see or believe. But our disagreements are over things that more learned men than us have been discussing for centuries. And the important stuff we all agree on: God is sovereign. He loves us. He rules over all, and He sets kings in place and takes them down. He loves us.

Did I mention He loves us?

I enjoy getting to know these gals. They are different from me. And I love our differences. We all love Jesus and want to learn more about the Word.

It's a good week.

April 20

Gossip

When someone tells you how a family member or friend did something awful, resulting in emotional pain and anger...

1. Remember there are two sides to every story
2. Be careful of taking sides or drawing conclusions
3. Consider what you know about the speaker
4. Consider what you know about the accused
5. Consider it may be none of your business.

When we are hurting, it is easy to let our guard down and to get caught up in issues that are not ours. Guard your heart. Don't pick things up that are not yours.

~~~~~~

April 24

Some days ....

Some days are harder than others.

We've had a few tough weeks: one adult child in ICU with pneumonia, one experiencing strange (and dangerous) behavioral side effects of seizure meds, ugly tax bill, car died, and few other struggles.

Some of this got better, eventually. Daughter out of hospital, meds changed and kid back to cheerful self, taxes paid, new used car purchased.

I'm not in much of a mood to write. I've chosen not to write about struggles my living children go through. I'm trying to respect their privacy.

It's raining and cold. Perfect day to sit and read a good book or watch a good movie. I'm grateful for the rain. Everything is green and we need any rain we can get in north Texas.

I have all I need, just not all I want.

Folks have posted new (to me) pictures and videos of Andrew this week. I love them. And I hate that he is not here to comment on them. I miss my son this week. He always had a story to tell, a hug to give, or a smile to share. He made me feel like a good mom. Especially when others don't.

April 30

Ill

I have been feeling out of sorts the past couple of weeks. I have a belly ache. I've had it for the past couple of months. But I didn't realize how much it was affecting me. Probably the results of taking an anti-inflammatory so long, due to my shoulder injury. Now it's getting much worse. I am amazed at how physical pain affects my mental state.

My life is busy and stuff happens. But my life is always busy and with a brood of chicks, even grown chicks, something is always going to be happening. The events of the last month affected me more than usual, not because they *are* more than usual, but because of belly pain. I feel down, critical, out of sorts.

This past weekend Ron asked on four occasions if I was okay. That's when it hit me: I am acting like I am sick or in pain. This is not how I want to act when he is home. I want to be kind and joyful and loving for him. But now I am ill. And Ron is being amazingly kind and joyful and loving. Bringing me foods that are good for my belly. Encouraging me. Holding me while I try to sleep. This is not surprising or unusual. It's the kind of guy he is: wonderful, loving, smart, funny, hardworking, talented, kind, fun...I should stop now before I make you want to gag. Suffice to say I love my guy!

I am confident that we will get this figured out. I went to doctor Tuesday and she put me a different stomach med. Blood tests run. Possibly an appointment with gastro doc next week and a scope. Not fun. But not life-threatening. Just painful. I thank God for good doctors and great insurance.

Here's the deal: Pain affects us. It affects every part of who we are and how we live. We often cannot see the pain others are experiencing. Many people we see each day have invisible physical illnesses: MS, migraines, heart disease, diabetes, and many others. Lots of folks live with chronic pain that we don't see. Others live with heartaches we cannot see: bad marriage, addiction, grief, poverty, infertility, financial issues, mental illness in those they love, conflict, fears, abuse, and much more.

So if someone is grouchy, mean, or simply unkind, give them kindness in return. You cannot know what pain they may be carrying or what challenges they may be facing. You may be the only kindness they experience today.

May 2

Gratitude and a Bit of Sadness

I am grateful for all my kids. (They are not kids anymore.)

I'm glad I get to be their mom. I proud of the men and women they have become and of the things they are doing. They are kind and generous. They are hardworking, loving, and fun. I'm proud that they have grown up and have lives of their own.

But I miss seeing them around the house. The noise! The laughs! Even the fights. I love how noisy our home was. I loved seeing them cook together and play together. I love how the Duncan boys were known as good workers if you had a project to be done. I loved seeing the girls help each other. I loved all the friends coming and going. The house was rarely quiet when they were all home, even during the night.

And I love how peaceful it is in now at the house. I can sit and study, read, or just think. We hear the birds singing and coyotes howling. We often wake to the donkey next door braying. Sitting on the front porch in the morning and evenings is so quiet and peaceful. And my house stays clean now!

I have a great relationship with most of my kids. I enjoy talking with them and hearing about the good things happening in their lives. I'm thrilled when new pictures are posted on social media or new stories about their exploits are shared. I love getting phone calls and texts. My grandsons call to talk even! At almost six, Elijah can carry on a long conversation. Three year old Colin is too busy sometimes, but he always says "thank you" when he gets a package from us. We get to see them all fairly often in our travels.

So don't get me wrong, I have a great life and lots of joy. But I miss Andrew. I wish I had....well too many things I wish I had done more of, or less of, or done better.

I've been feeling grateful...and a bit sad lately. Part of having a child die. Gratitude for all I had with him, for all I still have, and sadness because he's not here to be a part of the goings on.

Perhaps it's time for some tractor therapy. Or jelly beans. Or Texas chocolate sheet cake if anyone wants to make one for me.

Have a blessed day.

May 6

Attention all Wichita Falls Peeps who are staying up to monitor the storms tonight: I am very tired. I want to go to sleep. If a tornado heads my way, please call me to tell me to hide in the closet. That is all.

~~~~~~

May 9

TimeHop

TimeHop is a Facebook app that shows you status updates and pictures that you posted on this date in years past. This app was really messing with my emotions Friday. Here is a FB post from two years ago.

> "Why is it that when college kids come home between semesters they bring total chaos with them and all my other children do terrible things like go for ice cream late without me and stay up past my bedtime playing Old Blue Eyes very loudly?"

Andrew had come home for his last weekend. Ever. Mother's Day. He would leave that Sunday for his second season of Texas. He and his younger siblings had fun that evening. They loved playing vinyl albums from granddad Bailey's collection.

Here is another post from that same day.
> "Me: Where is Andrew?
> Peter: Maybe he went out with Margaret
> Me: Where is Margaret?
> Peter: Maybe she went out with Andrew
> My children are so helpful!"

My dear friend commented, "Now you know where he is, my friend." I love her for comments like this. I am so grateful for other parents who walk this grief journey with us. I miss my son today. This weekend will always be difficult. I am grateful for the time I had with him. I am grateful for my other kids. But I miss my son. Andrew loved me well and made me feel like a good mom.

May 9

Mother's Day

To all my friends under age 30:

Hey. You need to call your mom this weekend. Don't just call to tell her happy Mother's Day. Call to talk with her. Really talk to her.

Take time to think before you call. Call her when you are in a place to talk and listen; take time out of your busy life. Don't call when driving with friends, while at a restaurant or backstage.

Plan some things to tell her.
   1.   Tell her you love her because _____.
   2.   Tell her you remember that time she did _____ for/with you and you are grateful she did that.
   3.   Tell her you would like to do _____with her this summer or over the next year.
Then tell her what's going on with you. Tell her about your friends, roommate, and adventures. Tell her about what you plan to do in the next few weeks and what you are excited about. Ask what she has planned for the next week or so. Ask her about her favorite memories of her mom or childhood. Ask what she is excited about.

Listen to her. Take time to talk with her. She loves you even if she sucks at showing it.

If she messed up when you were growing up...oh well. We all do. She was doing the best she could with what she knew at the time. She may have made big, terrible mistakes. Forgive her mistakes and start fresh today. Give her a chance to do better in the future. (And BTW maybe you weren't that easy to parent.) You are an adult now. Learn to forgive others, including your mom, for their failures. Give them opportunity to grow and change. Don't hold grudges or expect the worst, even from your mom.

If she was a great mom, she may not know it or feel it. Tell her. Thank her. Be specific. Encourage her. Your mom encouraged you in many ways during your childhood. Now is your turn to also compliment and encourage her. Even moms are insecure and need love, kindness, and compliments.

Oh! And do it again the next week. Posting memes about Mother's Day isn't enough to show you love her. We need to hear it from you. And we need to hear it often.

May 11

Mother's Day Has Been Hard

Mother's Day has been hard for years. All those "Thank God for praying mommas" comments. And things like, "Our mothers made us who we are today!" Not for me. Not at my house. My mother was a drunk. An abusive, angry, bitter drunk.

In my early years, she was a good mom. She was PTA President, home room mom, etc. She helped other people and was well known in our community. She was a tennis champ. We lived in a beautiful home in the right area of town. We had wedding receptions in our home. Neighborhood parties were great fun! It was beautiful. On the outside.

But inside, in private, we had yelling, hitting, and anger every day. It got worse as the years went by. After my parents separated, it was worse still. I had days when I hid, when I was afraid. At our house the main rule was "Don't get mom mad. Especially if she's drunk."

I was the baby, her favorite. This is not a good thing. My siblings resented me and took out their anger on me. I remember hiding under my brother's bed because my sisters wouldn't dare go in to his room. I was stabbed with a fork, thrown over the banister, hit, and made fun of. I hated watching my mom hit or belittle or yell at my siblings knowing there was nothing I could do to stop it. Knowing they would get me back for what she did to them.

I remember one night when I was babysitting for one of my regular families. I'd sat for them for years. Every week or two. Every OU home game. I loved this family. The mom said she would drive me home. Mr. G always drove me home. But that night she said that she would drive me. I was concerned. Even more so when she pulled over on a side street and turned off the car. Meredith G then turned to me and with tears in her eyes said, "My mom was a drunk, too. I know what it is like growing up with an alcoholic mom. If you ever need to talk or need a safe place to go, call me. I am here. And I love you." Then we talked for a while.

This was the first time anyone acknowledged what I dealt with. My parents were divorced and I couldn't really talk with my dad about what happened at home, or I didn't think I could. I didn't think anyone else knew. They did know, and they cared. I saw over the next few years how many of them cared. I had Mama Lane, Mrs. G, Mrs. Clark and so many others show me love and encourage me. They showed me what moms can be. They opened their homes to me.

When I married Ron, I got an amazing mother-in-law. Rita was kind, loving, sweet, gentle, and full of grace. She taught first grade for 30 years. I learned so much from her. I learned how to be a good mom from her.

I worked full-time until I was pregnant with our fourth. A friend asked me why I worked rather than stay home. "Because I am afraid that if stay home, I will do to my kids what my mom did to us." My friend told me I needed to get help with that, to get counseling. I did. And I quit work. I became a stay at home my when Adam was born.

My mother accepted Christ before she died. She died in 1997. I know I will see her in Heaven. I am sorry she never quit drinking. I'm sorry she was so miserable and angry. I am not sorry that I forgave her years ago and we had a fairly good relationship in her final years.

I have a great relationship with my big brother, Uncle Bob to my kids. I've forgiven my siblings. I've asked their forgiveness. But the junk that happened when we were kids still impacts us today. I rarely see my sisters. (They were both wonderful to me when Andrew died and I am grateful.) A couple of my boys see one of my sisters often because they live close to her, and I am glad they do. She's a great gal. I pray that someday we may have a closer relationship, but that is not entirely up to me.

So, Mother's Day has always been hard.

Early in our marriage, Ron encouraged me to think not about the mother I had but the mother I wanted to be. I have failed many times. I made mistakes, huge mistakes. But I would ask forgiveness and try again. I raised seven amazing people. I am grateful for each of them. I am not a perfect mom, but I worked to change the family line. I did a better job than my mom did. And I pray that my children are better parents than we were.

Mother's Day is no longer hard because of my childhood. Last year was hard. Obvious reasons. This year I spent the day with Ron. We had dinner with dear friends in St. Louis Saturday night then got up and drove to Chicago. We rode a couple of hours on a nice trail through a nature refuge. Lovely weather for riding bikes with the man I love in a beautiful area makes for a nice Mother's Day.

Chapter Fourteen

Summertime!

May 12

Twelve Things I am Grateful for on the 12th

This month I am grateful for simple things. Things I would struggle to live without.

1. Breath
2. Trees
3. Water
4. My home
5. Electricity
6. Natural gas
7. Sewers
8. Healthy, clean food
9. Hair brush
10. Soap
11. Calculators
12. And finally...my husband. Today is his birthday. I can't imagine my life without him. Thirty-two years together this month. I pray we get thirty-two more.

What are you grateful for?

May 12

For those who did not notice, Ron Duncan turns 55 today. Like a good wine or cheese, he just keeps getting better and better.

God,

Thank you for giving him to me. For letting me travel this journey by his side. For helping us through the tough times, the tragedies, and the joyful times. And thank you that there has been more joy than not. I ask you to keep him in Your hand, order his steps, and lead him in Your ways daily.

Amen

May 14

Traveling, Again!

We are on the road again.

I love traveling with Ron.

We planned to head out Friday night, but severe storms caused us to stay home. We drove to St. Louis Saturday and met our friends the Burtons for dinner. They are amazing - loving, kind, honest, godly, transparent. My boys were friends with their sons when they lived near us. Kathy is a great friend to me. She listens and tells me the truth. And she made me chocolate cake even though she eats Gluten-free and vegan. We have been able to visit them often this past year since they are on the way to many of our destinations.

We slept late Sunday then drove to a western suburb of Chicago. We will be here all week. We packed our bikes for this trip, hoping to ride a bunch. Within an hour of arriving at our hotel, we got our riding gear on and drove to a nearby nature refuge. As I mentioned in my article Ill, I haven't felt well for a while so haven't ridden much. I was a bit nervous about riding the trail. It is crushed limestone and unfamiliar. But the ride was wonderful! The weather was a bit chilly and overcast, but dressing in layers helped us handle that. We rode almost 20 miles.

Riding with Ron is great fun. He is a much stronger and faster rider than I. But he is patient and encouraging. He rides at my pace while gently prodding me to improve. He constantly reminds me we can slow down or rest whenever I choose. We road about 30-40 minutes out then he suggested we turn back. "If we want to do more, we can go the other direction on the trail or we can be done when we get to the car," he suggested.

I love this about him: he is caring and aware of my needs while encouraging me to become better at whatever we are doing.

Our hotel is just a mile or so from one portion of The Great Western Trail, the trail we rode, but the car parking area is a few miles from our hotel. From where we were on the trail, Ron suggested we ride back to the hotel rather than to our car. He wanted to see if I was comfortable riding the route to the trail in case I want to ride by myself while he works this week. After leaving me back at the hotel, he rode alone the three miles back to the car. I adore the fact that he is willing to ride a few extra miles to be sure I am comfortable and able to ride this week.

We rode again on Wednesday. Twenty-two miles. Out on The Great Western Trail and back on the Great Illinois Prairie Trail. Are all the trails in Illinois "Great" something?

Thirty-two years together. We make a good team. We enjoy being together. We have great memories and hope for the future. We have faced hard times raising seven children - some hard times in our marriage, career changes, issues with our children, the death of four parents and one son. But through it all we have been committed to each other. Divorce was not an option. Serving God and trusting Him daily is required.

I am glad Ron invites me to travel with him and grateful that our situation allows it. I plan to journey with him until death do us part.

Next week we will be traveling to Wisconsin. I have never been to Wisconsin. I love new adventures!

~~~~~~

May 15

Hotel Etiquette

When the breakfast area is packed, do not set your plate down and block the muffins, bagels, toaster, and juice while texting. GET YOUR FOOD AND TEXT AT YOUR TABLE !!!! Whatever it is, it can wait long enough for you to walk 20 feet out of the way of every other hotel guest!

And don't take the only two chairs in the business center. One for you and one for your stuff?? NO! Put your bum in a chair and your stuff on the counter or floor!

Maybe I need a nap today. I am a little bit grumpy.

May 16

TEXAS 50th Season

Rehearsal for TEXAS started this past week. Andrew had the honor of being in the show two seasons (2012 and 2013). If you are ever in the Amarillo, Texas, area in summer, it is worth the time and drive to see this wonderful outdoor musical.

This week I wrote a quick note to my friends in the show, young and old.

> To all my friends in TEXAS 50th Season: Enjoy!
>
> Make new friends. Help the new kids feel welcome and show them the ropes. Have a blast. Rest when you need to, but don't sleep all your spare time away. Definitely participate in the fire training! It's a blast to be set on fire! Take care of your feet and your voice. Get some sleep! Call your moms. Text your dads (but not while driving). Snapchat your siblings. Find time to do laundry. Don't drink and drive. Be sure to have an Andrew Duncan Panty Raid. Share your toys, be kind, and get to bed before two on show nights. If in school, do you homework. Explore the area on Mondays, there's some cool stuff around there. Do the Shakespeare plays. Forgive often, laugh, and make great memories. It's going to be a great summer!
>
> Love you all, Momma Duncan

I suppose I should explain what an Andrew Duncan Panty Raid is. First, you need to know that Andrew was a bit clumsy off-stage. On the dance stage he was graceful and a talented dancer. But anywhere else, he could trip over his own shadow.

Now to explain the panty raid part....The adults (real responsible adults, not just folks over 21) help organize themed panty raids at TEXAS. They check to be sure all in the targeted dressing room are decent, and then have the guys or girls run through the other dressing area. For example, a Cowboys theme raid may include water guns. For the Andrew Duncan Themed Raid, the guys ran through the gals dressing area tripping on things, knocking things over, and falling down. They had one last summer. Yep, it was a success. They will have another one this year.

May 17

Bike Riding

In preparation, we rode eighteen to twenty miles Sunday and Wednesday. I am not very fast and was a bit nervous about riding to town, but those rides helped me gain confidence that I could do the Saturday ride. We had never done anything like this before. Our rides are usually around our home town or at cycling events with well-marked routes and sag wagons. This was going to be an adventure!

We checked the Web to be sure of our route. Ron checked the rules for taking bikes on the trains. We verified the train schedules to be sure which to get on to town and which to ride home. We double checked everything! Our phones were charged and we packed extra layers of clothes in case it rained on us.

Turns out it was raining early Saturday, so we left later than originally planned. We didn't head out until about 10:30. We parked our car at a nearby Metra station then rode the Great Western Trail to the Prairie Trail. After about thirteen miles we stopped for lunch in lovely Elmhurst. We ate a local Italian deli. Back on the trail for another nine miles to the Forrest Park EL station. We only got lost once. A quick train ride and we found ourselves by the Chicago Stock Exchange.

It was a bit harrowing riding through downtown traffic. Maneuvering through the crowds of people in addition to cars took great patience, but we did it. We made it to the lake.

I could hardly believe I was actually riding my bicycle with my love in Chicago! It was about 70 degrees and mostly sunny. Beautiful day. So much fun! We rode about ten miles along the lake shore then found a deli for dinner. Our Metra ride back to car was almost an hour. The train was comfortable and we enjoyed the time to rest. We had left the hotel at 10:30 and arrived back about 8:00. Total mileage ridden on my bike was about thirty-five.

Back at hotel, we hobbled to the hot tub for a relaxing soak. A couple of Tylenol and it was off to bed. I am grateful that I am able to ride a bike, and I am thankful for a husband who wants to spend the day with me. It was a wonderful day.

May 18

Some Days

Some days I am thrilled to see Andrew's friends growing up
    getting married,
        graduating,
            having babies,
                getting jobs.
                    These things make my heart sing!

I am glad they have healed and are moving on with their lives.

Other times these things bring me sadness
    tears
        pain
            grief.
                Reminders that he is gone.

I am not jealous or angry that he is not doing those things.
    Those things are not in the plan for Andrew.
    Early admission to Heaven was the plan.

But once, just once, I would like to see his smiling face in the pictures at
their wedding,
    their opening night
        their graduation
            their baby dedication
                their new apartment.
Just once.

Or maybe twice.

May 19

One of These Things is Not Like the Other...

I wish that Ron always came home to the picture on the left. Unfortunately, he too often comes home to the picture on the right.

Can you tell the difference between the two pictures? I'm not talking about the wet hair and no makeup in the second picture. Can you tell what is different about the first picture? What matters? I am talking about the smile! In the top picture, I am looking up and smiling!

It is a choice. The only thing that changed in the twenty minutes between taking the two pictures is that I took time to dry and style my hair and apply a bit of makeup...and I chose to change my attitude.

My attitude in the second photo:

I am in a hotel alone all day. We got to this hotel about eleven last night after Ron took a wrong turn, which means we didn't even get to bed before midnight, and Ron was up making lots of noise at 6:00. Not enough sleep for me. I have no car. No way to go anyplace but to walk. I have to check out by 11:00, but Ron won't be back to get me before six. So I have to hang out in the hotel lobby alone all day. Then we have to drive three hours to the next town and next hotel. Where I will sit alone all day tomorrow.

My attitude in the first photo:

I am traveling with my love! We had a great bike ride and fun dinner last night. We got here late, but the detour was an adventure. And no one was hurt by a driving a few miles out of the way. Ron woke me early, but I am grateful that my husband works so hard and cares about making his business a success! I got a little nap in after he left. It is so sweet to curl up under the warm covers for a quick nap after my love kisses me goodbye in the mornings! Late breakfast (cooked and cleaned up by someone else!) before checkout, then I'm off to explore the area around the hotel! A walk will be nice in this lovely Wisconsin weather! If I don't find anything fun to do, oh well! I have a few good books to read and a safe place to hang out while reading. I might even get another lesson of Nehemiah done this afternoon! And I am grateful for the quiet business center at the hotel. I can use their computers to check social media and, of course, write in my blog. Life is good on the road!

My attitude is a choice. Daily I choose life or death. Joy or sorrow. Grief or gratefulness.

What will you choose today?

~~~~~~

May 25, Memorial Day

Freedom

I have not personally known anyone who gave his or her life while serving in the military. But too many of my friends and my son grieve those they stood beside in school, boot camp, training, and battle and who paid the ultimate price for this country. I have friends whose sons or grandsons died in foreign lands fighting for this country, protecting our freedom.

Many remember and grieve their comrades who died too soon for our liking: some in battle, some in training accidents, some at their own hand. Soldiers, Marines, pilots who left family, wives, and children behind to carry on and keep their memories alive.

Today I pray for them, for the families, spouses, children, and friends left behind. I pray that the Comforter may bring them peace in their grief, that He may bring healing and joy to their lives. And I pray that we remember our freedom is not free. Many have paid the price for my freedom. I am grateful.

I am also grateful that Christ paid the price for my freedom from condemnation and sin. Freedom on this earth and spiritual freedom are not free, but both are available. May you choose freedom today.

Now the Lord is the Spirit,
and where the Spirit of the Lord is,
there is freedom.

2 Corinthians 3:17 | ESV

June 2

Running this Race

I ran my first triathlon in September 2011.

After weeks of caring for my mother-in-law as she fought pancreatic cancer, I had become exhausted in every way. I was honored to care for her in her last days. I could feel depression settling in and knew I had to fight it. I knew physical activity is a great way to fight depression, so I called a mom who I knew worked as trainer. Sarah invited me to join her class at the YMCA. I did. And five weeks later I had gone from overweight couch potato to overweight triathlete.

In my first race, I was slow. The winner of the event, Leanne, was finished, had loaded her bike into her car, and was chatting with friends before I even got off my bike. I still had 3.2 miles to go. I knew that would take me another hour. Leanne is a friend, so I walked up to congratulate her. When she saw that I still had the run to do, she offered to walk it with me. I love her for that. I knew I would be dead last and didn't want to walk alone. She encouraged me to jog a little as we went. A very little. I was last out of 77 people at the 2011 Y Tri. Sarah was there to cheer for me as I crossed the finish line.

A month later I did my second event, the Toyota Tri in Dallas. An open-water event. Having trained for 9 weeks, I was a bit faster and in a bit better shape. I knew I would be at the end of the pack, but was more comfortable with the whole thing. I did well in the swim portion, but was in the last wave to enter the water so I started out behind 1100 others. My bike time was okay, and I then I headed out for the run. At the end of the pack.

The first portion of the run was up a very steep, long hill. I was worn out when I started the run, and more worn out when I got to the top of that hill. So I walked. Slowly. I was walking slowly when a very fit young lady ran past me. Then she stopped to walk. We chatted. She walked with me then suggested we jog "the next 10 cones." (Traffic cones placed every ten yards mark the trail.) We walked ten, jogged ten over the next two miles. I was just about done in, but I was determined to finish.

I enjoyed chatting with this young woman and having someone to walk with. With a quarter mile to go, my new friend said, "Do you mind if I run the last part? Are you okay finishing by yourself?" Then she told me she is a personal trainer. She had planned to do the Olympic Distance and should have been ahead of me, but she had slowed on the bike portion to encourage another athlete. She had found me struggling and slowed to walk/jog with me. She enjoyed helping others finish their race. Turns out I beat eight people in that event. Eight out of twelve hundred. But I was not last! And I finished smiling.

I could not have finished either of those events without the help of women who had more experience, more training, and more strength than I had. They slowed down and ran, beside me to spur me on to the goal; they helped me finish the race.

As I finished the Toyota Tri, I thought about my walk with Christ. I have learned a lot and have grown strong in faith. I could simply keep going forward and finish my race. I believe God wants me to slow down when needed and walk beside another runner, to help them and encourage them. I believe that we must stop, to help others along this narrow road.

What does that look like? I'm learning still. But I think it means that I am to teach bible studies when asked, to let others lead while I encourage them by listening, to be available when a mom is struggling with her teenage son, and to give godly counsel to my friend considering divorce.

On my journey of healing after Andrew's death, I must walk beside others just beginning their journey. Painful as it may be to hear their stories, I must be willing to listen to bereaved parents, to pray for them, and to love them. In helping them in their healing journey, I continue to grow in my own faith and healing. Together we help each other finish the race.

After The Accident, Sarah called to see if I wanted to continue our run training to do the Y Tri for the third time. Sarah came to my house twice each week. Sometimes I could not do it. I could not get up and get my running clothes on. Other times, I cried the whole three miles. But Sarah was there, like clockwork. And Sarah was there at the finish line of the 2013 Y Tri cheering me on.

Ron and I both did the Y Tri that year. I don't know how many I beat or what place I came in. I don't know if I was last. I do know that many of those participating knew us and knew our son, and many shed tears that day. Many of the volunteers and spectators knew us as well. They hugged us and cheered us on. We felt loved. And we knew that with the help of those around us, we will continue to run this race and we will reach the goal set before us.

June 4

Soaring Stats

The past few days my blog statistics have been soaring. This happens every month or so. And I hate it!

You see, the reason my stats are soaring is because someone shared "What Bereaved Parents Want You to Know (but may not say)." Last month someone shared "What Parents with a Baby in Heaven May Want You to Know (but may not say)" causing my stats to soar.

People share these two articles on social media, usually because they have lost a child. That is why I hate to see my stats soar: I know another family has experienced the death of a child. I know another momma is grieving. A dad is feeling the pain of loss. Brothers and sisters have watched their parents bury their sibling. So I hate seeing my stats soar. And I pray.

Father,

You know what it is like to see Your Son die.

Because of Your great love for us, You freely gave Him to come into the world, to live, teach, laugh, and suffer. You gave Him to die for us. Jesus willingly came, and willingly He suffered and died for us. And because He lived, died, and rose again, we can have peace and eternal life. Because my son chose life in Christ while on earth, he now lives eternally in Heaven with You. Thank you for peace and healing.

For the hurting, grieving families who have buried a child this week or month, I pray peace, comfort and grace. Give them strength to make it through one more day. Help them. Comfort them. Draw them to You. Show them Your love, compassion, and mercy. Help them to seek truth and protect them from the lies of the enemy. Give wisdom to their friends, family and clergy that they may know how to love, support, and comfort the hurting parents and siblings. Give them all grace to forgive when needed and joy to laugh often.

Until we see You face to face, help us to live well and to love one another. Give us hope while we wait for the glorious reunion in Heaven.

In the name of Your Son Jesus Christ.

Amen

June 6

Visiting Churches

As Ron and I travel the country on business, we visit churches. We have been to forty-four states in fifteen months. The job-related travel means we are often away from home and away from our home church a couple of weekends each month. We attend a Baptist church at home. On the road we often attend PCA, Vineyard, or non-denominational churches.

I wonder what the pastors of the churches we visit think when they see me cry during worship. I wonder if they think me weird or overly emotional. Do they think I am one of those holy rollers who get all emotional about a move of God every Sunday? Do they think I am struggling in some way?

I wish I could print out my post on Tears in Church and hand it to the pastor and worship team as we enter the building. Then they might understand.

I wish I could tell them about our loss. And about our healing, joy, and peace. I wish I could tell them about all the parents I know who are still grieving their children. I wish I could help them know how to help us. I wish I could tell them why I still cry in church sometimes.

And I wonder who around me each Sunday has experienced this type of loss. Who in this church has a baby or a child in Heaven? Have they healed? Do they know the love and compassion and healing power or our Father? Have they let Him help them? Has this church loved them well?

I wish I could sit and chat with those parents. I wish I could listen as they share their stories. I wish I could tell them .... something, anything that would help them, comfort them, and strengthen them.

I will never know, never find out, never share. We visit once and then move on to the next city.

June 9

Special Days

Bereaved parents mention two special days on which they struggle: their child's birthday and the day their child died. These special days can be tough.

There are so many memories of past birthdays and happy times. How old would their child be if he had lived? How do they celebrate birthdays in Heaven? Thoughts of birthdays that will never be.

And there are many memories of the day they died. Visual memories of doctors or policemen. Sounds of medical alarms or rescue sirens. Funeral arrangements. Feelings and memories of calling friends to give them the bad news. Things people said. Or did not say.

For me, Christmas Eve is one of those special days. Andrew was our early Christmas present in 1992. Our fifth child.

August 12 is the other. It is the day of The Accident, though his official date of death is August 13 because the justice of the peace could not get to the scene and pronounce them dead for 45 minutes due to the remote location.

The last week of May and Second week of June are hard because of tech week for TEXAS and recital time. I love seeing the pictures and antics of the cast and crew. But again, I wish he was among them. So many pictures of young men and women in their dance costumes! Many of them danced with Andrew at one time or another. Pangs of grief grip my heart when I see these pictures and read these posts. I wonder if anyone remember my son. Do they think of him? Do they still laugh when remembering his antics?

And then I get a text or message from another mom or young person telling them miss him, they love him. And a friend posts a picture featuring his smile, like the one posted by a TEXAS cast member today. And my heart sings with joy.

June 10

Each time we go to a new doctor they ask how many in your family? Ages of siblings? Are they living or dead? How old were they when they died?

(College kids moving to new states means new doctors.)

I hate filling out those forms. I hate that my other kids have to fill out those forms. I hate that they have to put that their brother is dead on those forms.

~~~~~~~

June 11

I shared a video of Andrew dancing on social media. Here is the address of the YouTube video: https://www.youtube.com/watch?v=AystIHdz-Ak

I'm missing him today. And every day. I enjoy watching this video as the tears flow. I know he is now dancing before the Throne of Grace worshipping the Creator.

I am reminded how God won't give up on us. Even when the times get rough, He'll still be waiting. For us, for our spouse, for our other kids. He is waiting with open arms. With love, compassion, forgiveness and grace.

The Creator, the Healer, the Loving Father waits for us to turn to Him and say, "Help me! I need you now!"

If you have not yet turned to Him in your grief, won't you do so now? He is waiting. And He loves you.

June 12

Twelve Things I Am Grateful for on the 12th

1. Texas
2. Illinois
3. Tennessee
4. New York
5. Georgia
6. Oklahoma
7. Florida
8. Wisconsin
9. Michigan
10. South Dakota
11. Nebraska
12. Iowa

... And the other 30 states I have visited with Ron the past fifteen months.

I am grateful for this country.

I am grateful that I am able to travel with my husband as he goes on business trips.

We are empty-nesters with a college gal staying at the house to take care of things. Because Ron drives rather than fly, it costs nothing for me to ride along, and hotel rooms are the same price for one or two people. We travel a couple of weeks at a time then go home for a week or two.

I love traveling this way! We have seen beautiful things in each state and met wonderful people.

I help with driving, navigation, and whatever else he needs me to do. I spend days reading, walking, talking with friends, exploring and studying. Sometimes I help with business appointments. Lately, I've been helping with set-up and take-down at each appointment. We try to find fun things to do on weekends.

Last weekend we were in Iowa. What does one do in Iowa? Political events, of course! Ron found out that some of the GOP candidates were going to be at Joni's Roast and Ride just an hour from where we were staying. We arrived in time to have a great BBQ pork lunch and meet some nice Iowans. Senator Ernst and other Iowa officials spoke then the GOP presidential candidates each spoke. They were also walking around, shaking hands, and speaking with folks.

There was very little security evident. I was able to get pictures of each of the candidates and stood close to all of them listening to what they had to say as common farmers, moms, dads, businessmen, and students asked questions. Ben Carson, Mike Huckabee, Mark Rubio, Lindsey Graham, Rick Perry, Scott Walker and Carley Fiorina were shaking hands, taking pictures, and answering questions. They did not turn away anyone wanting a selfie with them. Including me!

We couldn't help but think about how awesome our political system is. Everyday people asking questions of men and women running for office, one of whom may very well be our next president. Most of these candidates did not come from wealthy or powerful families; they came from working-class parents, single moms, immigrants. They are living the American Dream.

If you looked at AOL News last Sunday, we were shown in the video that went with the article titled "Motorcycles and puppies: GOP contenders face off in Iowa." I'm not sure why they showed us out of the hundreds in attendance. Maybe because they caught on tape that we were from Texas and filmed Ron at Rick Perry's tent. Whatever the reason, it was fun to be in the news.

And no, I don't know who I will vote for. I'm not sure if it will be any of the folks we heard on Saturday, but I am glad I went. If you live in America, I encourage you to learn about all the candidates - republican, democrat, Green Party, independent, whoever is running. Be an informed voter. And VOTE! It is a privilege to live in this country and to participate in the political process. It matters.

The fact that we were part of this event on the 71st anniversary of D Day was not lost on us. Men and women have given their lives for us to have this type of freedom. I cherish it. I hope and pray you do as well.

July 1

Time Off

would anyone care?

would anyone notice?

if I took the month of July off?

just to ride my bike and read a few good books?

no cleaning

no cooking

no mowing

no writing

just sleeping

and eating

and swimming

and reading

and riding my bike

July 2

Attacked by Chickens

Last year I was attacked by a mob of killer chickens. Rotisserie chickens. At a local big box store. Sure, those chickens in their little plastic boxes look all juicy, tender, and innocent. But they are not! Well, they are juicy and tender. But they can be vicious!

There I was...minding my own business. I reached out to get one to take home for lunch...and they all attacked me! It was horrible! The noise! The squawking! The screaming! And, yes, all the noise came from me. The chickens didn't have mouths...or heads...or feet...or feathers. If they had feathers they would have been flying! The attack resulted in a serious burn on my arm. My arm is healed.

(By "attacked" I mean that I tripped on my own feet and fell into the shelf holding the chickens. My arm slid along the very hot shelf resulting in a serious burn. The folks at the big box store were wonderful and kind. They even called me to check on me.)

Praise God for healing! The Physician's Assistant had warned me that I might have some permanent damage because the burn was deep. But I don't! It took months for my arm to heal completely, but it did heal. It is completely healed. Not even a scar!

I still shiver when I walk past those chickens. And I NEVER turn my back on them. You just don't know when they might attack.

If you could have seen my heart a year ago, it probably looked as bad as my arm. But today...only a small scar.

Yes, grief still hits me in the gut sometimes. Sunday morning one song just hit me. I quietly sobbed. But I still had a smile on face. I love worshipping the Father with my church family.

Heaven is so real to me now! So beautiful to think about! And the glory of God to be seen there! I am grateful for His touch in my life. For His love, compassion, forgiveness and grace! And sometimes my emotions get me. But I am glad to feel them. They help me know I am still alive.

July 7

A fake. A fraud.

Sometimes I feel like a fake. A fraud. Sometimes...I am not strong. I am not happy. I do not have peace. I cannot see the light.

Then I remember that life is not always peaceful. We are each sad at times. We all have our moments of weakness. Our lives are sometimes dark.

These times do not define me; they are not who I am. They do not determine my future. They do not control my destiny.

I can choose happiness, joy, peace, and strength...after I feel the pain and have a good cry...I can reach out to Him who is always available. He is always near to the broken-hearted. He is joy. He is peace. He is my strength. He is Light. He is the Way, the Truth, and the Life.

~~~~~~

July 10

Within a year of Andrew's death in August 2013, four of our other adult children moved out to their own homes or off to college in another state. Empty nest big time!

I started traveling a bunch with my husband. We have grown closer through all of it. To each other and to Christ.

We home schooled through high school as well. Another major change: not only is our nest empty but I am no longer teaching my children after seventeen years of doing so and am no longer helping head up home school events in our community. It meant not seeing many moms regularly.

Blogging, traveling, reading, studying, and biking have become my main activities. Friends have changed mainly due to my change in parenting status.

My life is very different than two years ago. But I love it! I have joy and peace.

July 12

Twelve Things I Am Grateful for on the 12th

1. Freedom. Purchased by so many.

2. USMC. The men and women who serve in the Marines including my son. First in, last out.

3. U.S. Navy. Including my dad who served during the Korean conflict and for many years in the reserves.

4. U.S. Air Force. Many of our friends serve in the Air Force. I am grateful to have met such wonderful people since we moved to Texas.

5. U.S. Army. And our friend Caleb who began his army career this spring.

6. U.S. Coast Guard. I hope my sailor brother will never need to call upon them. But if he does, they will be there.

7. Police officers. They put their lives on the line every day. They often get a bad rap. The ones I know are amazing people. I believe most of them care and do a great job. I especially like the FB page of Bangor Maine PD.

8. EMT's. I could never do their job. The workers who arrive at accident scenes every day helping injured men, women and children. Never knowing exactly what they will find on a call. Bless them all.

9. Nurses. Caring men and women like my brother-in-law who works in pediatrics, my friend Liz who just graduated last week, and Patty who is starting her final year of school. All of these nurses started nursing school after age 40. It's never too late to choose a new career.

10. Our presidency. The office. I pray for him. I am grateful that our country has had so many peaceful changes in leadership, something many other countries never experience.

11. State and federal legislatures. And judicial systems. We have an amazing government system! It's not perfect, but it better than the other choices.

12. Local leaders and state officials. Texas is a great state in which to live and work.

What are you grateful for today?

July 13

Biking in the Adirondack Mountains

Yes, I am foolish at times.

"Let's ride bikes this weekend," he said. "In the Adirondack Mountains. It will be fun," he said. I did not think about how tough riding bicycles in upstate New York would be. You'd think that the word Mountains would have clued me in.

Our plan for Saturday evening was to do an easy ride from Glens Falls to Lake George. It is about twelve miles each way. We rode only about six or seven miles when I found myself worn out, shaking, and weak. I had Bonked.

"Bonk: *The miserable condition you suffer if you don't eat and drink enough on a ride. Symptoms include a pins-and-needles feeling in the arms and legs, light-headedness, disorientation and nausea."*[1]

I wasn't in quite as bad a shape as this definition describes; I was simply weak and shaky. However, I knew if we kept going I would experience a full-out Bonk. I might not make it back to the car without help - as in Ron leaving me in a shady spot to get the car and drive to pick me up.

I ride 25-30 miles a few times per week, so I found this very frustrating. And I did not understand it. I had hydrated and eaten properly. It was warm but not too hot. I was riding a different bike, but that should not have made such a big difference. I checked the brakes to be sure they weren't rubbing. We had adjusted my seat to the proper height before starting. The bike wasn't the issue.

Ron tried to encourage me to keep going. I just couldn't. I had nothing left. We had to rest and then turn around. We were not going to finish the ride to Lake George. We turned around to go back to the way we had ridden when I started picking up speed. Lots of speed. I went very fast for a little over mile. Without pedaling! Yep. We had just ridden UP what some cyclists refer to as a False Flat.

"false flat: *1. A surprisingly difficult section of road that looks flat but is actually slightly uphill. Usually, no matter how hard you pedal you go way slower than you think you should be going. 2. A stretch on a long hill that looks flat and tricks you into thinking you've reached the top when there's still more climbing to come."*[1]

I had never heard that term before. Now I had experienced it! We had been going uphill when we thought we were on a fairly flat trail. The trees, shadows and curves in the trail disguised the incline. The false flat right before I bonked was one of many that went on for about a half mile to a mile each. The trail was one incline after another as we discovered going *down* the trail. No wonder I was worn out!

We rode back the way we came and then rode around the very level town of Glens Falls making our total distance around sixteen miles. We had dinner at a lovely family-owned diner. The East End Eatery in Glens Falls, NY. The Toscana Pizza was amazing! The service was great. I highly recommend this place if you are ever in the area. After dinner we went back to our hotel for a soak in the hot tub and a good night's rest.

Sunday afternoon we tried again. And made it! I rode my bicycle through the mountains from Glens Falls to Lake George. Up and over the false flats and down the other side. We rode the inclines more slowly and took a few rest breaks. I made it to the top this time!

Downhill into Lake George was great fun! We ate lunch at a restaurant in Lake George. (Service was terrible. Food was okay. So I won't mention the name.) We rode around town for a bit then headed back up and over the mountains. Total distance ridden was just over twenty miles on Sunday. A short but very hard ride.

Along the trail were signs indicating a steep decline. I loved when we got past each sign! It meant the climbing was over and I could coast downhill for a bit. I was completely worn out by the time we got back to the car. We did it! We rode our bikes through the Adirondack Mountains!

My grief journey has caused me to bonk a few times. Times when I thought I was doing well, riding hard, and then found myself worn out and unable to move forward. I had to take time to rest. I even had to back up and start again a few times. But eventually I made it over each hurdle. I have found myself on the other side of that mountain. And I have found peace and joy.

Note: 1 From Bikeline.com glossary of cycling terms

July 13

23 Months

So many memories
    So many tears
        So many laughs
            So much love
                So much pain
                    So much joy
                        So much sorrow

As we walked to our hotel tonight after a nice dinner,
    I heard a song that was played
        during the slideshow at the memorial service.
            Amazing how my mood can change so quickly.
            The tears flow easily at times.
And I wonder...
    Does anyone remember?
        Do they think of him?
            Will he be forgotten by everyone but family?

And then I get a text.
    Or a photo.
        Or message from one of his friends.

Thank you, Lord, for his friends.
    And the love they show me.

~~~~~~

July 15

After many replied to the above post with stories, video, and pictures of Andrew, I wrote:

Thank you all! Batman, dance, loud laughter, smiles, TEXAS, and so many more things bring him to mind often. I miss that boy.

I look forward to seeing him again someday.

If you have not chosen life in Christ...won't you? He did. And because he did, I know he is dancing before the throne. I will join him in pure worship in Heaven. What a glorious day that will be!

July 16

How Many Children Do You Have?

Sarah and her husband have an elderly couple on their street with whom they have become friends. These neighbors have a wonderful driveway which is perfect for little boys to play in and ride their bikes. Sarah and her little boys like to go visit. The neighbors enjoy having them come over. Early in the friendship, Sarah asked Jean how many children they have.

"Three boys," was the answer. Jean went on to talk a bit about her sons. Then they were interrupted by a little boy squealing.

A few months later, they were playing with the boys in the yard. "I hear you speak about John and James and their families. But you never mention Michael. I wonder why. If I may ask," ventured Sarah.

"Well," answered Jean. "He died when he was young."

"I am so sorry," answered Sarah. "Do you mind talking about what happened to Michael? If you don't want to talk about, I understand."

"No, I like to share the story. But usually don't until we get know each other. It is a hard story to hear."

Jean went on to explain that he was murdered.

Michael had been playing in the backyard. She went to call him, and he did not come. He was not in the yard. She went to search the woods behind their home. Eight year old boys like to have adventures in the woods. (This was forty years ago when it was thought safe to let them.)

As she searched and called, he did not answer. This was unlike him. She began to search more frantically. At last she saw him, off in the distance, lying in the ground. She immediately knew something was very wrong. Before she got close, she heard a still, small Voice say, "No one will ever hurt him again. I have him now." And a complete peace came over her.

Jean found her little boy. Murdered.

The rest of the story.... Well... You can imagine the rest.

My point is, when Jean was asked, "How many children do you have?" she answered, "Three. I have three boys: Michael, John, and James."

She does not give details to those whom she has just met. It is a story that is precious to her. She treasures her memories of her son. They are not for sharing with just everyone. But she never leaves him out when asked about her children. She includes him when listing her sons.

When asked, I say that I have seven children.

I will always be mom of these seven, no matter where they live. I do not, however, always tell people that one of them died in a horrible car wreck with four of his friends. That is just too much information for some situations.

When introducing myself in a group setting, I often say that I am wife, follower of Christ, and mom of seven with three sweet grandsons.

If asked how old my children are, I usually say, "ages 19 to 31." Andrew was 20 when he died; in a few years I will probably say, "20-34." I'll figure that out later.

If anyone asks where my kids live, I say, "Michigan, Texas, Oklahoma, Tennessee, Georgia and Heaven." When I rattle it off quickly, most folks don't even notice the last location. Honestly, most people don't really listen carefully; they are usually thinking about their own answers or feelings.

If asked what my children do or what they are studying, I say, "The oldest two have graduated, Meredith is married and Lyz teaches preschool; Peter and David are at OU studying engineering; Adam coaches at an elite gymnastics gym in Michigan; Andrew was a dance and accounting major; and Margaret is a sophomore at Covenant College." It is rare that people ask for more details or notice the word *was*.

Handling Social Events

At a recent event for Team KMOC, we were asked to introduce ourselves. I said that I have "seven children who live all over the place." It was not the time to become the center of attention by saying that I am Andrew Duncan's mom. (He is well known in our community. At least his story is.) After the dinner, one family came up to talk. They asked if we are Andrew's parents. Their daughter had recently been awarded one of the Andrew Raymond Duncan Memorial Scholarships. We were thrilled to meet them! They appreciate the scholarship. It will help her as she goes to Abilene Christian College this fall. We do not select the recipients, but are glad to meet each one.

At a weekend business event just four months after The Accident, we sat at a table with six others. It was a black-tie formal dinner dance.

The entire weekend at this business event, we had avoided talking about what had happened; we did not want to be *the grieving parents*, even if for just a few days. And we did not want The Accident to be the center of conversation when Ron was trying to talk business. It felt good to pretend, to not have people giving us the sympathy looks, and to not have folks asking how we're really doing. We kept it secret. By choice.

We see many of these business folks and their spouses only at this annual industry event. They are business associates, not close friends. As a result, most had no idea what we had been through since August. They did not know our son had been killed. A very few did, and they were kind enough not to share what was our story to tell.

When asked how our family was, we had answered, "The kids are all doing well!" It was true. Even Andrew, who was in Heaven, was doing well. Better than the rest of us, in fact. This answer was sufficient all weekend...until the last night at dinner.

As we sat down with others at dinner, one man we had known for years, and whose daughter was a music theater major, commented, "You have a son who was a dancer. Is he still dancing?" An awkward silence followed. I looked at my husband for guidance.

Ron quickly smiled and answered, "Yes. Yes, Andrew is still dancing. It's just that now he is dancing in Heaven before the throne of the Father. He was killed in August. We are doing well through it all...How is your daughter doing in school?"

The man and his wife are also Christians. They understood. They said how sorry they were to hear about our son and took the cue to change the subject.

After dinner, the band came out to play for the dance. Usually we love to dance at this event with our friends. Not that year. The band members were young, in their twenties. A couple of the musicians looked very much like our son. One singer even had the exact same glasses Andrew wore. Before the end of the first song, tears were flowing. We left the large ballroom and tried to compose ourselves in the hall before going back in to dance a little.

More than a few folks saw us standing in the corner, crying, behind a big plant. As I think back, it is a funny image: Ron in his fine suit and me in my black and purple formal dress and pearls, behind a large plant!

I went to the ladies room to fix my make-up. I realized folks thought we must be drunk or fighting! A friend in the powder room was concerned about me. I told her why we were both crying, and others heard me. Before the night was out, everyone knew about The Accident. We were glad it had not been known until that last night of the convention

If you have lost a child, I encourage you to think about how you will respond to questions.

Since that awkward silence at the dinner dance, I have prepared answers for various questions about our kids.

Do you want to give details about your child's death? Or a short vague answer? What story do you want to tell if you are going to share about your child's death? Can you tell it in such a way to not make yourself the center of attention or make others very uncomfortable? Have you thought about how to share your story while honoring your child's memory? Have you discussed with your spouse when and where he is comfortable sharing the story?

It can be helpful to think through a short version of what happened. You can always add details if appropriate.

And think about *when* it is appropriate to give details. A business dinner or other event like I mentioned may not be the place to share details about your child's battle with illness or your child's murder. Sometimes it's best to simply say she passed without revealing that she took her own life or was murdered. Being considerate of the feelings of others and being aware of the situation does not mean you're hiding something or dishonoring your child.

I know moms who say something like, "I have five children: John is thirteen, Mary is ten, Josh is eight, Sarah is four, and Luke is forever three." Others say nothing about their child in Heaven. I know a mom who has had five miscarriages. She only mentions her living children. A few others ways to answer:

- We have four, one is still at home.
- I raised three terrific people.
- I am mom to two living children.
- My wife and I had four children. One died last year and the others are homeschooled.
- I had two children plus I claim my son-in-law. He is raising our two beautiful granddaughters!

How you answer the question "How many children do you have?" is a very personal choice. A choice I encourage you to consider before you find yourself in a tough spot.

I have shared how I answer some questions. There is no right way to answer, only what is right you and for your situation. But you should think about how you will answer questions. Talk with your spouse. He may have strong opinions on how to answer certain questions.

- How many children do you have?
- What ages are they?
- Where do they live?
- What happened?
- How did he die?
- What caused his illness?
- Do you plan to have more children?
- Did the driver die?
- Have you read the autopsy report?

Plan your answers. Practice them in the car, in the shower, in front of the mirror. It helps to be prepared.

Help your children know how to respond to questions.

Our children have been asked, "How many siblings do you have?" many times since The Accident. Especially when they went to new colleges. It was hard for them at first. They might tear up if they said anything about their brother's death. The awkward silences. They knew some people would ask for details. They did not want to be center of attention because of him. They did not want to be known as the kids whose brother died. They have each figured out how they will answer questions.

If you have other children perhaps you can help them think through how they want to answer questions. If your children are younger, you may need to teach them answers you feel are appropriate. If they are older, help them think through what they wish to say. And encourage them to practice.

For others

Some of the questions listed above should never be asked of strangers or new acquaintances at a business meeting or church event. If you are a friend of a bereaved parent or meet one of us at an event, ask open questions like "tell me about your family?" Then they can decide how much to tell.

Let your friend decide if they want to talk about their child. If you hear you friend tell others they have one child when you know their youngest died of cancer or took his own life, please do not correct her! Let her decide what to tell. This is especially true at social or church event where she may not want to become the center of awkward attention.

If you are not sure what to say, you may want to read "God did not need my son in Heaven" or "What not to say to a grieving parent.." Or any of the other posts found on my blog by clicking on the menu item "Helping the Grieving." You can search the Web for articles on helping grieving parents.

It is kind to mention their loss with a simple "I'm so sorry" and let the bereaved parents lead the conversation. Take cues from the parents, like the couple did at dinner that night in November. Ron asking about their daughter indicated that we did not want to go into detail about Andrew's death. They took the cue and quickly went on to another topic.

If a mom or dad indicates they have a child in Heaven, ask about his or her life, not their death. Most of us would much rather tell you how beautiful our child was and how he lived than talk about their death.

And if we do want to talk about their death, please listen. And love us well through your tears.

~~~~~~

July 17

I'm thinking about my life today. Last month I conducted my last Home School for High School Seminar. I have been doing these around the country for fourteen years. I am finished home schooling our children. We had said that I would stop doing the Seminars after our last one graduated. I am grateful that I was able to help other families home school. I enjoyed encouraging them to do what God had called them to do.

I wondered what I would do after that stage of life was finished. Now I know. It's not what I had imagined, but I like my life.

July 18

A reader commented on the post "How Many Children Do You Have?" She asked, "Tell me something that makes you smile about your loved one, please?"

My answer:

> Thank you for asking!
>
> His kindness! His kindness makes me smile. He was a goofy kid and often forgot to use a filter, but he was never malicious. Andrew was kind and thoughtful. He smiled all the time and brought smiles with him when he walked into a room.
>
> He was grateful for little things like a box of starbursts I sent to him at college, along with the summons for a speeding ticket. He was excited to open the box and find the bad news surrounded by colorful candy.
>
> In the midst of struggling with issues some our others were going through, Andrew made me feel like a good mother. I needed that sometimes. I could always call him and he would tell me about his life, his friends, and his adventures. And he always told me he loved me and was glad I was his momma.
>
> Thank you for asking me to share. I am smiling through my tears as I type this.

~~~~~~

July 20

Warning

A friend called to tell me my blog should come with a warning. So here goes....

> WARNING: Reading my blog may cause fluid to leak from your eyes. I hope it also causes you to smile often. And maybe even giggle.

Chapter Fifteen

Another Tragedy

July 20

Siblings Struggle

My youngest daughter started writing a blog this past spring. She doesn't use spell check as often as I would like, but I enjoy reading her thoughts on life as a college gal. In May she wrote about the movie "Big Hero 6" and her anger towards the driver of the car in which her big brother died. It gave me insight into her thoughts and feelings. It also encouraged me to continue to want to want to forgive those who hurt me.

The Bad Guy

by Margaret Duncan

I was the "Bad Guy"

(**Big Hero 6—spoiler alert**)

Summer is here! Well, mostly. School is out for most of Covenant, but I somehow though it a good idea to take Human Genetics over May term. We have class 9-3 each day then few hours of studying or homework to do in the evenings. Over all it isn't too bad. Class is interesting enough and the homework isn't terrible. It's just lot. But every once in a blue moon, I finish my work early and actually have the evening to enjoy myself. Last night I finished everything for the day, so I called up a few friends and we had a movie night. I decided a kid's movie would be a nice break from all the thinking I had been doing that day and give my brain a rest. Boy was I wrong.

We watched Big Hero 6. I'd heard it was good, but I actually had no idea at all what it was about. Well here's the basic gist: two brothers bond over being brilliant. The movie gets you super attached to the older brother and shows how great he is then he very abruptly blows up. Just like that. All is well, then boom, no more big brother. So time goes on and the younger brother, "Hero", finds a project the older one was working on that is basically a giant, puffy, robot that serves as a "personal health care provider." Hero works on improving the bot, but is interrupted because there's a bad guy trying to take over. Fast forward a while and we find out the bad guy is seeking revenge for his daughter's

299

death but turns out she is alive but needs saving. Oh also, the bad guy started the fire the brother died in. So Hero and his bot risk their lives going into the vortex thing-a-ma-jig to attempt to save the daughter. More people die and everyone cry, but in the end, the daughter, the bot, and Hero are all okay. Bad guy goes to jail and everyone lives happily ever after.

So I went through a roller coaster of emotion watching this. First, I always get overly attached to good big brothers in fictional stories. Reminds me of mine. Andrew and I were not "best friends" my any means, but I was quite fond of him. We were close enough that it really hurts that he isn't here and won't ever be again. I tend to relive the pain of losing my brother when anyone dies in a movie, much less a big brother figure. So from the start this movie and I were off to a bad start. I had already had a rough week in regards to missing Andrew. Now I am just about thrown over the edge.

Then the boy finds out the fire was set on purpose by the bad guy. The brother went into the building trying to save someone. He was doing something good. And he was killed. It wasn't an accident. There was no reason, no purpose in his death. Andrew was at a party and had been drinking, but a friend was to be his DD. The friend had a little to drink and thought he was fine to drive. He wasn't. He ran a stop sign and killed five people. I have been angry with the driver since day one. He had been drinking and chose to drive regardless without telling anyone else he had been drinking. His foolish decision cost his own life and the life of four others. Not cool. (Don't drink and drive kids.)

So the movie goes on and Hero figures out he can try to save the daughter of the man who caused the death of his brother, but his life will be risked in the process. He should be angry at the bad guy. Hero has every right to want to smash his face in. Why would he ever do something good for him? Especially something that could possible take Hero's life? What?? I thought were supposed to stay angry and seek revenge?

So, on my drive home I had some thinking to do. I tend to think out loud. This process started as talking, changed to ranting, and quickly escalated to yelling. "Why would you set the fire?! You killed him for no reason? How dare you take his life! How selfish are you?!" which, subsequently, turned into yelling at the driver of the car my brother died in, "How could you ever think it's okay to drive after you'd been drinking!? You killed my brother!! Did you ever think about that??!! Why were you so selfish?" I then switched to yelling at Hero, "Why would you risk your life for this person? He was the bad guy! He killed your brother! He wasn't worth your spit! Why would you love him like this?" That's when Jesus stepped in and softly whispered back, "For the same reason I gave my life for you."

My car was all the sudden very quiet.

I was the bad guy. I was selfish and wanted my own glory. I tried to take over my world and, in the process, set a lot of fires that hurt a lot of people. No, I haven't killed someone, but I have done enough other things to warrant God's full wrath. God should hate me. He ought to have left me for dead. But he didn't. While I was his enemy, Christ chose to not only risk but willingly give his life so I may be restored. How great is our God? By Christ having mercy on me while I was the bad guy, I have been given life. What would prompt God to love me in this way? I cannot explain how God's love works, but I am ever so grateful for it.

"Therefore, since we have been justified by faith, we have peace with God through our Lord Jesus Christ. Through him we have also obtained access by faith into this grace in which we stand, and we rejoice in hope of the glory of God. Not only that, but we rejoice in our sufferings, knowing that suffering produces endurance, and endurance produces character, and character produces hope, and hope does not put us to shame, because God's love has been poured into our hearts through the Holy Spirit who has been given to us. For while we were still weak, at the right time Christ died for the ungodly. For one will scarcely die for a righteous person— though perhaps for a good person one would dare even to die— but God shows his love for us in that while we were still sinners, Christ died for us. Since, therefore, we have now been justified by his blood, much more shall we be saved by him from the wrath of God. For if while we were enemies we were reconciled to God by the death of his Son, much more, now that we are reconciled, shall we be saved by his life. More than that, we also rejoice in God through our Lord Jesus Christ, through whom we

have now received reconciliation."

Romans 5:1-11 | ESV

But here is the part I would love to leave out. I often find myself grateful for God's forgiveness, but scarcely do I find myself desiring to forgive others as a result. But this is what we are told to do many times over. (Colossians 3:13b forgiving each other; as the Lord has forgiven you, so you also must forgive. Ephesians 4:32b forgiving one another, as God in Christ forgave you.) I recognize forgiveness is not a one and done thing. It's a process—or so I hear, I haven't tried it much—that starts with a desire and, I'm guessing, lots of prayer. Well, Jesus, I don't really want to forgive the man who caused my brother's death. But that's not my grudge to hold. I want to want to forgive him. Father, help me to love Clint even though he seems like the bad guy. show me how to love him as you loved me.

I love Margaret's honesty in this blog post. I enjoy reading her thoughts. She loves Jesus and knows Him as her Redeemer, Counselor, and Friend.

If you have anger towards someone for any reason, won't you consider forgiveness today? Even if you don't want to, you can choose to want to want to forgive them. Ask God to help you. He will.

Put on then, as God's chosen ones, holy and beloved, compassionate hearts, kindness, humility, meekness, and patience, bearing with one another and, if one has a complaint against another, forgiving each other; as the Lord has forgiven you, so you also must forgive. And above all these put on love, which binds everything together in perfect harmony. And let the peace of Christ rule in your hearts, to which indeed you were called in one body.

Colossians 3:12-14 | ESV

July 21

Topics of Conversation

On a recent twenty plus hour trip home, we discussed a variety of topics. Some topics were discussed very quickly. More like me asking a question and Ron saying "No." Others, like Lincoln's biography, were an ongoing conversation.

- Could I get plastic surgery to fix my droopy right eye lid?
- Should we stop to see the world's largest wind chime? Or The largest golf tee?
- Where should we eat?
- Who was in Lincoln's cabinet?
- Should I share my lemon pound cake? If not, can I still have half of your brownie?
- Can we go through Chattanooga to see the grandsons?
- What should we do next weekend in San Antonio?
- Can we go through the Starbucks drive-thru pulling a trailer to get an Indianapolis mug without getting wet?
- How do you practice safety during severe thunderstorms while pulling a large trailer down the interstate?
- What do they grow on farms around the USA?
- When should we stop for the night?
- Which Tim Keller Podcast should we listen to next?
- What about Mary Lincoln's decorating tastes?
- What name should Ron pick for his Waze character?
- Why is every hotel for fifty miles around St. Louis booked?
- Want to listen to Stuart Townsend?
- Why aren't there more Krispy Kreme stores along our route?

Yep, we are old and have been married a very long time.

July 22

Topics of Conversation, Part Two

Did you notice that grief and death were nowhere in the list of topics we discussed in our 20+ hour drive home last weekend? Yes, we remember our son. Yes, we still hurt and get sad sometimes. Yes, I think of him every day. But grief no longer overwhelms me. Death and grief are not the focus of my life. Actually, we rarely talk about grief, The Accident or sadness on our travels. If Andrew is mentioned, it is usually with a smile. Or even a giggle. He ~~brought~~ brings joy to our lives, as all our adult children do.

In Christ, we have hope, joy, and peace. Our son was a follower of Jesus. As a result, he is in the presence of Christ now. Someday I will join him there, because I, too, am a disciple of Christ. There is great joy and hope in knowing that I have eternal life.

There are times when we see something in our travels or read a post on social media that reminds us of our son, and Ron will comment. As I wrote last week, I cried in a hotel in New York after hearing a song from the memorial service. He held me while I cried and loved me well. But tears are rare these days. Joy, smiles and laughter are common.

We like to laugh and tell stories when we are together as a family. Our kids' lives are intertwined, so a story about one might include or lead to a story about the others. Andrew's name comes up often.

However, I try to be careful not to mention him right before we go to bed. I don't want us to be sad last thing before sleep.

I made an exception last night. I was looking for a video of Andrew getting pepper sprayed. Voluntarily. I found a video of him and one of his favorite partners dancing for the final in one of their dance classes at West Texas A&M University. I had never seen this video. I love the smile he gives her towards the end. Johanna and Andrew were dear friends. Watching it brought joy to us both just before we went to sleep.

July 26

Batman

Most of the time I have peace and joy. But...

At times ... rarely these days ... But at times, I feel a deep, aching sorrow over losing my son. A sadness flickers through my being. Usually lasting only a short time. Moments really. And I wonder if I am alone in missing him.

Invariably when this happens one of my friends will mention him or post a photo without knowing the dark place I am in. These kindnesses help. They bring me great joy and often a little giggle as I recall his antics.

It happened this week when three of his friends posed with serious faces dressed in Batman shirts. And Saturday night, they had an Andrew Themed Panty Raid at TEXAS. All in good fun, led by the real adults who make sure the girls are dressed prior to the guys running through the dressing room yelling cheesy pickup lines and tripping over things.

If you have a friend who lost a child, find time in the next week or so to send a message, note, or photo to let them know their child is not forgotten. Those remembrances bring healing. And show you care.

July 29

How Did He Die? Part Two

Why do so many people ask, "How did he die?" Why are they concerned about what happened? I'm not an expert or trained counselor, but I have a few ideas on the subject.

Some people ask out of genuine concern and love. As imperfect as they are, they want to love us and help us. To these people, I spill my guts. I tell them what happened. All of it. It is sometimes messy. Tears, and snot, and stuff. But they love me anyway. I am thankful for these friends.

Sometimes it's asked out of simple curiosity or ignorance of what to say to a grieving mom. If the former, we can deflect the questions by saying something like, "Oh, I'd rather not discuss that." I usually just say, "drunk driving accident", as if that explains everything. It doesn't. If the later, we can help educate folks by teaching them or posting good articles on what to say and how to help. In the early days of grief, we can't help others know how to love us. We are too broken. But as we heal, and as time passes, we will have learned a few things. And we can share those lessons with our friends so we can all love the next bereaved parents just a bit better.

But I think a deeper reason people ask how he died or what happened is that, in their minds, they think, "If I know how another mom lost her son, I can prevent that from happening to my kid. To my family. To me."

If it was illness - I'll get a better doctor than they used
Accident - I will watch my kid more carefully than they did
Stillbirth - my kids were all born healthy and I'm done having kids
He fell mountain climbing - my daughter will stay off mountains
Drugs - my kid would never use drugs
Murder by abuser - my daughter will be more careful who she marries
Suicide - my kid is a Christian, he would never take his own life
Drowning - mine will always wear a life vest

Really!? Your child will ALWAYS wear a life vest?? *Always?*

You see, if they can explain the whys, maybe they won't have to face the fact that it can happen to them. And yet... Anyone of us could face the horror of losing a child. I know. I face it every day.

It makes me want to shout: "No!!! No, you cannot prevent all accidents. Your child will not always wear a life vest nor will he always be careful not to get in a car with a buzzed driver. I know lots of people who are great parents and yet their child died. More prayer or a better team of doctors or bigger hospital would not have saved our kids. Yes, some of our kids were Christians and they became addicts or alcoholics; your child could become one, too, and if she does, you will love her through the whole horrible thing."

And I want to shout, "love your child and introduce him to Jesus! Trust God and pray and love your kid. And know that he is not really yours; he was loaned to you for a little while. He is God's. And God can be trusted with him. No matter what happens. He is a loving, compassionate, gracious God. He loves your kid. In life and in death. And He loves you! Turn to him now!"

So, If you are a bereaved parent who is tired of the question, "How did he die?", surround yourself with people who can love you well. With folks who will listen to you talk about how your son lived, not how he died.

If you don't have those folks in your town, well, you can found us here. In WWW. We will listen. And we will love you. Consider going to a moms mini retreat, dads weekend, or parents weekend. Or find a Grief Share group in your community.

And if you are a friend of a bereaved parent, instead of inquiring about death details, try asking, "Could you tell me about your child? What were his favorite toys? What was she like? How can I contribute to a memorial charity?" Love your grieving friend. Love her well.

~~~~~~

July 23

One of Andrew's favorite dance professors, who wrote us a very kind note after The Accident, recently posted about another student, Jake, getting an offer from a big dance company out of state for after graduation.

Andrew would be completing his second bachelors this December. His dance degree. He would be auditioning and planning his new adventure.

And ... cue tears...

August 3

Another TEXAS Tragedy

I have been trying to think of what to share about what happened this weekend. It was horrible. And beautiful. A terrible thing happened. And we saw God work. We were a part of His work. God worked in a beautiful way.

This is a long post. Before you read it, you may want to get a cup of coffee. And maybe some tissue. Get comfortable. As I share my heart.

Weekend Plans

Ron had meetings scheduled in Colorado Springs for Monday, August 3. We didn't want to drive the whole way on Sunday and be tired Monday, so we decided to drive on Saturday. This would allow us to attend church in Colorado Springs and then explore the area and even ride our bikes. That was the plan.

We had been planning for weeks. But early last week I felt like we should go Friday night. We should drive part way and stay the night in Amarillo. It would mean paying for an extra night in a hotel, but I felt like God was showing me we should go Friday. Now I know why.

I told Ron I would like to go to Canyon to see some of the kids from TEXAS. He was okay with that.

We have stayed close to Kris Miller, the executive director, and to many of the kids from the 2013 season. You may have seen pictures they sent me. I love when they send me pictures. I enjoy seeing what is happening in their lives today. They loved our son and the others killed in The Accident. They love us still. They message me with stories and tell me when they think about Andrew. We are excited to see them graduate, get new jobs, and live. We enjoy getting to see them a couple of times each summer.

Ron and I discussed our options. We have a lifetime pass to the show. All we have to do is call ahead to let them know we are coming. Margaret and I saw the show back in June. We didn't call to tell them we were coming this time. We never made reservations for the show; we just felt like we were not supposed to see it. But we wanted to love on the cast and crew. We did not understand it, but that's what we knew we were to do.

We planned to leave the house around 2:00. This would allow us to go to the Canyon and see folks before the show. Then we would head back to Amarillo to sleep, get up early the next day, and drive to Colorado. We would arrive in time to ride bikes in Colorado Springs. That was the plan. Or so we thought.

Weekend Reality

Those who know me know that if we plan to leave at two, I want to be *on the road* by two. I sometimes get upset if Ron is late when we are leaving town, even if it isn't his fault. This is something I have been working on for years. (I never claimed to be a perfect wife. This is one of my many failings.)

Friday afternoon Ron's meeting at work ran late. We would be late leaving town. And I did not care. I wasn't upset at all! This should have been a sign to me that something was different. Something was very different, but I did not notice it until much later.

We took our time packing. I read a book. We fed the dogs. We finally left the house about 6:00. Four hours late ... and I was just fine with that. We were not going to make it to Canyon that night, but since we hadn't yet told anyone we were coming they wouldn't miss us.

We were talking and laughing and having a wonderful time as we drove towards Colorado via Amarillo. We stopped to grab a bite eat. We weren't in a hurry.

Then I checked Facebook a little before 8:00 pm.

Another Death, Another TEXAS Tragedy

I saw the news. It had been posted by one of the cast members more than an hour earlier. There had been an explosion at TEXAS. One person was missing. The show was cancelled for Friday night.

I turned to Ron and said, "They are dead. I know there is another kid dead. We have to go." He agreed that we should go if we were needed. He set the GPS to Canyon. We were two hours away.

Ron told me to call Kris Miller to ask if we could help and ask if we should come. We didn't want to be in the way. He said, "YES! Please come! We need you!" We did not know what we could do, but knew we had to go. I began to pray

We knew Kris would be dealing with investigators, media, parents, and a devastated cast and crew. The cast and crew are mostly kids ages 19-25. We thought we might be able to help Kris by simply showing him love. We would be available for whatever he asked of us. He asked us to go where the kids were.

We know many of the cast and crew. They were Andrew's friends. Some have stayed in our home. One young man, Austin, grew up with my boys. I am friends with his mom. He went to West Texas A&M University (WT) in large part because of his friendship with Andrew. He took his first ballet class there after The Accident. Now he is majoring in dance and dancing in TEXAS. Now he had lost another friend.

I love these kids. I knew they were hurting. They are so young! They were far away from home. They had lost five friends just two years ago. And now they had lost another. They would be in shock. They would need comfort. Ron and I wanted to love them, hold them as they cried, listen to them, and pray for them. We wanted to be Jesus with skin on for them. So we drove to Canyon. We arrived a little after ten Friday night.

Hugs

Within moments of my posting on social media asking for prayer, I began getting texts from mommas all over the country. They were concerned about us. These were mommas whose children worked at TEXAS. Their children were facing another horrible tragedy. And yet, they were concerned about me! They were sending me virtual hugs. I assured them that Ron and I were okay. It was a shock and we were upset, but we were going to be okay. We were not reliving the events of 2013. We have experienced healing from God. We knew this was not about us or what happened two years ago. They reminded us to take care of ourselves. I told them we were driving to Canyon to help in any way we could.

We were concerned about their kids and the staff of TEXAS. I contacted Austin's mom to see how she was doing. I told them each that I would give their child a hug. Lots of hugs. And I would let them know what was going on.

We arrived at the WT Baptist Student Ministries building where the cast and crew had gathered. And I did just what I told those mommas I would do: I gave each of their kids a huge hug first from their own momma and then one from me. Many of the kids had already left, but we stayed and talked with those who were there.

I had posted on my FB page asking for prayer for peace and wisdom as to what we should say. We felt a great peace. We mostly said, "I'm sorry. I love you. You will get through this. We will help." Then we listened as they shared and held them as they cried.

And I received a beautiful "hug" from Laura. Her daddy was killed in an accident when she was very young. She was part of the show in 2013. She has experienced too much death. But she has a beautiful faith. She told me stories of my Andrew from their Bible study these two summers. I will be forever grateful for "hugs" like that which I get from our TEXAS family. I love hearing new stories about our son from his friends!

After a couple of hours and many tears, we left and headed to the hotel. It was past midnight.

While driving we got a call from Kris. We had not yet seen him. He had been at the office dealing with the press ... and calling the young woman's mom. He had had to talk with five sets of grieving parents two years ago. He never wanted to do that again. But he made another call Friday night. This time to the mother the 21 year old stage manager who had died in an explosion a few hours earlier.

Kris asked me to call her. I did. I'm glad I was available. It was hard. And that is all I will say about that. It was a private conversation between two grieving moms.

We also turned around and went to the office instead of going to the hotel. Kris sounded like he was hurting. Bad. We went to see him. We hugged him. We told him how much we loved him. We cried with him. He and Ron talked. He asked us to come to the meeting of cast and crew scheduled for ten Saturday morning on the WT campus. They would be talking about what happened and if the show would continue. Kris wanted Ron to speak to the kids. And to everyone else.

At the hotel, I sent a message to the parents of the other four killed in 2013 and to the young man who survived The Accident. I expressed our love for them. I told them we were in Amarillo and would keep them posted.

We were not going to be in Colorado Springs early enough to ride bikes on Saturday. We were going to be in Canyon, Texas. Just where He wanted us.

Saturday Mourning

We arrived at the fine arts building at WT for the meeting. We saw a number of kids we hadn't seen the night before. More hugs. More tears. And a bit of laughter as they shared their memories of their friend and the Texas Angels.

One of the other Texas Angels moms had called me that morning. "Where do I go? What can I do?" She had asked. She drove in to be with the kids.

The meeting started. On stage, men in charge of the organization that produces the show spoke to the group. Kris spoke. They talked about stuff that had to be discussed. Details. Information. More details. What they knew at this point. What would happen this morning, later today. Who was investigating. Etc. Everyone was hurting, still in shock. Many had not slept. They had lost a friend.

The crew had worked hard putting out the fire just after the explosion and had worked late into the night. They had lost a fellow crew member. You can read about what a great job they did. They had done what needed to be done. A group of young people who did exactly what they had been trained to do and were now grieving.

A few kids stood up in the audience and expressed their thoughts. At times it was tense. Everyone was emotional.

Then Kris asked Ron to speak. He got up, turned and asked me to join him on stage. We had prayed. During the night Ron had carefully considered the message he wanted to share. I had not planned to speak. I planned to stay in the audience. I was hurting too much to help. But my husband asked me to join him, so I did.

He spoke a bit about our son, even drawing some laughter as we remembered Andrew's antics. And he shared some of how it hurt to lose him and the four others. He shared our pain, our grief. He also shared that we have found peace, joy, and comfort from a loving God. He spoke to the cast and crew. He spoke of their pain, their grief. He connected with them. He spoke of a God who can heal and help.

"A teacher I like to listen to once said, 'well off (blessed) are those who mourn,'" Ron shared. "He meant that those who mourn can be well off - we can all be well off (blessed) - because the Kingdom of God is now available to everyone. The Kingdom of God is not just for a special group of religious people. Even spiritual losers (poor in spirit), the meek, and those who mourn can find peace and joy in Christ. The kingdom is available to us all."

Ron spoke of not going it alone, but reaching out to each other and helping each other get through this. He also spoke of feeling it all. Feel the pain. Grieve, cry, hurt. And then walk through it. Walk through it together.

He encouraged them to LIVE! "Honor your friend by living well and doing what you are passionate about," he told them. "Dance, sing, do what you love. That is how we heal from tragedy: we live!"

He reminded them to eat, rest, and care for themselves. I don't remember everything he said. But it was beautiful. It was heartfelt. It was healing and helpful.

I spoke as a momma. I encouraged them to reach out to God through their tears. I told them not to try to drink or drug away the pain. It won't help. Really, it won't. I shared the love of Christ with them, told them that God can and will help them through this. They can trust Him. We both testified about our own grief and healing journey. I don't remember all I said either. I was brief. I hope it helped.

I do remember the feeling that we were in God's will, being led by the Holy Spirit to speak words of life, words of joy, words of peace, and words of hope through tears. It was a beautiful thing. In the midst of a horrible thing. We are both humbled to think of how God used us. And how He has healed us and blessed us.

After we spoke, the other mom shared just a few thoughts. Her words were full of love and pain. We hurt for these kids. We hurt for this grieving family.

Then more business was discussed. The tech crew, who had been the first responders, expressed that they needed a day to rest but wanted the show to go on. More was said by cast and crew members. It was hard. It was beautiful to hear the hearts of these young people as they supported one another.

It was decided that the Saturday show would be cancelled and they would perform on Sunday. The show would go on and they would honor their friend and the other TEXAS Angels by doing what they loved, by performing, and by living!

Then a gal, who plays one of the leads and teaches voice at WT, led the cast and crew in singing "It Is Well with My Soul" a Capella. The voices sounded like angels. I stood by the wall and wept. Ron sang out in his amazing, beautiful tenor voice. The room was filled with music. Healing had begun. God was glorified.

At the end I prayed over the group. I prayed as a momma who loves them all. Because I do. I love them all dearly.

After the Meeting

We stayed a while to talk with the staff and with the cast and crew. We stood by a wall at the edge of the auditorium and waited for anyone who wanted talk to come to us. This was not about us but about them. They are hurting. They are grieving. We were available but did not want to impose.

We wanted to show them a loving, compassionate God by being loving and compassionate. Many came up to thank us for coming and for sharing. They told us stories of their friend. We hugged and cried and listened to their pain.

Then we drove to Colorado Springs.

Sunday

I cannot adequately express how I feel. I am writing this Sunday night. I am still overwhelmed with emotion as I think about this weekend.

We attended Colorado Springs Vineyard Fellowship this morning. I sobbed through worship. It was beautiful. I have used that word a lot. I don't have another word to describe it. "Beautiful" seems almost out of place during such a terrible tragedy. I was full of joy, sorrow, hope, pain, compassion, grief, and peace all at once. I am grateful that this body welcomed us, two strangers in their midst, as I sobbed through worship. I am grateful for a loving God. I am grateful for the Body of Christ.

Tonight I hurt for the young woman's parents. And for her siblings. For her friends. I know what her parents are facing in the next few months. I know some of what they are all facing. It will be hard. Grief is hard. But God is available to help and comfort them along the way.

This was a horrible weekend. A hard weekend. Yet we saw beautiful things happen. The cast and crew will go on grieving. The young woman's family will grieve. They will hurt. And we will continue to pray for them all and will reach out to them. And they will, I hope and pray, heal in time. They will remember a lovely 21 year old who died in a horrible accident. And I pray they will remember her with joy.

God is Good

What an understatement! He is compassionate, gracious, merciful, and loving.

I am humbled to have been used by Him. I am grateful for the healing I have experienced these past two years. I am willing and available to share the healing I have received with others who mourn. I want to be used by God. I want to see Him move through us in the lives of others who grieve the loss of a child, a sibling, a friend. I saw a glimpse of what that might look like this weekend.

Through pain and tragedy, I have joy and peace. I am married to a most amazing man who, through his own pain, spoke words of life from his heart to a room full of devastated young men and women. I serve a God who loves beyond measure. I serve a God who knows we live in a broken hurting world and envelops us in His grace and mercy.

Monday

I have spent the morning praying, reading and writing. I have edited this post to try to make it shorter. Trying to put into words all that happened the last three days. I am still amazed. I have talked with some of the kids and prayed for them all.

Sometimes I feel like I don't know much. What do know is that Jesus is still Lord. Even in the midst of tragedy. He still loves, still heals, and still saves. He is the King of Kings, Lord of Lord, Mighty God, Counselor, and Prince of Peace. He is the same yesterday, today, and forever. He loves us. He IS love. He is the Bread of Life. He is the Way, the Truth, and the Life.

And for all of this I am thankful.

Yes, it is well with my soul.

And ... Cue sobbing

You read about my weekend, the TEXAS tragedy. It was a tough weekend. But it was not about my grief. We were being led by God to try to help others, and it was hard.

Yesterday was a full day. A very busy day. Today ... I sobbed.

Sometimes, in my grief journey, I just need a good cry. Sometimes nothing major has happened, nothing special set it off. I just need to cry. Today was different. Today there was a reason for my tears. I have been through a lot these past four days.

The past few days were tough. We saw God working. We saw people hurting. We loved them and tried to be led by the Holy Spirit. We drove. We worshipped. We played a bit. We had dinner with old friends then drove some more last night. We did not rest much. Parts were awful, parts were beautiful. But they were tough days.

Here's the deal: When I know it's coming - the tears, the sobbing, the intense emotions - I find a safe place. A place where I can sob and pour my heart out to my Father. Then I rest.

Today was one of those days. I was alone in a hotel with no place I had to be. I ate a good, healthy, late breakfast. I listened to Chris Tomlin and read a great book about another dad's grief journey. I sobbed, I prayed, I worshipped. Then I slept. I awoke refreshed and joyful.

"Consider others more valuable than yourself"

I have learned I need to hold it together sometimes. For others. There are times I must be brave and strong. I must care for others who are hurting. But I cannot do that too long. I cannot hold it together while hurting for too long. That is not healthy. It is not healthy to hold emotion in too long.

It is healthy and healing to feel the emotions and to share them our Father. He knows. He understands. He cares. And He loves. But I must find a safe, appropriate time and place to feel it all and to sob.

So that's what I did today. It was beautiful.

Chapter Sixteen

The Second Anniversary

Life Goes On

August 9

This week will be ....I have no words. The anniversary. God is still good.

~~~~~~

August 10

Three years ago today he moved to Canyon. Andrew loved it there. He loved his school, teachers, friends and dance partners.

Thank you for loving him. Thank you for sharing your memories with us.

And he was working towards two degrees. Two bachelors. Smart kid.

God is still sovereign. He is good and kind.

~~~~~~

August 11

Riding Alone

In the last four years, since I first got off the couch and became more active, I have almost always exercised with a buddy. Weights, yoga, running, biking - all with partners. Swimming is the only thing I enjoy doing alone. I have only gone on one bike ride by myself.

I won't say it's a fear, but I am very averse to riding alone. It scares me. Ok. So it's a fear. Today I overcame that. I rode a strange route in a strange city. Alone.

I rode more than twelve miles out from the airport hotel to the Salt Lake Marina then back. Upper 80's. Strong headwinds on the way back. NO shade anywhere along the route. I was tired and hot when I got back. All my water was gone. But I did it! And I was still smiling. Kind of.

This really is a big deal for me. Especially this week when I would rather stay in bed and hide my head. I'd like to sleep through the next few days. But as Ron said last Saturday to a group of amazing young people, "the best way to honor those we have lost is to LIVE!"

I choose life today. How about you? Will you choose life?

August 12

Twelve Things I Am Grateful for on the 12th

Two years.

I am trying to write this monthly feature.
"Twelve Things I'm grateful for on the 12th" began 13 months ago.
It is good to count my blessings.

But this month...trying to write it...
I can't.

Forgive me, dear readers.

I am grateful for many things. I really am. But...

Today I grieve.
Today I remember my son.
Today I remember....

> His joy.
> His laughter.
> His voice.
> His pickup lines.
> His stomping through the house.
> His clumsiness off stage.
> His beauty and grace on stage.
> His kindness.
> His lack of filters.
> His hugs.
> His stories.
> His phone calls.
> His goofy smiles.
> His love.
> His life.

Mostly, I am remember that he knew Christ as Savior.
He knows Him now face to face in all of His glory.
I miss him.
I love him still.

Two years ago tonight The Accident ended my son's earthly life.

August 13

To Parents Who Have Lost a Child

Two years ago today my life changed forever. Two years ago last night The Accident happened.

It was about 11:45 that five young people died. Amanda, Clint, Eric, Andrew, and Julian. All talented, kind, beautiful people. The Justice of the Peace did not get to the site for about 45 minutes so the official date of death is 8/13. Both days are hard for Julie and Gabe Diaz, June Bush, Victor Starz, Kimberly Starz, Debbie and Henry S. Harrison, Ron and me. Please lift us all up in prayer today.

June and some of the folks from the show TEXAS will be placing crosses at the site today. Five crosses. We cannot be there but are grateful she is doing this for our five Texas Angels.

I am so grateful for those of you in the While We're Waiting group. You have helped me heal. Your stories, love, encouragement and prayers have helped me live with joy even in the midst of sorrow.

Our Father is loving, compassionate, merciful, and gracious. I do not understand the why's of what happened. I don't like it that Andrew is not with us on earth. But I know the character of God and I trust Him. I know my son was a believer in Jesus Christ. I know he is in the presence of Christ even now and will live eternally.

Yes, I still have sad days. But most of the time I have peace and joy. Peace and joy that can only come from knowing a good and beautiful God.

For those of you just beginning your grief journey please know that the Holy Spirit, the Comforter is available to you. He can teach you, lead you, comfort you and help you.

Time spent doing the next right thing and following God can heal your broken heart. It may take longer for some, and it will look different in each of us. But healing can happen. You can know peace and joy again.

May you all be blessed today and every day in the name of Jesus.

September 30, 2015

Healing

As I look back over those first two years – reading posts, blog articles, and my personal notes – I am struck by how raw my wound was and how excruciating daily living was. I see the pain, the sorrow, and intense grief I experienced in those first months. I see how simple tasks were extremely difficult. I remember how hard it was dealing with the paperwork and the decisions we had to make. And I am in awe that I no longer walk in that pain. I no longer walk in a fog of constant sorrow and grief.

There is a void in my life that only Andrew filled. I miss his laugh, his stomping through the house, his hugs, and his stories. Nothing will ever replace my son in my life. I still have moments and even days of sadness. Some memories still bring tears. I see his friends dance, graduate, get new jobs, or get married, and these things bring a twinge of regret that I don't get to see Andrew do those things. I hate that his nephews won't know him like they will know their other uncles and aunts. Yes, I will grieve my son until I die.

However, those early days of sorrow so deep that I physically ached are gone. The days of doubt, sobbing, and aching have passed. Seeing an old picture of all four of my boys together no longer takes my breath away. I no longer count the days, weeks, or months since I saw him last or since the date of his death. I no longer cry each time I see a picture of him or hear his name. I no longer wake up with my pillow wet from my tears. Death is no longer a central theme in my thoughts.

Pictures and stories of my son bring a smile. I enjoy looking back at his Facebook, seeing photos of him with his friends, and hearing stories of their antics. I rejoice at seeing his friends growing and living. I know that they were changed for the better by having Andrew in their lives, and I know that they have not forgotten him.

Friends, family, and of course grandchildren bring me joy. I have peace. I sleep well. Sometimes I dream of Andrew, and I am glad. I ride my bike, travel with Ron, and mow my property. I read great books, study my Bible, and enjoy movies and TV. I play with my dogs, visit with friends, and go out to eat. In short, I live.

I know I have forgotten things about Andrew, stories he told, little things. I see pictures and wish he were here to tell me the backstory. I miss Andrew.

I know my son lived. He lived well. He still lives.

My heart is no longer broken. I no longer ache all over. I no longer think of death, dying, grief, and pain much of the time. Yes, there is a void. Yes, there is a scar. Yes, I have experienced loss. But in Christ I have found peace, joy, and strength to go forth and do the next right thing.

This is what I mean when I say my broken, shattered heart has been healed by a loving, gracious, living God. When I say that I have found healing after The Accident, I don't mean that I no longer grieve.

As you try to comfort a mother or father who has experienced the death of a child – a child of any age and by any cause - remember that they will grieve their child forever. Or at least until we join them in Heaven. Please know that their birthday and the date of their death will always be difficult days. Even when it doesn't look like they still grieve, please know that they miss their child.

Mention our children. Share your memories. Acknowledge our pain.

And pray for us. Pray that we find joy. Pray that we have happy memories. Pray that we find healing in a loving, living God.

"Let not your hearts be troubled. Believe in God; believe also in me. In my Father's house are many rooms. If it were not so, would I have told you that I go to prepare a place for you? And if I go and prepare a place for you, I will come again and will take you to myself, that where I am you may be also. And you know the way to where I am going."

John 14:1-4 | ESV

Appendix

Andrew Raymond Duncan

From the moment Andrew Raymond Duncan stepped onto a stage, his life was transformed. The energy of a live audience and Andrew's energy for life matched perfectly.

One of his first productions was the musical *101 Dalmatians* with his 4-H club Actors Creating Together, and he spent his high school years immersing himself in every performing arts organization he could find, including Opera Breve, Wichita Theatre, Backdoor Theatre, and Applause. Some of his greatest joys in life and his most beautiful friendships were forged through performing. Some of his favorite roles were Macavity in *Cats*, Thenardier in *Les Miserable*, and Prince Charming in three different shows: *Snow White, Sleeping Beauty*, and *Cinderella*.

Andrew loved musical theatre. He could act and sing but knew his weakness was dance, so Andrew began ballet, jazz, tap and other classes at the age of 16 at Dance Etc. He fell in love with dance, and it became his passion. Andrew spent the summer of 2011 in *The Great Santa Clause Bank Robbery* in Cisco, Texas and the summers of 2012 and 2013 as a dancer in the musical *Texas!* at Palo Duro Canyon State Park. He was thrilled to have paid acting gigs. During the 2012-2013 school year, he performed with the Amarillo Lone Star Ballet in *The Nutcracker, The Legend of Sleepy Hollow*, and *Cleopatra*, fulfilling his dream to work with a professional dance company.

Besides the performing arts, delivering pick-up lines to make every girl he knew feel special, and telling horrible jokes, he was involved in his youth group at Fairway Baptist Church and Boy Scout Troop 15, where he earned the rank of Eagle Scout.

Andrew was born in Bristol, Tennessee on December 24th, 1992. He was the fifth of seven children born to Ron and Kathleen Duncan. Early in life, Andrew struggled with a speech problem and learning difficulties, both of which he overcame with determination, hard work, and the love of his parents.

He was loved by his siblings, and he adored them as well. The Duncan boys were a force to be reckoned with when they decided to take on a new adventure. Andrew and Margaret loved dancing together at the Casablanca and at every wedding they attended.

Andrew was homeschooled through high school. He began attending Vernon College when he was fifteen and continued to take dual credit courses there and at Midwestern State University until he graduated high school in 2011.

He was a student of West Texas A&M University and a former student of Midwestern State. At West Texas, he majored in accounting and dance. He knew that he could not dance forever, but also knew that every dance company and theatre needs a business manager. Accounting would allow him to be a part of the arts even when he could no longer perform as a dancer. He attained the Dean's List at both WTA&M and MSU.

Andrew's life ended suddenly on August 13 of his junior year in an automobile accident on highway 287 near Dumas, TX. Andrew had been riding home from a cast party with his friends. Five of the six passengers in the vehicle were killed immediately.

Andrew knew God was his Master Choreographer. He loved life, loved to dance, loved his friends, and loved to laugh – loudly and distinctly. Though he sometimes forgot to use filters, Andrew was kind and considerate to all. It was hard to stay in bad mood when Andrew was around; he brought joy everywhere he went.

He was, indeed, a Prince of a son, a Prince of brother, and a Prince of a friend.

Forever Our Prince

Andrew Raymond Duncan

December 24, 1992 to August 13, 2013

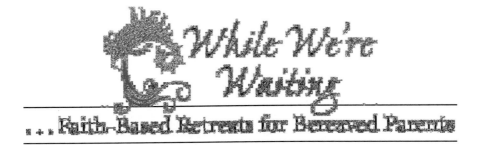

Facts about the While We're Waiting Ministry

While We're Waiting was co-founded in April of 2011 by Brad and Jill Sullivan, whose 17 year old daughter, Hannah, went to Heaven in February of 2009 after a year-long battle with brain cancer, and Larry and Janice Brown, whose 36 year old son, Adam, a member of Navy SEAL Team SIX, went to Heaven in March of 2010 when he was killed in Afghanistan. Board members include Tiffany McCain, whose daughter, Lily, was stillborn in 2008, and Charles and Christy Swain, whose 17 year old son, Ryan, drowned in 2013.

The mission of While We're Waiting is to bring bereaved parents together in order to provide a faith-based network of encouragement and support as they grieve the loss of their children. Our goal is always to point grieving parents to our only true source of comfort, Jesus Christ. Our desire is to encourage parents to live well while we're waiting to be reunited with our children in Heaven one day, bringing glory to God in the process. This goal of bringing bereaved parents together is accomplished primarily through our retreats.

We currently host three types of retreats for bereaved parents:

- Weekend-long retreats for couples/singles
- Weekend-long retreats just for dads
- One-day mini-retreats just for moms

At all of our events, we share our children's stories and discuss topics relevant to bereaved parents. We pray for each other and we encourage one another. We may shed some tears, but we also share in times of laughter as we discuss the hope we have in Jesus Christ. We may have many more years here on earth before we see our children again. Our desire is always to determine how we can live well "while we're waiting" to be reunited with our precious children in Heaven.

All of our events are offered at no charge to the attendees. A voluntary love offering is accepted at each event. We attained 501(c)(3) status in August of 2012, so all donations are tax deductible. No one receives any salary for their work with While We're Waiting, and all donations go straight to the operations of the ministry.

Our retreats are typically held in the Hot Springs, Arkansas, area, but we occasionally do events "on the road." We have hosted events in Picayune, Mississippi; Wichita Falls, Texas; Huntsville, Alabama; and other parts of Arkansas.

At the present time, we are using borrowed facilities for our retreats. However, we have seen the need to offer our While We're Waiting events more often due to the fact that they are filling up months in advance and we have waiting lists for all of them. Therefore, we are in the early stages of building our own retreat facility. Fifty acres in Hot Springs has been donated to the ministry, and this is where we are planning to build. The property is situated between two thoroughbred farms on the outskirts of the city, and is a beautiful site, with a pond and lots of mature trees. There is an older house on the property, which is being completely renovated. A large kitchen/dining area and ten hotel-style bedrooms will be added, so participants in our events will each have their own private bedroom and bath while they're staying with us. We have committed to building the While We're Waiting Refuge debt free, and we have faith that God will supply all that we need. We anticipate holding our first retreat at this location in October of 2016.

Registration for our events is through our website at www.whilewerewaiting.org.

In addition to our retreat events, we host two faith-based support groups just for bereaved parents in Arkansas. One meets on the last Wednesday night of each month at Hot Springs Baptist Church in Hot Springs, Arkansas, and the other meets on the second Wednesday night of each month at Cross Church in Springdale, Arkansas. One of our dreams is to have "While We're Waiting" chapters around the country. These would be support groups like those hosted by Compassionate Friends and Bereaved Parents USA, but with a basis in our faith in Jesus Christ as the one and only healer of broken hearts.

While We're Waiting hosts three Facebook groups. One is a public page, which can be found and followed by anyone by searching for "While We're Waiting." Another is a private page, with membership limited just to parents who have lost children. It can be found by searching for "While We're Waiting – Support for Bereaved Parents" and requesting to join. An encouraging quote or Scripture is posted daily on each of these pages, but the private page allows for conversation between parents who have experienced the death of a child. We also host a page just for bereaved siblings. It is also a private group, and can be found by searching for "While We're Waiting – Support for Bereaved Siblings" and requesting to join. A young pastor who lost his only sibling seven years ago is the moderator of that group.

The While We're Waiting Team loves to share their stories and the While We're Waiting ministry with churches and civic organizations.

For more information about While We're Waiting, please contact Jill Sullivan at jill@whilewerewaiting.org.

About the Author

Kathleen Duncan has been married to her husband Ron for 32 years. They met and married while attending the University of Oklahoma where Ron earned a degree in mechanical engineering and Kathleen earned an accounting degree. Kathleen is a Certified Public Accountant, but has been a stay-at-home wife and mom for the past 24 years, working only part-time during tax season.

Their seven children range in age from 20-31 - Margaret (Maggie), Peter, Andrew, Adam, David, Elizabeth (Lyz), and Meredith, who is married to Mark. Their children live in Texas, Oklahoma, Michigan, Tennessee, Georgia, and Heaven.

Ron and Kathleen have lived in five states and now call fifteen acres in North Texas their home. When they first moved to Texas, they tried raising chickens but ended up with a few fat coyotes. They enjoy playing with their two dogs, a yellow lab named Lady and a fat, black pug named Lyla. They also enjoy watching the hawks, deer, turkeys, and other wildlife from the back porch and riding their bikes. When Ron's work requires visiting customers (which is much of the time), Kathleen often joins him in his travels. They have visited forty-seven states in the past two years.

Ron and Kathleen educated all of their children at home. For fourteen years she taught Home School for High School seminars around the country helping home school families navigate high school and the college application process.

Kathleen's hobbies include reading, studying the Bible, swimming, biking, and mowing their property. But her favorite hobby is visiting her grandchildren.

To read more of Kathleen's continuing
Journey through Grief into Grace,
go to

www.KathleenBDuncan.com

Or

"Like" her Facebook Page
Kathleen B. Duncan, My Journey through Grief into Grace

www.facebook.com/KathleenDuncanblog

Books by Kathleen Duncan

My Journey through Grief into Grace
ISBN-13: 978-1516976638

What Bereaved Parents Want You to Know (but may not say)
ISBN-13: 978-1517528591

God's Healing in Grief
ISBN-13: 978-1621196143

My Journal of God's Healing in Grief
ISBN-13: 978-1621196327

Index of Blog Articles

Kathleen .Duncan

Have you lost a loved one?

The pain and grief run deep, and you wonder how you're ever going to make it. You feel broken, helpless, and you've lost hope.

You need healing for your heart and healing in your grief.

God's Healing in Grief

An Inductive Bible Study written to help you discover answers from God's Word about grief.

- What "comfort" can I expect from the Lord and how do I get it?
- How can I possibly find joy and peace when my child, spouse, or parent is dead?
- How can we truly heal when nothing can go back to "the way it was" before they died?

This 18-lesson study contains Bible study activities to help you learn Truth straight from the Bible. It's designed for you to come to a place of healing by studying for yourself what Scripture says about these important topics. The lessons learned in this study will help gently bring you to the solid foundation of Christ and the true comfort found only in God and His Word.

Order at precept.org

Kathleen .Duncan

Discover what God says about death, dying, and life after death.

Many people are intrigued by what lies beyond death's door, but we live in an age bombarded with many conflicting views. How can we be sure of what is true?

In this eye-opening study you'll examine the Bible's answers about death and what comes next. As you confront the inevitability of death in the context of the promise of heaven and the reality of hell, you will be challenged to examine your heart-and in doing so, find that, in grabbing hold of the hope of eternal life, the sting of death is replaced with peace.

Heaven, Hell and Life After Death is part of Precept Ministries International's 40-Minute Bible Study series. These revolutionary, *no-homework, 6-week studies* are an easy introduction to inductive study. They have proven great for small groups and have a unique format that includes Scripture alongside the text. Zoom in on the issues you care about and learn to think about them as God does. These focused, self-contained studies guide you into God's Word one topic at a time, 6 weeks at a time, with no homework.

Order at precept.org

44635678R00194

Made in the USA
San Bernardino, CA
19 January 2017